"HIGH-TOPPED SHOES" AND OTHER SIGNIFIERS OF RACE, CLASS, GENDER, AND ETHNICITY IN SELECTED FICTION BY WILLIAM FAULKNER AND TONI MORRISON

Tommie Lee Jackson

University Press of America,® Inc.
Lanham · Boulder · New York · Toronto · Oxford

Copyright © 2006 by
University Press of America,® Inc.
4501 Forbes Boulevard
Suite 200
Lanham, Maryland 20706
UPA Acquisitions Department (301) 459-3366

PO Box 317
Oxford
OX2 9RU, UK

Library of Congress Control Number: 2006923753
ISBN-13: 978-0-7618-3497-7 (paperback : alk. paper)
ISBN-10: 0-7618-3497-4 (paperback : alk. paper)

For my beloved son Kofi Ulysses Bofah

In memory of my parents Rev. Thomas Jackson, Jr. (1921-1989),

Bertha Clarke Jackson (1920-1995),

Maternal grandfather and namesake Lee Clarke (1882-1951)

Contents

Preface

The impetus for the study has been, in criticism, the myriad allusions to the links existent between William Faulkner and Toni Morrison. For example, Missy Dehn Kubitschek in her work *Toni Morrison: A Critical Companion* identifies the narrative technique of juxtaposition as one shared by modernists Faulkner and Morrison and cites *As I Lay Dying,* by Faulkner, and *Sula,* by Morrison, as examples of their experimentation. On *Sula,* Kubitschek writes:

> Morrison, who wrote her master's thesis on two modernists, Faulkner and Virginia Woolf, uses juxtaposition as a structuring device in *Sula.* Though relatively short for a novel, *Sula* has an unusually large number of chapters, eleven. This division into small pieces creates an intended choppiness, the uncomfortable sense of frequently stopping and starting. The content of the chapters accentuates this choppy rhythm. (50)

John Kennedy makes another parallel of Morrison to Faulkner in his review of the novel *Paradise.* Kennedy observes that the opening chapter "Ruby" "contains wonderful writing, Faulknerian, with rich, evocative and descriptive passages" (377); however, similar to Kubitschek, a pursuit of such parallels was peripheral to the focus of the criticism, namely, an overview of a particular work, or works, by Morrison. The study situates the works by Faulkner and Morrison alongside one another to ascertain the extent to which they refract one upon the other. It also address a need that Morrison has identified in interviews—a criticism rooted in black cosmology, as the moorings of her literature reside there: "I am yearning for someone to see such things—to see what the structures are, what the moorings are, where the anchors are that support my writings" (McKay 151).

Moreover, the study aims to adorn the blueprint established by aforementioned reviewers, critics, and others to ascertain both the nature and the extent of the cross fertilization between two authors whose literary careers have unmistakable parallels. In 1958, Faulkner was affiliated both with the University of Virginia and Princeton University, with the former as a writer-in-residence; the latter, as part of his duties associated with the Council on Humanities (Karl

987); Toni Morrison, since 1989, has been Robert F. Goheen Professor in Humanities at Princeton University. In addition, to their respective affiliation with Princeton University, the two authors have the same publisher, Random House.

Strategy

The study draws upon the small but growing body of criticism that pairs Faulkner and Morrison. The following book-length studies link the authors in a sustained fashion: *Unflinching Gaze: Morrison and Faulkner Re-Envisioned*, edited by Carol A. Kolmerten, Stephen M. Ross, and Judith Bryant Wittenberg; *Producing American Races: Henry James, William Faulkner, Toni Morrison*, by Patricia McKee; and *Balancing the Books: Faulkner, Morrison, and the Economics of Slavery*, by Erik Dussere. Moreover, the study uses the theoretical model identified by Gates in *The Signifying Monkey: A Theory of Afro-American Literary Criticism*. Therein Henry Louis Gates, Jr. addresses what he sees as a genuine need: the development of a critical model autonomous to African American culture rather than an imported critical model: "While this latter mode of literary analysis can be a revealing and rewarding exercise, each literary tradition, at least implicitly, contains within it an argument for how it can be read. It is one such implicit argument or theory about the black tradition that I wish to discuss in this book" (xix-xx). Notwithstanding the resemblance of black texts to Western ones, Gates proffers that the resemblance always bears a difference, "a black difference that manifests itself in specific language use. And the repository that contains the language that is the source—and the reflection—of black difference is the black English vernacular tradition" (xxii-xxiii). Such texts are referred to as "mulattoes" due to their double-voiced utterance. Therein lies the challenge for the critic of African American literature, according to Gates: to read the literature as a comparatist: "Anyone who analyzes black literature must do so as a comparatist, by definition, because our canonized texts have complex double formal antecedents, the Western and the black" (xxiv). In pairing Morrison and Faulkner, the writer is mindful of the potential pitfalls that such a comparison entails, namely, making one author the ideologue of another. Thus emphasis has been placed on artifacts in the literature and the negotiation by the authors of those signs. Restrictive claims of a predominant limning quality are muted by a foregrounding of the reverberative and revisionist aspects of selected works by the Faulkner-Morrison ensemble.

Description

One such artifact is that of "High-topped shoes." "High-topped shoes," synonymous in many instances with brogans, "shoes made with wooden or thick leather, soles pegged to a sturdy leather upper" (Barthelemy 189), become a signifier of "the livery of slavery and oppression" (Barthelemy 193); concomitantly, identifiable by their iconic reproduction in the literature with race. **Chapter 1** examines the motif in Faulkner's *Light in August* and *Sanctuary;* also, in Morrison's *Sula* and *Song of Solomon* to make evident the extent to which identities are individually as well as socially constructed.

Another sign to be explored in selected literature by Morrison and Faulkner is that of incest, particularly in *The Sound and the Fury, Sanctuary,* and *Absalom, Absalom!,* by Faulkner; also, *Love, Paradise,* and *The Bluest Eye,* by Morrison. The obsession of Quentin Compson and Henry Sutpen with Caddy and Judith, respectively, drives them toward destructive acts of murder and suicide. By the same token, the in breeding among the nine founding families of the all-black town of Ruby, population 360 (45) produces a similar anathema, namely, extinction. Thus the motif of incest in Faulkner and Morrison becomes connotative of the exclusivity associated, respectively, with race and class. Lyall H. Powers, author of *Faulkner's Yoknapatawpha Comedy,* has written on the implications of the motif in Faulkner's works:

> What is everywhere implicit in the Yoknapatawpha Saga . . . [is] that the incestuous attitude of the pseudoaristocratic Southerners is introverted, reductive, and finally self-destructive, is indeed the emblem of, or synecdoche for, the typical Southern attitude in general. (119)

The trope of incest is symbolic also of a narcissistic will to power as the use of the female slave for reproductive ends not only benefited the slaveholder economically but asserted also the proprietary claim of the slaveholder over the female slave at the same time that it demoralized the black man helpless to defend the black woman's virtue. According to Thadious Davis, the nullification of the slave as person has residual effects that persist in the present, in the presumptions of blacks' inferiority that constituted the moral and legal foundation of slavery:

> In particular, the presumption of inferiority has hampered the progress of blacks in seeking equal access to education, housing, and employment, despite repeated efforts of 'remedies.' It is no coincidence that inferiority is one of the precepts Higginbotham and Anne F. Jacobs have distilled from the relevant colonial and antebellum Virginia statutes into 'the legal and moral foundations of American slavery and early race-relations law': inferiority, property, and powerlessness. (16)

The polysemous definition of the motif incest in selected American literature is the focus of **chapter 2.**

An investigation in **chapter 3** into the ramifications of Biblical names in African American culture establishes a contrast to Faulkner whose race and class signifiers are largely archetypal, such as his use of the name Clytemnestra for Thomas Sutpen's mulatto daughter in *Absalom, Absalom!.* On the other hand, in *Song of Solomon,* Morrison describes the historical practice by African Americans to select Biblical names for their offspring. The random selection of names from an open Bible explains names such as "First Corinthians" (31), "Pilate" and "Magdalene" (18) from *Song of Solomon.* In addition to the choice of Greek names, such as Clytemnestra, which communicate the Olympian aspirations of the slaveholder/father Thomas Sutpen, Faulkner also has the practice of re-cycling his fictional names, such as "Nancy" both in the short story "That Evening Sun" and the drama *Requiem for a Nun,* thus cloaking the Black characters in anonymity.

Importantly, the names in Faulkner's and Morrison's body of work also hint at a connection between the two, as characters in both *The Sound and the Fury* and *Paradise,* respectively, are accorded the name "Deacon," suggestive of their function in the works as cultural custodians; however, more significant is their use of names and themes derivative of African and African American folklore. The influence of folk culture on Faulkner and Morrison, respectively, is the focus of **chapter 4.**

The storytelling tradition of the South fueled the young Faulkner's imagination. The stories told by the hunters around the campfires, by Callie Barr of the Civil War and Reconstruction, as well as by the blacksmith who entertained the young Faulkner with tales "involving wolves and other varmints of the Tallahatchie Bottom" (Blotner 31) inevitably found their way into Faulkner's literature. An analysis of the folk elements in Faulkner's literature is the subject of **chapter 5.**

Chapter 6 of the study relates the ambiguous pronominal references in Faulkner's *Sanctuary* and *Absalom, Absalom!* and Morrison's *Paradise.* Frederick R. Karl in *William Faulkner: American Writer* has observed that the ambiguous pronominal references are used by Faulkner, in part, to enhance the reader's participatory role in the invention of the novel and to mimic actual dialogue: "By confusing pronoun references, Faulkner hoped to draw the reader . . . into the actual scene where references can be gleaned from gesture, look, body language. Even after revision, *Absalom* is still full of such confusions, deliberately so, and often to the advantage of greater intensity" (561). Similarly, Morrison has noted in an interview the emotions readers supply are integral to the creative process (Tate 164). Hence, an examination of the pronominal references in the novels *Sanctuary* and *Absalom,* by William Faulkner, and *Paradise,* by Morrison, would shed light on the vital role of the reader to the authors' craft.

Significance

William Faulkner is not known simply as a regional author. In fact, the impact of Faulkner on writers abroad has been documented. Frederick R. Karl credits Faulkner's devotion to his craft, creation of a mythical kingdom, and experimental literary technique for his influence on Latin American authors (1017-18). The imprint of Faulkner on the literary consciousness of American authors has also been established. To be sure, Morrison considers the transcendent nature of Faulkner's prose as a model for her own work: "Faulkner wrote what I suppose could be called regional literature and had it published all over the world. It is good—and universal—because it is specifically about a particular world. That is what I wish to do" (LeClair 124).

Morrison is also an author who straddles a number of traditions. Missy Dehn Kubitschek avers in her work *Toni Morrison* that despite the link of Morrison's works to a number of traditions—African American, American, the Novel—"she remains one of a kind" (6). She observes too that Morrison completed formal study of American literature at Cornell University with an M.A. thesis on two modernist writers, Virginia Woolf and William Faulkner" (17).

The objectives of the study will be not only to identify discernible imagistic, narrative, and thematic patterns, but, in so doing, to ascertain the sources of the authors' fiction. The study constitutes a dialogue that Erik Dussere predicts, given the connections between Morrison and Faulkner, will intensify in years to come: "[I]t is perhaps common knowledge by now that Morrison wrote her M.A. thesis at Cornell on themes of alienation in Faulkner and Virginia Woolf—and it seems clear that the Faulkner-Morrison connection will be the subject of much more discussion, academic and otherwise, in the years to come" (2).

Acknowledgements

During the completion of this study, I have been the beneficiary of the largess of a number of individuals who deserve my expression of gratitude: the graduate students enrolled in the William Faulkner Seminar during the fall 2000 (they were exacting readers, and the dialogue begun there sparked the investigation that follows); also, colleagues who examined drafts of the manuscript, either whole or in part. Professor Andrew Baskin, Editor of *The Griot,* offered valuable editorial advice on chapter one. Dr. Pearlie Peters, Rider University, gave unstintingly of her time, reading and commenting on a bulk of the manuscript. Her advice on Zora Neale Hurston was invaluable.

A year-long sabbatical in 2005-2006 provided me the unencumbered time needed to mount a final charge toward the project's completion. Hence, I thank faculty, staff, and administrators of St. Cloud State University. I thank the Editorial team at University Press of America, Inc., a Member of the Rowman & Littlefield Publishing Group, for shepherding the manuscript through production.

My beloved son has been steadfast in his support; his Olympian spirit is a source of inspiration.

Permissions

Introduction

The Southern author, William Faulkner, casts a long shadow. Indeed, he is recognized by George Garrett in the article "The Influence of William Faulkner" as a pioneer who "blazed trails, broke ground, opened up new country for the American novelist" (426). Given Faulkner's mastery of technique and years of writing without becoming redundant, Garrett contends that virtually all young writers have been inspired by Faulkner and virtually all young writers have been influenced by him in one way or another. On the indebtedness of the Southern author to Faulkner, John T. Irwin, author of *Doubling and Incest/ Repetition and Revenge: A Speculative Reading of Faulkner,* had the following to say: "The regional debt is, obviously, to the South, since no one born in the South in this century and interested in literature can avoid, at some time or other, confronting the very personal significance of Faulkner's work to an understanding of his own way of life" (20).

The influence of Faulkner is not confined to Southern authors alone, as writers from other regions emulate Faulkner's narrative techniques that, according to Garrett, show the effect of Faulkner's employment as a screenwriter: "cuts, dissolves, and fades—are at work in his prose fiction, as well as camera-like angles—pans, high shots, close shots, long shots, etc., montage effects, and finally even the continual present time of the framed celluloid world" (425). Garrett ultimately identifies Faulkner not only as a model of craftsmanship, but also as a model for "behavior as a novelist. He kept going, kept writing in spite of indifference and hostility, praise and blame for the wrong reasons. And through it all he preserved his sanity, his humor, his courage, and his integrity" (427).

Exemplary of Faulkner's artistic integrity was the refusal to accept an advance from Doubleday to pen his own version of Mark Twain's *Huckleberry Finn.* Despite persistent money worries, Faulkner had declined the offer of a

$5,000 advance from Doubleday, one that would have relieved him, temporarily, from the Hollywood hack work he loathed, but one that he could not justify since the idea had not sprung full-blown from his own creative consciousness. In a letter to his agent, Harold Ober, Faulkner had registered the reason for his rejection of the Doubleday offer: "I have too much respect for my ancient and honorable trade (books) to take someone's money without knowing neither of us will be ashamed of the result" (*Selected Letters* 202).

Faulkner's apocryphal Yoknapatawpha County became a model for Ernest Gaines' fictional Bayonne (Babb 4; Carmean 19), a setting based upon the River Lake Plantation in Pointe Coupée Parish, Louisiana, Gaines' birthplace (Babb 1). In interviews, Gaines has often credited Faulkner for the development of his ear for language:

> "I have learned as much from Faulkner's language—handling of the language of both Blacks and the Southern whites—as from anyone else . . . . I have no interest in Faulkner's philosophy. I could no more agree with his philosophy no more than I could agree with [former Alabama governor] Wallace's. But this man taught me how to listen to dialogue; he taught me how to leave it out. You can say one word and if you say it right and build up to it and follow through, it can carry as much meaning as if you had used an entire sentence." (qtd. in Babb 12)

Valerie Babb has noted in her work that, similar to Faulkner, Gaines addresses in his works the peculiar legacies of slavery: "The casting of the Cajuns is both an element of negative change and the representatives of a new southern order replacing the old reflects the influence of an author whose style Gaines greatly admires, William Faulkner" (12).

The influence of Faulkner is not confined to Southern authors alone. American author James Baldwin expressed admiration for Faulkner; however, in the aftermath of Faulkner's remarks in 1956 in an interview with *The Reporter* that made clear the writer's allegiance to white Mississippians opposed to integration, Baldwin came to realize the role of art as a catalyst for social change and abandoned, according to David Leeming, "sentimental literary preferences" (117).

The African American author Ralph Ellison has expressed repeatedly his admiration for Mark Twain and William Faulkner, respectively. In his view the two became guardians of those democratic principles mocked in the condition of Blacks that the nation could only reconcile through a provision of rights denied them (104):

> I felt that except for the work of William Faulkner something vital had gone out of American prose after Mark Twain. I came to believe that the writers of that period took a much greater responsibility for the condition of democracy and, indeed, their works were

imaginative projections of the conflicts within the human heart which arose when the sacred principles of the Constitution and the Bill of Rights clashed with the practical exigencies of human greed and fear, hate and love.

Ernest Gaines, James Baldwin, and Ralph Ellison have acknowledged Faulkner's influence. Contrastingly, reviewers have asserted Faulkner's influence on literature by Toni Morrison albeit Morrison has identified Faulkner's prose style as worthy of emulation. Paul Gray, writer for *Time* magazine, observed that "In the Nobel sweepstakes at the moment, Morrison looks to be a lot closer to William Faulkner, whom many critics regard as this century's greatest American novelist, than to [Pearl S.] Buck and Steinbeck" (64).

Critics often identify the two modernist authors Faulkner and Virginia Woolf as models for Morrison's prose style. For example, Missy Dehn Kubitschek likens the novel *Sula*, in its elliptical style, to the works by Faulkner and Woolf:

> Morrison, who wrote her master's thesis on two modernists, Faulkner and Virginia Woolf, uses juxtaposition as a structuring device in *Sula*. Though relatively short for a novel, *Sula* has an unusually large number of chapters, eleven. The division into small pieces creates an intended choppiness, the uncomfortable sense of frequently stopping and starting. The content of the chapters accentuates the choppy rhythm. Almost every chapter shifts the focus from the story of the preceding chapter by changing the point of view character or introducing sudden, shocking events and delaying discussion of the character's motives until later. (49-50)

In interviews, Morrison has correlated her narrative prose style to the call-and-response of the black church; also, to the repartee of jazz musicians. However, Louis Menand argues that the multi-vocal narrative fiction of Morrison has roots in the modernist tradition:

> Morrison has listed this technique as one of the characteristics of what she calls "Black Art." It derives, she says, from the call-and-response style of black preaching, and also, presumably, from the give-and-take of jazz playing. But the technique has a literary source: it comes out of the modernist fiction of Woolf, Joyce, Hemingway, and Faulkner. Morrison wrote a master's thesis, at Cornell, on Woolf and Faulkner back in 1951, and her novels reflect their influence, plus, beginning with "Song of Solomon," the influence of Gabriel Garcia Marquez. Her achievement is to have adapted that modernist literary tradition to her own subject matter, which is the experience of African American women, and thereby to have made it new. (80)

Indicative of the modernist tradition is, according to Daniel Singal, the reversal of social and racial stereotypes. This reversal is seen as early as Faulkner's New Orleans sketches, namely, in the "Sunset" wherein the Black desperado, intent on returning to Africa, mistakes those in pursuit of him, those who speak Cajun dialect, as cannibals and shoots them in self-defense (60). This reversal is seen also in the novel *Mosquitoes*, wherein the sculptor Gordon is depicted as emblematic of masculine energy, quite in contrast to the popular image of the artist as effeminate. In a letter to Malcolm Cowley, Faulkner claimed that his style stemmed from the Southerner's love of oratory; art, on the other hand, was deemed of the second order:

> Oratory was the first art; Confederate generals would hold up attacks while they made speeches to their troops. Apart from that, 'art' was really no manly business. It was a polite painting of china by gentlemen. When they entered its domain through the doors of their libraries, it was to read somebody's else's speeches, or politics, or the classics of the faintly school, and even then these were men who, if they had been writing men, would have written still more orations. (*Selected Letters* 216)

Indeed, Frederick R. Karl in his biography on Faulkner considers that Faulkner's largest contribution to modernism is the introduction of a variety of temporal modes, among them the withholding of information and the telling and re-telling of characters' histories, that had as its equal "abstractionism," since what these artists sought to do was to introduce "new forms of seeing and hearing":

> The assault on objects as the enemy of creativity became part of [Faulkner's] weaponry as a writer, in his emphasis on the withholding of information, in the distribution of facts so that they never seem collected or resolved, in his collapsing of historical detail so that it appears and reappears differently shaped at different times. While this is not quite "abstractionism"—impossible to achieve in a verbal medium—it is an approximation of what cubists and then nonrepresentational painters were attempting to do on canvas. (244-45)

The Faulknerian method of telling and re-telling, a method that creates the impression of interior montage (Karl 246), is apparent in *The Sound and the Fury*, as the second generation relives the rivalries of the first generation. Witness Quentin, Candace's daughter, who assumes the role of her mother in her bitter feud with her uncle Jason, a contestation symbolic, in the view of Karl, of a rivalry between promiscuity and continence:

> The scenario of retelling and redoing is a familiar one in Faulkner: Jason saves, holds on, puts away, does not spend—a typically anal personality—whereas she spends, wastes, gives it away—a typical

orality. Money is merely another way of representing a sexual
conflict at the deepest levels. The struggle is between withholding
and wasting, sexual continence and promiscuity. (330)

Similarly, the doubling impact of the multiple narrators in Morrison's *Paradise*
accentuates their collective identity as detritus. The twenty-seven-year-old
Mavis Albright considers herself a murderer following the deaths of her twins
Merle and Pearl by asphyxiation. Fearful of reprisals from her husband Frank
and their eleven-year-old daughter Sal, Mavis fled Maryland in the 1965 mint
green Cadillac that Frank had forbidden her to drive. Importantly, the trope of
pariah becomes a signifier of the female condition in the novel. The mergence of
the female voice is apparent in Consolata's view of the women—Mavis, Grace,
Seneca, and Pallas—as indistinguishable one from the other: "What she knew of
them she had mostly forgotten, and it seemed less and less important to
remember any of it, because the timbre of each of their voices told the same tale:
disorder, deception and, what Sister Roberta warned the Indian girls against,
drift" (221-22). Karl identifies Faulkner's "convolutions of narrative" (251) as
one of a number of Faulkner's modernist strategies:

Stream, interior monologue, withholding of information, long,
intense silences, extraordinary attention to language, free association
of sentences and entire passages, revelation of character through
language, burial of authorial voice, creation of a multiplicity of
voices in a given text—all become inseparable from Faulkner's
desire to make you see in particular ways. (251)

The proliferation of italics in Toni Morrison's novel *Love* to indicate
interior monologue and to signal shifts in perspective are hauntingly similar to
their use in Faulkner's *The Wild Palms* and *The Sound and the Fury* to register
time shifts as well as shifts in perspective. In addition to signaling interior
monologue and shifts in perspective, the italics in *The Wild Palms* signal
conversations not witnessed, but imagined, as the one imagined by Harry
Wilbourne, Charlotte's consort in adultery, between the estranged couple
Rittenmeyer and Charlotte (226-27). In a letter to his Random House editor Ben
Wasson, Faulkner had articulated his frustration with publication restraints that
disallowed the use of colored ink, since he considered its use would have
clarified his intention to portray the subjective consciousness of the idiot Benjy:
"I think italics are necessary to establish for the reader Benjy's confusion; that unbroken-
surfaced confusion of an idiot which is outwardly a dynamic and logical coherence"
(*Selected Letters* 44). The use of italics in Morrison's *Love* largely indicates the
ruminations of the ghost L., an omnipresence in the novel who gives the book its
title and, among the chorus of voices in the novel, who validates as "truth" the
suspicion circulated as rumor, namely, that Cosey, rather than having fallen
victim to a heart attack, was instead the victim of a murder (17; 201).

The multi-vocal narrative voice in the literature of both Faulkner and Morrison is revelatory of theme, namely, the relativity of truth. As Faulkner pronounced on 8 May 1958 during a question and answer session at the University of Virginia on *Absalom, Absalom!*
:

> I think that no one individual can look at truth. It blinds you. You look at it and you see one phase of it. Someone else looks at it and sees a slightly awry phase of it. But taken all together, the truth is in what they saw though nobody saw the truth intact. So these are true for Miss Rosa and as Quentin saw it. . . . It was, as you say, thirteen ways of looking at a blackbird. (273-74)

Contradictions abound likewise in Morrison's novel *Paradise* that readers often cannot reconcile. For example, the number of founding families is cited variously as fifteen (187) and as nine (188), thus underscoring the "thirteen ways of looking at a blackbird." The conflicting accounts of the raid at the Convent likewise suggest that "All seeing is perspectival; no one sees all" (Weinstein xx):

> As for Lone, she became unhinged by the way the story was being retold; how people were changing it to make themselves look good. Other than Deacon Morgan, who had nothing to say, every one of the assaulting men had a different tale and their families and friends (who had been nowhere near the Convent) supported them, enhancing, recasting, inventing misinformation. (*Paradise* 297)

The multiple narrators in Morrison's eighth novel *Love* likewise challenge the reader to reconcile the conflicting accounts of Bill Cosey following his mysterious death. The narrator Vida is not impartial as she idolizes Cosey for rescuing her from the cannery and providing her with a job as receptionist at Bill Cosey's Hotel and Resort as well as with a wardrobe: "It was Bill Cosey who paid for two more [dresses], so she would have a change and the guests wouldn't confuse the wearing of one dress as a uniform" (33). Thus she excuses Cosey, who at fifty-two married the eleven-year-old Heed the Night and slanders Heed as an opportunist. The now sixty-six-year-old Heed who re-unites with her childhood friend Christine, also her granddaughter, after a foiled attempt at forgery to fortify her claim to the estate, expresses resentment over being sold to the highest bidder (185). Sandler Gibbons, Vida's husband who had been befriended by Cosey, approaches 'truth' as he sees coercion rather than choice as responsible for the marriage (147): "What was she [Heed] supposed to do? Run away? Where? Was there someplace Cosey or Wilbur Johnson couldn't reach?" Even the character L who confesses in her interior monologue to poisoning Cosey, her former employer to forestall his disinheritance of the Cosey women—Heed, May, Cosey's daughter-in-law, and Christine—in favor of his mistress, can dispute neither his devotion to his late wife Julia and their late son Billy Boy nor his philanthropic deeds: "You could call him a good bad man, or a bad good man. Depends on what you hold dear—the what or the why" (200). The chapters, entitled variously "Friend," "Stranger," "Benefactor," "Lover," "Husband," "Guardian," "Father," and "Phantom," announce to the reader the individual vantage point from which the history of Cosey is being re-constituted and refracted.

    Faulkner and Morrison are linked not only in terms of narrative technique, but content as well. Jill Matus in her work *Toni Morrison* asserts that the delicate balance of individual needs and communal demands is a concern shared by Faulkner, Morrison, and Virginia Woolf alike:

> What interests Morrison in these two writers is the accounting of alienation—the relative costs and gains. *Sula*, too, is an assessment of isolation and conviction, and how these states inflict identity. Like all Morrison's works it is about the negotiations and relationship between the inside and the outside. (61)

The allegorical nature of Morrison's novels, namely, Morrison's seventh novel, *Paradise,* is linked to Faulkner's *The Sound and the Fury.* According to Louis Menand, the novel *Paradise* recalls the Biblical story of the Exodus, which is likewise the sub-text of Faulkner's *The Sound and the Fury:*

> These novels [*The Sound and the Fury* (1929) and *As I Lay Dying* (1930)], too, have allegorical subtexts almost entirely hidden from view: in "The Sound and the Fury," it is the Easter story; in "As I Lay Dying," the story of Exodus. The difference is that Faulkner's Biblical allusions are bitterly ironic; they make for farce, not for uplift. In Morrison they are never ironic. She really does see the fallen world as infused with spirit, and she wants to hold out hope, not to validate resentment or despair. (80)

Paradise is the third installment of a trilogy that deals with three different types of love: motherlove in *Beloved;* romantic love in *Jazz;* and spiritual love in *Paradise* (Menand 78). Set in the 1870s through the 1960s, the novel spans a century that began following Reconstruction when Blacks moved from the South to the North and mid-western territories such as Oklahoma, where the action of the novel takes place, in order to found all-black communities. The fifteen founding families settled first in Haven, Oklahoma, but only after they had been spurned, due to their blue-black blood, by other homesteaders in Fairly, Oklahoma. Known as the "Disallowing," this history of rejection is re-enacted annually in a Nativity play at Christmas: "This rejection will reverberate through the next hundred years of the outcasts' collective memory as the Disallowing" (Gray 65).

    An inter-textual reading of Faulkner's and Morrison's works discloses not only correspondent narrative prose styles and content, but as well correspondent plot lines that cannot be dismissed as merely coincidental, one of which is the insult in *The Sound and the Fury* and *Absalom, Absalom!* and *Paradise,* whose unexpected source magnifies its potency and becomes a catalyst that drives the respective story lines. For example, worse than the theft of $3,000 by Quentin, Candace's daughter and Jason's niece, in *The Sound and the Fury,* is Jason's humiliation at the hands of his seventeen-year-old niece. Angered that he has been cheated out of his inheritance by the sale of Benjy's pasture to finance Candace's wedding and Quentin's Harvard education, Jason projects his displaced anger at his parents onto his brother's namesake Quentin for that loss. Jason also blames his niece Quentin for the divorce of Candace from Herbert Head inasmuch as her illegitimacy caused the dissolution of the marriage that rendered void the bank job promised to him by Herbert Head. Of no account to Jason is Quentin's entitlement to the money, sent to Mrs. Compson by Candace for her daughter's maintenance and stolen by Jason who substitutes bogus checks for the real ones to prevent their destruction by Mrs. Compson who intones at the ritual that has gone on for 15 years, "We Bascombs need nobody's charity. Certainly not that of a fallen woman" (138). Blinded by his own fury, Jason can only rage to the sheriff that he has been swindled by a "b---h" (189)! Meanwhile, the sheriff is adamant in his refusal to intervene without proof, which Jason cannot provide without self-incrimination, that Quentin is the culprit that he alleges her to be:

> "I wouldn't lay my hand on her. The b---h that cost me a job, the one chance I ever had to get ahead, that killed my father and is shortening my mother's life every day and made my name a laughing stock in the town. I won't do anything to her," [Jason] said. "Not anything."
> (189)

On the other hand, "[e]ngraved into the twins' powerful memories" (14) is the insult from an unsuspected source, as a result of their blue-black features, as the 158 wayfarers of newly-freed men and women made their way from Mississippi and Louisiana to Oklahoma upon the open invitation to settle in Negro towns under construction: "[F]or ten generations they had believed the division they fought to close was free against slave and rich against poor. Usually, but not always, white against black. Now they saw a new separation: light-skinned against black" (194). Haven had been founded as a consequence of the insult that came to be known as "the Disallowing." The wayfarers had ventured forth a second time after World War II when they recognized the cold reception provided returning soldiers by sons of the Confederacy as the second Disallowing. Ruby, named in memory of the twins' sister and mother of K.D., Kentucky Derby, was founded in response to the second Disallowing:

> Those that survived that particular war came right back home, saw what had become of Haven, heard about the missing testicles of other

colored soldiers; about medals being torn off by gangs of rednecks
and Sons of the Confederacy—and recognized the Disallowing, Part
Two . . . So they did it again. And just as the original wayfarers never
sought another colored townsite after being cold-shouldered at the
first, this generation joined no organization, fought no civil battle.
They consolidated the 8-rock blood and, haughty as ever, moved
farther west. (194)

Toni Morrison makes clear in *Paradise* that the slaughter of the Convent
women at the end of the novel constitutes the third "Disallowing." Referred to as
"detritus" (4), or "throwaway people that sometimes blow back into the room
after being swept out the door," their primary flaw is that they are not "8-rock"
(297). Thus the basis for the exclusion of the 8-rocks from Fairly, Oklahoma,
ironically, becomes the basis for their exclusion of the Convent women from
Ruby. The novel, in its evocation of a storied past, parallels the incantatory
prose of Faulkner's *Absalom, Absalom!* that bestows onto the past an active
presence:

Maybe Zechariah never wanted to eat another stick-roasted rabbit, or
cold buffalo meat. Maybe, having been routed from office by whites,
refused a homestead by coloreds, he wanted to make a permanent
feature in that open land so different from Louisiana. Anyway, while
they set up temporary quarters—lean-tos, dug outs—and hauled
wood in a wagon with two horses the state Indians lent them,
Zechariah corralled some of the men into building a cook oven. (99)

The Oven is a symbol that embodies the past of the fifteen founding families.
Constructed in 1890, the Oven knitted together the wayfarers as it provided
them both sustenance and monumentalized their Herculean efforts to conquer
new territories. Inasmuch as it heralded them as God's elect, it defied a past of
servitude. The twins' memories are of

Unembellished stories told and retold in dark barns, near the Oven at
sunset, in the afternoon light of prayer meetings. About the saddles of
the four black-skinned bandits who fed them dried buffalo meat
before robbing them of their rifles. About the soundlessness of the
funnel that twisted through and around their camp; the sleeping
children who woke sailing through the air. The glint of the horses on
which watching Choctaw sat. At suppertime, when it was too dark for
any work except that which could be done by firelight, the Old
Fathers recited the stories of that journey: the signs God gave to
guide them—to watering places. . . . (14)

In the seventies, however, the Oven has become a source of dissension among
the talk-back youth and their elders, also between the ministers Pulliam (Zion)
and Misner (Calvary), over the meaning of the words enshrined on the lip of the

Oven that the youth aim to re-write in order to envelop a new consciousness. The mid-wife Lone remarks the graffiti on the Oven that expresses the ideology of the warring camps: "No longer were they [the young people] calling themselves Be the Furrow of His Brow. The graffiti on the hood of the Oven now was 'We Are the Furrow of His Brow'" (298).

The past is embodied in the ghost of Bill Cosey that inhabits the abandoned hotel in Morrison's eighth novel *Love* and that betokens his active presence, albeit he has been dead some twenty-five years. Fittingly, it becomes the burial ground for Heed whose childhood was desecrated by "[the] good bad man, or [the] bad good man" the Cosey women, through their relinquishment of personal power, helped to create: "We could have been living our lives hand in hand instead of looking for Big Daddy everywhere" (189).

In the same way that the Oven in *Paradise* and the Hotel in *Love* literalize the past, an "absent presence" in Faulkner's fiction is a preoccupation with the loss by the Confederacy that gets played out in lower registers in the private agonies of individual characters. Witness Rosa Coldfield of *Absalom, Absalom!* who goes to live with her niece Judith and Judith's half-sister Clytie at Sutpen's Hundred to await the end of the War and Sutpen's return. Greeted with the news of Henry's disappearance following the murder of Bon, Henry's half-brother, Thomas Sutpen begins for the third time to create his design and, in an act of desperation, proposes marriage to his sister-in-law Rosa Coldfield (160): "[H]e was old (he was fifty-nine) and was concerned (not afraid: concerned) not that old age might have left him impotent to do what he intended to do, but that he might not have time to do it in before he would have to die." However, the forty-three-year-old Rosa Coldfield, twenty years old at the time fifty-nine-year-old army veteran Thomas Sutpen proposed marriage, was not prepared for the caveat of male progeny as his condition for wedlock. Her obsessive outrage that has arrested her emotional and physical development stems not entirely from the source of the insult, namely, from a man deemed the Coldfields' social inferior, but likewise from a susceptibility caused by desire:

> Yes, Rosa Coldfield engaged at last who, lacking the fact that her sister had bequeathed her at least something of shelter and kin, might have become a charge upon the town: and now Rosa Coldfield, lose him, weep him; found a man but failed to keep him; Rosie Coldfield who would be right, only being right is not enough for women, who had rather be wrong than just that; who want the man who was wrong to admit it. And that is what she cant forgive him for: not for the *insult*, not even for having jilted him: but for being dead. (170)

Rosa Coldfield's preoccupation with a blighted past parallels that of Ike Caslin in "The Bear." Importantly, however, the past assumes a literal presence (similar to that of the Oven and the Hotel in, respectively, Toni Morrison's *Paradise* and

Love) in a silver cup that is a legacy of the fathers that has become a repository of IOU's to generations past and present:

> there had been a legacy, from his Uncle Hubert Beauchamp, his godfather, that bluff burly roaring childlike man from whom Uncle Buddy had won Tomey's Terrel's wife Tennie in the poker-game in 1859--; no pale sentence or paragraph scrawled in cringing fear of death by a weak and trembling hand as a last desperate sop flung backward at retribution, but a Legacy, a Thing, possessing weight to the hand and bulk to the eye and even audible: a silver cup filled with gold pieces and wrapped in burlap and sealed with his godfather's ring in the hot wax, which (intact still) even before his Uncle Hubert's death and long before his own majority, when it would be his, had become not only a legend but one of the family lares. (300-301)

In addition to echoing themes, namely, the past as an active presence in *Paradise, Love, The Sound and the Fury*, and *Absalom, Absalom!*, Faulkner aficionados are struck also by the use of titles, such as "Deacon" in *The Sound and the Fury*, as a substitution for names. The twins Deacon and Steward Morgan of *Paradise* are accorded names correspondent to their symbolic roles as custodians of family and cultural history. In the same vein, the character in *The Sound and the Fury* is emblematic of the stock character in plantation fiction associated with a nostalgic past. In *The Sound and the Fury*, Deacon has been made the custodian of a letter, written by Quentin prior to his suicide, to be delivered to his roommate Shreve with instructions for the removal of his goods from their dorm room (63): "He [Deacon] was looking at me now, the envelope white in his black hand, in the sun. His eyes were soft and irisless and brown, and suddenly I saw Roskus watching me from behind all his whitefolks' claptrap of uniforms and politics and Harvard manner, diffident, secret, inarticulate and sad." As will be argued in chapter "High-topped Shoes," Morrison often invests the symbols of Faulkner, often equated with stereotype, with positive value.

Chapter 1

"High-topped Shoes": Signifiers of Race, Class, and Gender in Selected Fiction by William Faulkner and Toni Morrison

Evidence of Toni Morrison's familiarity with William Faulkner's literature abounds. The language of *Beloved,* for instance, echoes that found in Faulkner's *Light in August.* After Hightower's delivery of Lena's baby, Hightower returns to his abode following a two-mile walk from the scene of the delivery to prepare breakfast, after which he immediately falls asleep. Faulkner writes that "Anyone pausing to look down into the chair would have seen, beneath the twin glares of sky in the spectacles, a face innocent, peaceful, and assured. But no one comes, though when he wakes almost two hours later, he seems to believe that someone has called him" (383). The language finds an echo in *Beloved.* Following Sethe's desertion by Paul D, the fellow slave from Sweet Home with whom she is re-united, Morrison expresses Sethe's attitude of non-defeat in the following manner: "Anyone feeling sorry for her, anybody wandering by to peep in and see how she was getting on (including Paul D) would discover that the woman junkheaped for the third time because she loved her children—that woman was sailing happily on a frozen creek" (174). In addition to the language that echoes Faulkner's, the imagery in some of their respective works is strikingly correspondent to one another, namely, the imagery surrounding Raby in Faulkner's short story "Evangeline" and Sethe in Morrison's *Beloved.*

The short story "Evangeline" contains the germ for the novel *Absalom, Absalom!* Thomas Sutpen obtained land from Native Americans, either through swap, deceit, or blackjack, and upon it built a grand estate designed by a French architect. There he lived for five years after his return from the war with his daughter Judith, "who was a widow without having been a wife, as they say" (584), and with Raby, the half-sister of Judith and Henry Sutpen, who is described as "pretty near whiter than she is black" (585), and who has a Sutpen last name. At the time of the story's narration, Raby resides in a nearby cabin filled with female great-grandchildren, grandchildren, and children. It is she, according to the newspaperman narrator, who has told stories of the goings on at Sutpen Mansion: Bon's visit with Henry, also a student at the University of Mississippi, to Sutpen Mansion, where Bon met Judith who became enamored with him, "prototype of what today would be a Balkan archduke at the outside" (587); Henry's visit to New Orleans with Bon and Henry's sudden return coupled with the plea to Judith that she break off the engagement (588): "She refused to send back the ring and she dared Henry to tell what was wrong with Charles, and Henry wouldn't tell. Then the old folks tried to get Henry to tell what it was, but he wouldn't do it." Even following Henry's attempt to murder Bon, after his invited stay at the Mansion by Sutpen, Henry refuses to explain the cause of his estrangement from Bon and his opposition to their engagement:

> "Say what he has done," [Judith] tells Henry. "Accuse him to his face." But still Henry won't tell. Then Charles says that maybe he had better clear off, but the colonel won't have it. And so thirty minutes later Henry rides off, without any breakfast and without even telling his mother goodbye, and they never saw him again for three years." (589)

After three years, Henry and Bon are reconciled and Judith and Bon marry before their separation caused by the war. Only at the end of the war is Bon killed, according to Judith, "by the last shot of war" (591). The narrator in "Evangeline" seeks to determine the nature of the ghosts at the Sutpen Mansion guarded by a line of police dogs and by Raby, a black woman with a mask-like face and "with eyes that had no whites at all; from a short distance away she appeared to have no eyes at all. Her whole face was perfectly blank, like a mask in which the eye sockets had been savagely thumbed and the eyes themselves forgotten" (595).

On the significance of Raby's eyes in "Evangeline," Frederick R. Karl writes in *William Faulkner: American Writer (A Biography)*: "Faulkner, as always, is excellent on eyes. Like a painter, he observed eyes perhaps more intensely than he did any other organ" (442). The "savagely thumbed" eye sockets of Raby in "Evangeline" become the "punched out wells" of Sethe in Morrison's *Beloved.* Collectively, the works by Faulkner and Morrison, respectively, give to the characters a haunting presence as they betoken the characters' memories of an unspeakable past. Paul D, a fellow slave from Sweet Home, describes Sethe after being re-united with her in Cincinnati (9):

> And though [Sethe's] face was eighteen years older than when last he saw her, it was softer now. Because of the hair. A face too still for comfort; irises the same color as her skin, which in that still face, used to make him think of a mask with mercifully *punched-out eyes.* (italics added)

The imagery surrounding Raby in "Evangeline" and Sethe in *Beloved* coincides; likewise, the character Stamp Paid of *Beloved* has a name seemingly inspired by Faulkner's character Hightower of *August.* Both have betrayed their marriage covenant through inaction; however, both consider their suffering as having mitigated any past wrongdoing. Hightower's silent plea to be left alone comes following Lucas Burch's repeated attempts to involve him in the affairs of Lena Grove and Joe Christmas:

> [Hightower] could feel the counter edge against his stomach. It felt solid, stable enough; it was more like the earth itself were rocking faintly, preparing to move. Then it seemed to move, like something released slowly and without haste, in an augmenting swoop, and cleverly, since the eye was tricked into believing that the dingy shelves ranked with flyspecked tins, and the merchant himself behind the counter, had not moved; outraging, tricking sense. And he thinking, "I won't! I won't! I have bought immunity. I have paid. I have paid." (292)

Stamp Paid, formerly Joshua, in *Beloved* relates to Paul D that he had renamed himself Stamp Paid following his flight to freedom, one precipitated by his inability to protect his wife Vashti from the clutches of his master's son. That loss he considers payment for his past ineffectuality. In Cincinnati, after his flight, the indebtedness he has created in others as a result of his work as an Underground agent likewise justifies the name: "Dispensing with that formality [a knock on the door] was all the pay he expected from Negroes in his debt. Once Stamp Paid had brought you a coat, got the message to you, saved your life, or fixed the cistern he took the liberty of walking in your door as though it were his own" (172).

In addition to the characters Beloved and Stamp Paid whose descriptions recall those of Raby and Hightower in Faulkner's "Evangeline" and *Light in August,* respectively, the "high-topped shoes," or brogans, are a common motif with multiple significations in the fiction by both Morrison and Faulkner.

The inspiration for the chapter has been the essay "Brogans," by Anthony Barthelemy. A metonym for the old order, Barthelemy likens the brogan to the bound foot of Chinese women, as the practice became a signifier of the subservience of women (190). The negativity that accrues to the brogan, as shown in Faulkner's *Light in August,* accounts for, in Barthelemy's view, the contempt displayed by freedmen for the brogan and its representation. Barthelemy contrasts the views of Ernest Gaines toward the brogan in his novels; the brogan is often indicative of mental shackles that must be overthrown by the wearer. Given the treatment by Barthelemy in his article, the focus herein will be on its treatment by Toni Morrison, as well as August Wilson and Zora Neale Hurston, African American authors who likewise provide disparate views on the brogan and hence serve as interlocutors to Faulkner.

The fugitive Joe Christmas in Faulkner's *August* races to escape the bloodhounds of the lynch mob that pursue him by substituting his town shoes for hand-me-down brogans worn by a black woman. The discovery of the exchange is made after the bloodhounds lead the sheriff and his men to the cabin occupied by Blacks:

> She was wearing a pair of man's shoes, which a member of the posse identified as having belonged to the fugitive. She told them about the white man on the road about daylight and how he had swapped shoes with her, taking in exchange a pair of her husband's brogans, which she was wearing at the time. (312)

The brogans, described as black, become signifiers of blackness. The hand-me-down nature of the brogans suggests a legacy of alienation, poverty, pathology, and even death. Inasmuch as Joe Christmas is described as nearly white in appearance, the author's association of him to the pathological may be viewed as evidentiary of the characters' and, by extension, of Faulkner's fear of miscegenation. According to Robert Dale Parker: "Miscegenation, or the fear of it, and the viciousness that fear can lead to, directly (as in Henry's murder of Bon) or indirectly (as in Joe Christmas's murder of Joanna Burden), are the reverberating secrets of *Light in August"* (6).

"The shoe symbolized for the freedmen what the Fifteenth Amendment to the Constitution sterilized into the phrase 'previous condition of servitude,'" writes Anthony Barthelemy in "Brogans." Joe and Violet Trace of Toni Morrison's *Jazz* left Vesper County, Virginia, in 1906 as part of the Great Migration North. Other emigrants came from Georgia, while still others escaped from locales such as "Springfield Ohio, Springfield Indiana, Greensburg Indiana, Wilmington Delaware, New Orleans Louisiana, after raving whites had foamed all over the lanes and yards of home" (33). Transplanted, the emigrants assumed new identities as they sought to shed old ones, namely, those associated with their Southern past and its legacy of slavery. Thus the newly arrived posted letters to relatives left behind, inviting them to the City, but with the instruction, "don't bring no high-top shoes" (32). Symbolic of their City identities were "the leather of their soles" (32), as associated too with Christmas in Faulkner's *Light in August,* Levee of August Wilson's *Ma Rainey's Black Bottom,* and Marcus Payne of Ernest Gaines' *Of Love and Dust.*

In August Wilson's play *Ma Rainey's Black Bottom,* which is set in Chicago during the 1930s, the "clodhoppers" (40), or brogans, as worn by Toledo, are signifiers of a Southern past inseparable from violence and dispossession. A transplant to the North, Levee aims to shed his shedding past by substituting his "old shoes" for a pair of $11.00 Florsheims. Levee's attempt to escape the horrors of his Southern past is understandable. After all, he had witnessed as an eight-year-old the rape of his mother by Southern whites incensed by his father's ownership of property to which they sought claim. His scars therefore are both physical and emotional: "Levee raises his shirt to show a long ugly scar" (1.69). Levee's murder of fellow band member Toledo, who has "the nerve to put on a suit and tie with them farming boots" (1.40) and who accidentally scuffs Levee's Florsheims while wearing his clodhoppers, is indicative of the firm hold of the past upon Levee's psyche as he, in a moment of rage at the white producer Sturdyvant who has reneged on his promise to Levee to record some songs that Levee has written, fails to discern the difference between the victim and the victimizer; also, the present and the past. According to Peter Wolfe:

> It doesn't matter to Levee that Toledo's act was an accident or that he apologizes for it. Levee strikes out in "a transference of aggression" [. . .] because he lacks any other available target. His dreams of sophistication and prominence, symbolized by his new shoes, have been punctured by a farming boot, sign of a rural southern past he equates with the rape of his mother, the murder of his father, and a knife wound that nearly killed *him.* (52)

On the other hand, Mary L. Bogumil, author of *Understanding August Wilson,* argues that the purchase of Florsheims by Levee and his replacement of the old ones signal his break from the jug band music associated with the South and his identification with a swing music that was beginning to evolve: "Younger musicians like Levee are now proposing to drop 'this old jug band' in favor of his swing version of 'Ma Rainey's Black Bottom,' which is a discordant rupture of the tonal harmony typifying traditional blues, for a new, rhythmically sophisticated blues seems to be evolving, re-vitalizing and competing with the more traditional forms" (21).

The black musical tradition, namely, the blues and jazz, helps to constitute the "concord of sensibilities" (131) that Ralph Ellison has associated in "The World and the Jug" with the African American tradition. In the article, Ellison had chafed at the criticism by Irwin Howe that his novel *The Invisible Man* lacked the messianic zeal of Richard Wright's *Native Son.* Ellison had responded that the novelist writes out of his/her experiences as filtered through the consciousness of self, culture, and literature. Unique to the American Negro tradition, according to Ellison, was not "the irremediable agony" (130) that others had proffered, but a stoicism borne from struggle: "American Negro life [. . .] is, for the Negro who must live it, not only a burden (and not always that) but also a discipline—just as any human which has endured so long is a discipline teaching its own insights into the human condition, its own strategies of survival" (112). Inasmuch as the music, particularly the blues, contains the spirit of tragedy imbued with lyricism, it mirrors the African American condition of struggle and triumph. Ellison describes elsewhere the avant-garde jazz saxophonist Charlie "Bird" Parker as possessing the mocking skills of the bird whose nickname he bears:

> For although [Parker] *usually* sang at night his playing was character-
> ized by velocity, by long-continued successions of notes and phrases,
> by swoops, bleats, echoes, rapidly repeated bebops [. . .] by mocking
> mimicry of other jazzmen's styles, and by interpolations of motifs
> from extraneous melodies, all of which added up to a dazzling dis-
> play of wit, satire, burlesque and pathos. ("On Bird, Bird-Watching,
> and Jazz" 223)

Accordingly, Morrison's mimicry of the well-worn trope of "Negrohood," the high-topped shoe, or clodhopper, becomes analogous to the "woofing" of Charlie "Bird" Parker played against the downbeat of August Wilson, Zora Neale Hurston, and Ernest Gaines who likewise are steeped in the African American tradition.

Antithetical to the brogans, or high-topped shoes, of plantation workers John and Freddie of Ernest Gaines' *Of Love and Dust* are the "low-top shoes" of ex-convict Marcus Payne. His flamboyance, characterized by pink shirts, two-toned dress shoes, and brown-striped pants, becomes emblematic of his quest for authentic self-hood. As a result of Marshall Hebert's intervention, Marcus is acquitted by the court of Hotwater's murder. Marcus is presumed therefore to do the bidding of Marshall Hebert, his beneficiary into whose custody he has been released and who wishes to annihilate his overseer Sidney Bonbon whom Hebert has used as a hired gun and who could implicate Hebert. Accosted by Marshall with the proposition of murder, Marcus proffers a counterproposal: induce Bonbon's pursuit by his flight with Louise, the wife of Bonbon with whom Marcus is having an affair. As Marcus reasons to Jim Kelly, the central consciousness from whose perspective the novel is narrated" "I ain't no hunting dog to go round killing people for nobody else" (197). The ending is soon told as the scheme backfires. Marcus is double-crossed by Marshall and ultimately murdered by Bonbon. Albeit Marcus has been murdered, his victory has been the courage of his refusal, a fearlessness that sets him apart from the fear branded in others such as Bishop and Aunt Margaret in face of the omnipotence of the plantation owner, "this big thing" (269), whose social and economic power both manipulates and controls their destiny. Importantly, the iconoclastic nature of the character has been imparted from his "low-cut shoes." In addition to his "low-cut shoes," Melissa Babb has enumerated other features of Marcus that set him apart from others:

> Though a black field-worker, [Marcus] rejects the symbols he feels mark him as a creature of servitude and shows his contempt for the plantation order by replacing the khaki pants usually worn by field-workers with a pink shirt and brown pants, the straw hat with a cap, and the brogans with black-and-white "low-cut" shoes. Dressed to project an air of defiance, he scorns Bonbon's attempts to "break" him. Jim frequently describes Bonbon mounted on his horse following Marcus so closely that Marcus feels the animal's breath on his neck, and each description preludes an increased resolve on Marcus's part to rebel and exact revenge through involvement with Bonbon's mistress, Pauline. His dress and his arrogant behavior signal to Bonbon and others that he will not adapt to the plantation system at the expense of what he perceives to be his self-esteem and manhood. (66-67)

The rejection of Marcus in *Of Love and Dust* of the Negro stereotype via his "low-cut" shoes is apparent. On the other hand, the association by Faulkner of the brogan with "Negrohood" is clear. Indeed, so confident is Faulkner that the reader of his novel *Sanctuary* would identify properly the ethnicity of Ruby Lamar, the partner of bootlegger Lee Goodwin, that all explicit referents to her ethnicity are omitted. Instead, her ethnicity, as well as that of Lee Goodwin, whose brogans she wears, is conveyed through the common signifier of blackness, the second-hand brogans: "A woman stood at the stove. She wore a faded calico dress. About her naked ankles a worn pair of man's brogans, unlaced, flapped when she moved" (8). On the ownership of the brogans, Faulkner provides the reader with the following textual evidence: "I [Popeye] wont tell them that Ruby Lamar is down in the country, wearing a pair of Lee Goodwin's throwed-away shoes, chopping her own firewood" (9). Only in chapter eleven, following Lee Goodwin's false arrest for the murder of Tommy, does Faulkner make explicit reference to Goodwin's ethnicity: "Goodwin [jerked] up his black head, his gaunt, brown, faintly harried face" (111). The anti-thesis to Ruby Lamar is the 18-year-old Temple Drake whose difference in caste, as well as ethnicity, is signified by her high-heeled slippers:

> She [Temple Drake] picked up the dress and tried to brush them with her hand and with the corner of her coat. Then she sought the other slipper, moving the quilt, stooping to look under the bed. At last she found it in the fireplace, in a litter of wood ashes between an iron fire-dog and an overturned stack of bricks, lying on its side, half full of ashes, as though it had been flung or kicked there. (86)

Indeed, a similar class division among characters is underscored by August Wilson in his drama *Ma Rainey's Black Bottom*. Set in Chicago in 1937, blues singer Ma Rainey seeks to appeal to urban Blacks; concomitantly, to retain those Southern fans responsible for her popularity. Meanwhile the sideman Levee, a trumpeter, aims to infuse the jug band music with a more progressive, or modern, sound and has provided to the manager Cutler a new arrangement for the tune "Ma Rainey's Black Bottom," one that Ma Rainey rejects. He also aims to assemble his own band and to secure a recording contract from the producer Sturdyvant. In his words, "I'm gonna be like Ma and tell the white man just what he can do" (94). Thus his newly purchased Florsheims signal his bid to elevate his status from sideman to bandleader. James C. McKelly in his article "Hymns of Sedition: Portraits of the Artist in Contemporary African-American Drama" has observed that the set is "the symbolic embodiment of those hierarchies within which nascent African-American artistic production must fight for birth" (99). One might add that the shoes, as donned by the principals, also are a metonym for the stratification among artists as well as expressed ideology. Toledo dons clodhoppers, brogans, or farm boots. Yet among the sidemen, he is the one to whom one might accord an African sensibility. It is he who links Slow Drag's license with Cutler to his African invocation of ancestors to achieve expected ends:

> TOLEDO. That's what you call an African conceptualization. That's when you name the gods or call on ancestors to achieve whatever your desires are. (1.32)

Contrastingly, Ma Rainey occupies the upstairs studio where she belts out her tunes: "The studio itself, on a level above the band room, is Ma's turf, where the material and arrangements played by the band must suit her, and where she demands the respect of the producer, if she is to perform" (McKelly 99). Likewise she appears on stage wearing "a full-length fur coat with matching hat, an emerald-green dress, and several strands of pearls of varying lengths" (48). She wears also "sharp toed shoes," which have created for her foot problems she relates in her music (1.60). To be sure, footwear in the play becomes not only symbolic of "roots," as seen in the case of Toledo, but of the intra-racial caste system that becomes a microcosm of the larger society.

In Faulkner's *Light in August,* the "bootblack's" failure to discern an obvious clue to Christmas' racial identity stresses the common association of hand-me-down brogans to Blacks (331): "Even when the bootblack saw how he had on a pair of second hand brogans that were too big for him, they never suspected." The brogan is a stigma of the poverty, or lowly origin, of the wearer, but as Barthelemy has noted in the article "Brogans," the stigma of the wearer extends to the shoemakers, many of whom, from the late 1700s throughout the Civil War and beyond, were women and whose wages were among the lowest in the manufacturing industry:

Some shoe bosses would give consignments of brogans to women.
Because brogans were constructed from materials of inferior quality
and designed for other than ladies and gentlemen, production of this
coarse footwear did not require the kind of skilled workers necessary
for making fine boots and fancy shoes; thus those employed in manufacturing the brogan usually received the lowest wages among shoemakers [. . .]. Some shoe bosses offered the women only onions or
store credit for their labor. (181)

Not only is the brogan a symbol of the poverty of the wearer and the female shoemaker; the unshod foot is depicted likewise in Faulkner as emblematic
of poverty, irrespective of race. In the short story "Mountain Victory," referred
to by Edmond L. Volpe as "one of Faulkner's great short stories" (146), Faulkner describes a loyalty between master and servant that discloses by contrast the
disloyalty of the Union soldier to the cause of freedom, as he becomes at the
same time liberator and executioner. The daughter of the mountaineer, described as having unshod feet, is stunned by the sacrifice the Confederate major
makes for his manservant; he had used the sable lining of his cloak to supply
Jubal, his manservant, with footwear. Another sign of the major's loyalty is the
compromise the major makes to his personal safety rather than desert Jubal, his
manservant, who is reviled by the very Union soldier who fought for his liberation. Contrastingly, the mountaineers are either unshod or wear brogans, a symbol of caste. On the importance of footwear, Edmond L. Volpe has summarized
in *A Reader's Guide to William Faulkner: The Short Stories:*

The continual attention upon footwear reveals the differences between the two social worlds. In the third scene, Jubal polishes Weddel's dancing slippers, which have been crudely soled. Weddel dons
these slippers for supper in the barren cabin with its crude iron table-
ware [. . .] . The daughter expresses her fascination with the alien
world that the stranger represents by being self-conscious, suddenly,
of her bare feet [. . .]. Weddel's humane treatment of his servant is
given dramatic force by the girl's shocked elation when she discovers
that the major has cut strips from the sable lining of his cloak to provide warm footwear for his black servant. (148)

Similar to the unshod feet of the daughter in the short story "Mountain Victory,"
those of Lena Grove are likewise an indicator of caste. Orphaned at twelve,
Lena Grove in *August* has lived with relatives in a log house that has few ameni-
ties; her unshod feet therefore are indicative of this deprivation:

When she was twelve years old her father and mother died in the
same summer, in a log house of three rooms and a hall, without

screens, in a room lighted by a bug-swirled kerosene lamp, the naked
floor worn smooth as old silver by naked feet. (2)

When Lena goes to live in the sawmill town of Doan's Mill with her brother,
who is twenty years her senior, he bequeaths to her a pair of hand-me-down
shoes, "shoes unlaced about her ankles" (5), a gesture that betokens a legacy of
poverty that ties her figuratively to Joe Christmas and Ruby Lamar of *Light in
August* and *Sanctuary*, respectively; also, to the unnamed female of *The Wild
Palms*. As Lena departs her brother's home following her pregnancy, she carries
with her a bandanna handkerchief that contains the following: "thirty-five cents
in nickels and dimes. Her shoes were a pair of his own which her brother had
given to her. They were but slightly worn, since in the summer neither of them
wore shoes at all. When she felt the dust of the road beneath her feet she removed the shoes and carried them in her hand" (4).

The female in *The Wild Palms*, by William Faulkner, is neither named nor
her ethnicity provided; yet she wears a pair of "unlaced brogans" (148), a moniker that identifies her, similar to Lena Grove, as "hillbilly." Moreover, she gives
birth in the skiff during the ravages of the 1927 Mississippi flood, another moniker of a prolix nature identifiable in Faulkner as well with those of her ilk. Finally, her stoicism, a manner that recalls that of Lena Grove in *August,* pairs her
likewise with the convict who considers questions tantamount to a request for
favor. After the two are rescued by the steamboat crew from the raging Mississippi River, the convict refuses to ask the steamboat's location. Inasmuch as the
other evacuees aboard the boat are identified as speaking a foreign tongue, the
convict's reticence may be interpreted too as evidentiary of his outrage at a relief effort that fails to make distinctions based on race, a reflex action that in the
face of calamity becomes absurdist.

Brogans are associated not only with females, but with the dirt farmer
Anse of Faulkner's *As I Lay Dying* whose homemade shoes as a youth had produced a deformity that rendered it almost impossible for him to wear the brogans that he currently owns. Anse's son Darl relates that

> Pa's feet are badly splayed, his toes cramped and bent and warped,
> with no toenail at all on his little toes, from working so hard in the
> wet in homemade shoes when he was a boy. Beside his chair his bro-
> gans sit. They look as though they had been hacked with a blunt axe
> out of pig-iron. (11)

The "man's heavy shoes" (46) that establish caste also bestow on the characters an earthen quality, i.e., the heavy, man looking shoes that Lena wears are
covered in dust (9), and make them analogous to those described by Faulkner as
"hillbillies" (391) in *August*. Lena Grove belongs to the same class as the mountaineers of West Virginia, identified by Faulkner with the Sutpens in *Absalom,
Absalom!,* whom Faulkner distinguishes not only by their houses which "didn't

have back doors but only windows" (233), but too by their "vicious prolixity" (235): "creatures heavy and without grace, brutely evacuated into a world without hope or purpose for them, who would in turn spawn with brutish and vicious prolixity, populate, double treble and compound, fill space and earth with a race whose future would be a succession of cut-down and patched and made-over garments bought on exorbitant credit"; also, by their hand-me-down brogans. Sutpen's nameless sister is described in the self-same terms as Lena Grove in *Light in August,* wearing "a calico dress and a pair of the old man's shoes unlaced and flapping about her bare ankles" (236), and Ruby Lamar in *Sanctuary:* " A woman stood at the stove. She wore a faded calico dress. About her naked ankles a worn pair of man's brogans, unlaced, flapped when she moved" (8). In *Light in August,* expressive of female affinity resultant from caste is the egg money that Mrs. Armstid, the wife of the farmer who provided Lena a lift, gives Lena. Mrs. Armstid, similar to Lena, is depicted as "manhard, workhard" (14) by the ravages of life:

> The gray woman not plump and not thin, manhard, workhard, in a serviceable gray garment worn savage and brusque, her hands on her hips, her face like those of generals who have been defeated in battle. (14)

The fertility of Mrs. Armstid also likens her to Lena; she is described as having "[borne] five children in six years and raised them to man- and woman-hood" (13). Near the novel's end, Lena gives birth in a Negro cabin that is associated in Hightower's view with fecundity. Thus Lena's poverty, as signified by the "man's heavy shoes," and fecundity, as signified by the Negro cabin in which she gives birth, align her not only with those described by Faulkner as "hillbillies," but as well with the Blacks in the novel:

> It seems to him that he can see, feel, about him the ghosts of rich fields, and of the rich fecund black life of the quarters, the mellow shouts, the presence of fecund women, the prolific naked children in the dust before the doors; and the big house again, noisy, loud with the treble shouts of the generations. (385)

Lena's innocence, as represented by her journey from Mississippi to Alabama in search of Lucas Burch, the father of her unborn child, under the presumption of marriage, also links her to Faulkner's stereotype of "the Negro." According to Karl, "[Faulkner] saw Negroes as the salt of the earth, in many ways far superior to whites—but he saw them in their place, serving, childlike people waiting for guidance. He foresaw change, but did not figure on how many generations would have to pass, how many contemporary Negroes would have to be sacrificed in that transition" (634).

That shoes are made analogous to identity are evidenced in Faulkner's description of the shoes worn by Mr. McEachern, Christmas' foster father, that are suggestive of age (139): "McEachern took from the wall a harness strap. It was neither new nor old, like his shoes. It was clean, like the shoes, and it smelled like a man smelled: an odor of clean hard virile living leather." Earlier McEachern was described as middle-aged, a description congruent with Faulkner's description of his shoes (132-33): "Hair and beard both had a hard, vigorous quality, unsilvered, as though the pigmentation were impervious to the forty and more years which the face revealed."

The ambiguity that engulfs Joe Christmas with respect to his identity suggests itself in his attire. That is, he is given a "Negro job" at the sawmill removing sawdust; however, his street clothes belie his "Negrohood" that is personified by the job:

> [. . .] he turned his back upon it [country road] and went on in the
> other direction, in his soiled white shirt and worn serge trousers and
> his cracked, dusty, town-shaped shoes, his cloth cap set at an arrogant
> angle above a threeday's stubble. (213)

The substitution by Joe Christmas of the "town-shaped" shoes for the brogans at the point of flight, following the alleged murder of Joanna Burden, would indicate the confusion of the character relative to his identity rather than as John Pilkington has noted, Joe's acceptance of his blackness: "Thus, the wearing of the Negro shoes appears to parallel and perhaps symbolize Joe's increasing commitment to the Negro race" (146). Daniel J. Singal in his construal of Christmas' attire is closer to the mark; he identifies Christmas' attire as emblematic of the character's identity crisis: "[Christmas's] appearance in this way reflects the agonizing tensions within him that he can neither resolve nor escape for the simple reason that they provide him with his sole basis for self definition" (176). Another assessment of the brogan comes from Anthony Barthelemy. He associates the brogan, as worn by Christmas, with doom. In the cabin owned by Joanna Burden, where Christmas lives with Lucas Burch, alias Joe Brown, Christmas seems aware of his destiny as he thinks, "something is going to happen to me. I am going to do something" (97).

Indeed, Faulkner relates Joe Christmas repeatedly to the pathological, as can be seen in the five-inch-blade razor with which he sleeps and his threats of murder following Brown's taunts and obscene laughter respecting Christmas' affair with Burden. His return to Mottstown where his identity is known and his escape from authorities while in their custody also point to a character being driven by unseen forces toward destruction (437): "His plunge carried him some distance before he could stop himself and climb back out. He seemed indefatigable, not flesh and blood, as if the Player who moved him for pawn likewise found him breath." Faulkner likewise suggests that the assault upon his foster father who, suspicious of Joe's deceit, had surprised Christmas at a dance, appeared to have been scripted: "He could not have known where McEachern had left the horse, nor for certain if it was even there. Yet he ran straight to it, with something of his adopted father's complete faith in an infallibility in events" (193-94).

Joe Christmas, a mulatto, is an archetypal Faulknerian character. Frederick Karl describes Popeye of *Sanctuary* as "a transformed Joe Christmas" (374). Daniel J. Singal contends that "One can see Faulkner groping toward Joe Christmas as early as *Sanctuary*, where Popeye, a man with pale skin who is somehow always perceived as 'black,' goes on to commit an especially repulsive rape of a white woman" (185). Indeed, not only is Popeye born on Christmas Day (296), the same birthday as Joe Christmas, but his emotional dwarfism mirrors as well that of Christmas in *August*. The rejection of food prepared for him by Mrs. McEachern, following his whipping by Mr. McEachern for Joe's failure to memorize Scripture, is played out again in his later rejection of the food prepared for him by Joanna Burden. So accustomed has Christmas become to maltreatment that he responds negatively to acts of mercy: "Thus Joe suffers on the one hand from uncharitable treatment, and on the other from his learned inability to respond to Charity, to gestures of love" (Powers 98). Contrary to the socialization process that has transformed Christmas into a pathological murderer, Faulkner suggests in *Sanctuary* a genetic condition that has altered irreparably Popeye's sensibilities: "[Popeye] had no hair at all until he was five years old, by which time he was already a kind of day pupil at an institution: an undersized, weak child with a stomach so delicate that the slightest deviation from a strict regimen fixed for him by the doctor would throw him into convulsions" (300).

Doc Hines, Joe's grandfather in *August*, shares a similar pathology with Popeye of *Sanctuary* and Joe Christmas of *Light in August;* however, his is linked to an obsession with race purity, as he is described repeatedly as someone driven toward fanaticism by his determination to cauterize the symptom of miscegenation. The desperate measures of Doc Hines, the father of Milly, to contain the blood contagion parallel those of Henry Sutpen in Faulkner's *Absalom, Absalom!*. Henry Sutpen had reconciled himself to incest resultant from a possible union between Bon and Judith; however, unacceptable to Henry was the miscegenation likewise resultant from their possible union. Hence to forestall the marriage, Henry had murdered his friend and brother Bon. In a similar fashion, Doc Hines in *August* murders cold-bloodedly Milly's paramour whom Doc Hines suspects to be Black, although he is rumored to be Mexican (355), and allows his daughter to perish during childbirth rather than seek for her medical attention (358), and, subsequent to Christmas' arrest for the murder of Joanna Burden, calls for the lynching of his grandson whom he considers Lord's abomination: "It's the Lord God's abomination, and I am the instrument of His will" (360).

Percy Grimm, a civilian dedicated to the practice of mob law, also shares with Doc Hines a pathology driven by a determination to maintain the myth of racial purity. Thus he likewise seems driven by forces beyond his control (439): "It was as though he had been merely waiting for the player to move him again, because with that unfailing certitude he ran straight to the kitchen and into the doorway, already firing [. . .]." His characterization likewise as a pathological killer suggests the contagion that is racism, as it is transmitted from Doc Hines to Grimm as though it were a communicable disease. Grimm not only murders Christmas on the uncorroborated testimony of Joe Brown, Christmas' partner in the bootlegging trade, but Percy Grimm's castration of Christmas evinces a mentality, similar to that of Doc Hines, which construes miscegenation a worse crime than murder:

> But the Player was not done yet. When the others reached the kitchen they saw the table flung aside now and Grimm stooping over the body. When they approached to see what he was about, they saw that the man was not dead yet, and when they saw what Grimm was doing one of the men gave a choked cry and stumbled back into the wall and began to vomit. Then Grimm too sprang back, flinging behind him the bloody butcher knife. "Now you'll let white women alone, even in hell," he said. (439)

The irony of Percy Grimm's murder and castration of Joe Christmas is that Grimm murders Joe under false delusions. Grimm has mistaken Joanna Burden to be a symbol of the cult of whiteness when, in point of fact, her blood lines, similar to those of Joe Christmas, were mixed. In a conversation with Joe after the two had become lovers, Joanna, the daughter from her father's second marriage, had identified her namesake as her father's first Mexican wife Juana (238); the bloodlines of her maternal grandmother, her father Nathaniel's mother, similarly as "murky": "His [Joanna's half-brother's] name was Calvin, like grandpa's, and he was as big as grandpa, even if he was dark like father's mother's people and like his mother" (234-35). Joanna Burden's alliance with the black community, as signaled by her representation by a black attorney, and her role as benefactress to Negro colleges would indicate her eschewal of the very whiteness deemed integral to her being that those such as Percy Grimm aim to protect. As one black boy put it, in response to Joe Christmas' remark regarding the danger to her incumbent from her isolation: "Who going to harm her, right here at town? Colored folks around here looks after her" (214). Thus both characters enhance severally the features of one another. Just as Joe Christmas shifts back and forth between the black and white worlds, Joanna shifts from a nymphomaniac to a matron, a transversal symptomatic of an individual in the throes of an identity crisis. Critics such as Robert Dale Parker therefore do an injustice to the novel by perceiving of Joanna Burden in isolation from the other females in the novel; also, from Joe Christmas:

> [. . .] Joanna [. . .] is repeatedly described as manlike (221-22, 227, 242, 244, 251). In the social world of this and most other novels that means she is or is perceived as a woman who has failed *as* a woman—the same suggestion as in the word spinster [. . .]. She lives apart from the town socially as she does geographically, so that no one in town knows or even would dare visit her (48, 81, 275). Mean-

while, as an active benefactor she lives a life she could well be proud of, but she lives it with zero (white) social sanction and zero novelistic sanction from Faulkner. The suggestion is that she comes to see herself as others apparently see her, as not a failed person but a failed woman, and in response she desperately tries to act out the full range of roles she thinks she has failed to live up to. As Joe thinks—Joe who at this point accepts the rule of role for women—"She's trying to be a woman and she don't know how" (227). She succumbs to type, in other words, as a defense against the excessive *burden* of having defied type for so long. (109)

One could add to Parker's assessment that not only is Joanna Burden described as manlike, but so too are other females in *August*, such as Mrs. Armstid, and to a lesser degree Lena Grove, a characteristic that affirms their group identity. Edmond L. Volpe, in his work *A Reader's Guide to William Faulkner: The Short Stories*, associates the masculine characteristics assigned to some of Faulkner's female characters, such as Mrs. Gant of "Miss Zilphia," with trauma (82-83): "Mrs. Gant is portrayed as a warped psyche. The impact of her trauma on her natural being is developed by descriptions of her as increasingly rigid and masculine." Importantly, Miss Zilphia, the daughter of Mrs. Gant, and Joanna Burden of *Light in August* have had willed to them a legacy of repression that Faulkner associates in his works with Calvinism. The emotional dwarfism of Miss Zilphia is implicated in her association with dolls. Unable to escape the psychological hold of Mrs. Gant, Miss Zilphia had returned to her mother's home, despite the groom's objection. The sudden death of Mrs. Gant, however, had not precipitated the groom's return as she had hoped, thus her resort to fantasy (378): "Nothing was worth that. 'Nothing,' she said, crying quietly in the dark, feeling tranquil and sad, like a little girl at the spurious funeral of a doll; 'nothing.'" Correspondingly, symptomatic of Joanna Burden's trauma are her delusions of pregnancy, despite the fact she is middle-aged; likewise, her nymphomania, which is followed by guilt, reflects that of someone in the throes of a religious crisis. Indeed, Joanna Burden's attempt to mimic roles expected of her mirrors that of Joe Christmas who suffers from an identity crisis resultant from confusion related to ethnic origin.

Miscegenation, or the threat thereof, that compels both Doc Hines and Percy Grimm toward destructive behavior may be viewed as a double-barreled motif for race mixing, or integration. Faulkner's fear of the latter prompted a kind of hysteria similar to that of the characters he created. On matters of race, Frederick Robert Karl in his work *Faulkner: An American Writer* identified Faulkner as a Southerner with a devout allegiance to his place of origin and all that ancestry entailed. In the infamous interview with Russell Howe, Faulkner is purported as having said: "But if it came to fighting I'd fight for Mississippi against the United States even if it meant going out into the street and shooting Negroes. After all, I'm not going out to shoot Mississippians [meaning whites]" (qtd. In Karl 933). This allegiance to the South often complicated Faulkner's views on integration, which were contradictory, if not irrational. Evidence of these contradictions is Faulkner's public stance on school desegregation following the Supreme Court's 1954 landmark decision that barred "separate but equal schools." Faulkner lamented the system-wide school failure, both for blacks and whites; however, in the essay entitled "A Letter to the Leaders of the Negro Race," he exhorted the NAACP "to go slow, stop for a moment, let events catch up to the rhetoric" (941). One might conclude, as Karl does, that the cause of Faulkner's illogic was an attempt to appease both sides on this issue (925):

> Faulkner agrees that the "best" Negroes no more want integration with white people than do the "best" white people. He defines his position, and we must note how he has shifted it from the talk a little earlier: "since there is much pressure today from outside our country to advance the Negro, let us here give the Negro a chance to prove whether he is or is not competent for educational and economic and political equality, before the Federal Government crams it down ours and the Negro's throat too." Here justice and equality for the Negro as an absolute value no longer obtains; what matters is taking the best possible position because of outside pressure. He adds he feels the Negro simply wants justice—to be left alone by the NAACP and by whites threatening violence. Negroes who do not wish integration must join with white people like the club members who oppose injustice and violence. In that meeting of minds, the South could tell the federal government to keep out of its affairs. To reach this position, Faulkner has twisted himself out of all recognizable positions.

Conceptualized as a murder mystery, *Intruder in the Dust,* published in 1948, contains the views of Faulkner on race problems in the South more than half a century following the War that theoretically liberated slaves from bondage. Lucas Beauchamp is the mulatto son of Carothers McCaslin and hence second cousin, or blood relative, to Carothers Edmonds. Carothers McCaslin is the great grandfather of Carothers Edmonds whose father, first cousin to Lucas Beauchamp, had deeded to Beauchamp the ten acres on which Beauchamp, now widowed, resides. This genealogy is important as Lucas is framed for the murder of Vinson Cowrie, one of a seven-male Cowrie clan from Beat Four susceptible to violence, the Town itself complicit in his arrest as Beauchamp refuses to accommodate himself to the role assigned him (18). The distinctiveness of Beauchamp, that is, his rejection of the role assigned him, is marked by contrast.

Contrary to "the overalls and the brogans" (*Intruder in the Dust* 96) that proclaim the identity of the Negro in Faulkner, Beauchamp comports himself in a black broadcloth suit, starched white shirt and custom-made beaver hat, set at a rakish angle, on the singular occasion that he comes to town to pay his annual land taxes. Other outward trappings associated with the McCaslins and, by extension, the Old South, are the gold toothpick, which adorns Beauchamp's upper breast pocket, and the "fawty-one Colt," the weapon inherited from McCaslin and donned as an accessory by the Southern plantocracy to which he is heir (226). Indicative of Beauchamp is also an aloofness that the Town finds insufferable. Four years ago he had helped rescue Charles "Chick" Mallison, nephew of lawyer Gavin Stevens, from a frozen creek, an act for which he refused compensation and one that "Chick" continues to try and placate, a compulsion that explains his presence in the jail cell. As a result of Beauchamp's instruction to the sixteen-year-old Charles Mallison to exhume the remains of the murdered man to ascertain truth, namely, that the murder weapon which killed Vinson was not the one belonging to him (69), "Chick," along with Miss Habersham, foster sister of Beauchamp's late wife Molly, effects Beauchamp's liberation; concomitantly, he unmasks the murderer—Crawford Cowrie, brother of Vinson.

A novel bifurcated as a result of its competing aims to entertain as well as to pass as serious literature, the disputations of lawyer Stevens become a poor substitute for dramatic action. Nonetheless, his conflicted views on the issue of race, specifically, the responsibility of the South to forge its own solutions, even as it glorifies the past, are consonant with those of the author, despite his published disclaimers. Richard Gray in his work *The Life of William Faulkner: A Critical Biography* has remarked the fissure between image in the novel and the rhetoric associated with Stevens and, by extension, the author:

> *Intruder in the Dust* may talk about change through accommodation; as the portrait of Lucas suggests, however, its fundamental investment is in conservation and restitution—the maintenance of the past rather than the management of the future. This is not to accuse Faulkner of disingenuousness, as some early, liberal critics of the novel did. There is no doubt that, however muddled his views on race might have been, he was in regional terms a moderate, who hoped to see the condition of Southern blacks significantly improved over time. Equally, it is clear that he tried to inject those views into *Intruder in the Dust*, using Gavin Stevens to articulate them—and to tell the North, not least, that the South was entitled and needed to solve its own problems. The fact is, though, that the fundamental drift of the novel is towards the pieties and practices of the past. (298)

Faulkner's contortions on the issues of racial equality are attributed to Southern views of honor. According to Erik Dussere, Southern plantocracy differentiated between business debts and debts of honor, the system of honor often perceived by Southerners as distinguishing them from their Northern kin. Satisfaction of debts of honor is deemed a precondition to the termination of a relationship. Conversely, a failure to discharge a debt of honor is to bind individuals interminably. Thus Faulkner posits slavery in his literature as a bond, or sin to be expiated by whites; however, he resists federal legislation of equality for blacks, considering that the matter rested wholly with Southern whites. According to Dussere, therein resided the problem, as the closed society that Faulkner defends has served as the very foundation for inequality, or dishonor. Thus Faulkner is caught in the double bind of defending the structure that he purports to repudiate:

> Preserving it [Southern honor] necessarily means acknowledging and settling the debt of honor, and in setting out this thesis Faulkner's fictions seek to preserve it. Preserving it necessarily means acknowledging and settling the debt of honor, and in setting out this thesis Faulkner is faithful to the old traditions, both by casting the problem of race in terms of debt and by opposing his debt of honor to an alternate, Northern conception of debt. (67)

A similar confusion on the race question is contained in *Light in August.* John Pilkington has identified as a major weakness in *August* the perception by many that Faulkner failed to elicit the readers' sympathy for Joe Christmas, a failure that may stem from Faulkner's inconsistent handling of the character reminiscent of his own views on integration, or race mixing. The character Joe Christmas, for instance, is identified as both a martyr and a pathological killer: "Often Christmas is not a much-to-be pitied, suffering victim; at times he is a vicious criminal loose in society" (156). Anthony Barthelemy in the article "Brogans" observes another example of Faulkner's inconsistent handling of character when he remarks that the black brogan is not only a signifier of blackness, but of death as well and questions the oddity of Faulkner's identification of death as an uncommon fate.

This duality, attributable to his role as 'other' also characterizes Charlotte Rittenmeyer of *The Wild Palms,* by William Faulkner. A mother of two, Charlotte has abandoned her children and husband in order to live out what she considers an idyll with medical intern Harold Wilbourne. To the extent that she rescues him from a hum-drum existence, she may be considered Christ-like: "Those like Charlotte who attempt to transcend that tension [between the desired and reality] by taking on a Christ-like role may succeed in pioneering new social norms and briefly taste the ineffable. But, like Christ himself, they must inevitably pay the 'price' by an outraged society that cannot tolerate the revolutionary they portend" (Singal 239). However, to the extent that Wilbourne is incarcerated for murder following a botched abortion, which she insisted he perform, she is deemed a Lilith. According to Frederick Karl, "In her needs, [Charlotte] consumes men; she is not only Helen of Troy, but the Venus's fly trap embodied. Although Faulkner's presentation of Charlotte is sympathetic to her kind of energy and leadership, she is the Biblical Lilith or Eve" (601).

In contrast to the dichotomy in the abovementioned fiction by Faulkner, who utilizes the "man's heavy shoes" (46) as a motif for a legacy of poverty, toil, pathology, and, as Barthelemy has noted, a symbol of death, at the same time that he invests these characters with affirmative values, in *Sula,* by Toni Morrison, the man's shoe becomes the essence of the character's sexuality. As has been observed, Major Saucier Weddel of "Mountain Victory" dons "mended dancing slippers" (758) to partake of the vittles offered him and his manservant by the Virginia mountaineers, footwear that distinguishes him from his hosts. In *Sula,* by Toni Morrison, Eva, the mother of Hannah, who has lost mysteriously one leg, wears "a black laced-up shoe that came well above her ankle" (31), one that accentuates her "one glamorous leg" (31). Also, Hannah Peace of *Sula* wears men's slippers, belonging presumably to one of her many lovers among the boarders who occupy the Peace home. The twist, though, is that the man shoes Hannah wears tease the imagination by downplaying the sexuality she exudes. Thus Morrison plays on the man shoes motif identifiable with caste and suggests its multiple significations; the man shoes that Hannah wears become a mark of territoriality similar to the spots by the canine of its terrain. Hence Morrison explodes the myth of man shoes that in the Faulknerian universe renders the female characters abstractions, such as the Earth Mother, and accords them distinction as sexualized beings. Trudier Harris argues in *Fiction and Folklore: The Novels of Toni Morrison* that Morrison's "primary folkloristic technique is reversal, where outcomes consistently fall short of expectations" (11).

The technique of reversal is evidenced as well in Morrison's *Song of Solomon* and Zora Neale Hurston's *Their Eyes Were Watching God,* respectively. Witness Milkman's abandonment of the thin-soled Florsheim shoes (229) and his assumption of the borrowed brogans when he goes on a hunt with the men of Shalimar: "Calvin seemed to be the most congenial of them, and followed the introductions with a command to King Walker to 'get this city boy some shoes for his feet.' King rummaged around, spitting tobacco, and came up with some mud-caked brogans" (274). Witness too Janie Starks' dress of "blue denim overalls and heavy shoes" (*Their Eyes* 200) as she picks beans alongside Tea Cake in the Everglades. There folk tales that feature John de Conquer are told (232), and Janie communes with the Bahaman drummers whose music communicates a common ancestral bond (206): "[D]uring the summer when she heard the subtle but compelling rhythms of the Bahaman drummers, she'd walk over and watch the dances. [. . .] She got to like it a lot and she and Tea Cake were on hand every night till the others teased them about it." Contrary to Joe Christmas of *Light in August,* wherein the assumption of brogans signifies his confusion relative to identity, the "mud-caked brogans" that Milkman wears and the "heavy shoes" that Janie wears become a symbol of their indoctrination into the fellowship of man and, concomitantly, their re-connection to their Southern and, by extension, their African roots. It is during the hunt that Milkman is able, for the first time, to commune with nature and the land of his ancestors: "Down either side of his thighs he felt the sweet gum's surface roots cradling him like the rough but maternal hands of a grandfather" (282).

The contrast between the authors' respective outlooks may be seen with regard to their points of view. Wilson has written in the Foreword to *Ma Rainey* that he is concerned in the play with the blues and the musicians who have spawned the blues: "It is with those Negroes that our concern lies most heavily:

their values, their attitudes, and particularly their music" (xvi). On the other hand, Robert Dale Parker has observed that Joe Christmas is seen mainly from the outside, "as if to suggest he is all compulsion and no consciousness. Our few glimpses into his thoughts are revealing only enigmatically" (92). The argument of abstractionism has also been made by Thadious Davis who has written the following in her work *Faulkner's "Negro": Art and the Southern Context:*

> *Light in August* does not delve into "Negro" consciousness of self as "Negro"; nor does it present Joe Christmas as a black man. Joe's characterization encompasses a level of abstraction and generaliza- tion which undermines his humanity, no matter whether he is black or white. Joe is almost purely a symbolic persona in what appears at least on the surface to be a realistic novel. Arguing that Joe's very lack of individualization is a part of Faulkner's thematic messages evades the issue. (176)

The same argument of abstractionism may be made of Lena Grove in *Au- gust* and Dilsey of *The Sound and the Fury,* respectively. Lena is a major char- acter, yet her consciousness is never illuminated. Readers ascertain her third hand, primarily through Byron Bunch (371), as he relates to Hightower her search for Lucas Burch (45) at the sawmill where he works and his unwitting revelation of Burch's alias as Joe Brown (90, 74); his procurement of a room for her to safeguard knowledge of Brown's true identity (76), occupation and Brown's implication in the murder of Joanna Burden (94).

Walter Taylor makes a similar argument relative to the obfuscation of Black characters, more specifically, Dilsey in *The Sound and the Fury*. A sym- bol of endurance, Dilsey assumes tragic proportion only in relation to the white Compson family she has adopted as her own, not her black family. Taylor ar- gues in *Faulkner's Search for a South:*

> The experiences of Dilsey's black family had been, in their own way, as tragic as those of the white family she thought herself a member of; but Faulkner seemed almost indifferent to Roskus, Dilsey's hus- band, or Frony, her daughter. Superstitious, arthritic Roskus seldom appeared. Faulkner suggested in Benjy's narrative that he has died, but that was about all he had to say on the subject, and Dilsey, her mind on the tragedy of her relationship with the Compsons, never mentioned her dead husband once on Easter 1928. (149-50)

The former streetwalker and mate to Lee Goodwin in *Sanctuary* is likewise an enigma. Similar to Lena, Reba is seen from a male perspective, namely, that of the lawyer Horace Benbow who seeks to exonerate Lee Goodwin from mur- der charges: "The woman finished her story. She sat erect in the chair, in her neat, worn gray dress and hat with the darned veil, the purple ornament on her shoulder. The child lay on her lap, its eyes closed in that drugged immobility.

For a while her hand hovered about its face, performing those needless maternal actions as though unawares" (262). As a result of the third-hand account of Lena Grove, Richard Gray in *The Life of William Faulkner: A Critical Biography,* identifies the narrative treatment by Faulkner as indicative of his treatment of female characters in his fiction:

> Original inspiration she [Lena Grove in *August*] might have been, but she is consistently denied her own subjective space; she is seen through an elaborate screen of male stories, the reports of men who react to her and discuss her fate. There is no attempt made at an interiorizing approach; nor any suggestion that men make her up, reinvent her as they perceive her. Instead, following a route that is worn down with familiarity by now, the author/narrator looks at Lena as an object and then celebrates her for the apparent possession of qualities that have, in fact, more to do with his exteriorizing approach than with any genuine discovery of her: the qualities, that is, of serenity or placidity, unimpatience and a supposed freedom from anxiety. (190)

It cannot be said that the "exteriorizing approach" applies to the handling by Morrison of her characters, as the narration ranges from the consciousness not only of the principal female characters, Sula and Nel, in *Sula,* but that of the male character Shadrack as well, whose loss, as a result of his World War I experiences, presages on the one hand that of the individual characters and on the other the wider loss of the community of Medallion, as the community is being razed to make room for a Medallion City golf course. Importantly, Shadrack wears too "high-topped shoes" (12), an identification that because of its link to Eva Peace, suggests for the reader Shadrack's feminized being caused by the horrors of war that he has experienced. His loss therefore prefigures that of Nel at the end of the novel. Morrison describes Nel's recognition that her greater loss has not been Jude, but rather her friend Sula (174): "And the loss pressed down on her chest and came up into her throat. 'We was girls together,' she said as though explaining something. 'O Lord, Sula,' she cried, 'girl, girl, girlgirlgirl.'"

Toni Morrison gives inverted meaning to the "high-topped shoe" in *Beloved* and *Paradise* as well. Baby Suggs is a cobbler who was taught the trade by the "husband" Suggs she claimed (142). Thus she is linked to him by trade; also, by a past of servitude associated with the footwear she mends: "[Baby Suggs] took the shoes from him—high-topped and muddy—saying, 'I beg your pardon. Lord, I beg your pardon. I sure do'" (153). Her role as cobbler who repairs is similar to that of Paul D in the novel, largely restorative, as she "pass[es] messages, heal[s] the sick, hide[es] fugitives" (137) at a way station of the Underground Railroad identified as 124. Similarly, Paul D, upon his arrival at 124, drives away the ghost of Beloved from the premises and begins to repair the damage wrought: "He was up now and singing as he mended things he had broken the day before" (40). Collectively, they function as healers as they nurture Sethe, following the aftermath of her escape from Sweet Home, in her journey toward wholeness. Moreover, they are the antithesis of the four horsemen—schoolteacher, one nephew, one slave catcher and a sheriff—(148) who likewise don "high-topped shoes" (138), signifiers of their role as destroyers, whose mission, aided and abetted by the 1850 Fugitive Slave Act, results in infanticide; the 1850 Fugitive Slave Act made unlawful the protection of fugitives in northern territories. Following the celebration at 124 to honor the arrival of the fugitive slave Sethe and the baby Beloved, Baby Suggs, mother to Sethe's husband Halle, has a vision of doom: "[Baby Suggs] squeezed her eyes tight to see what it was but all she could make out was high-topped shoes she didn't like the look of" (138). Thus the ambiguity in the novel hinges in part in the view that the savagery of infanticide cannot be divorced from the savagery of slavery and the legislation that undergirds it: "The Society managed to turn infanticide and the cry of savagery around, and build a further case for abolishing slavery" (260).

Furthermore, this inversion of stereotype exists in *Paradise*, by Morrison. One of the twins, Deacon, in *Paradise* is made distinctive from the other, Steward, by his black high tops (235). Members of the New Fathers in Haven, Oklahoma, the nine original families view themselves as authentic due to their unadulterated blood. In this context, the black high tops that Deek wears, rather than a source of shame, become iconic of their pride in their 8-rock blood, or authenticity.

The dialogue with Faulkner by Toni Morrison is not new. According to Herman Beavers, author of *Wrestling Angels*, the African American novelists, expressly Southern ones, are invariably captivated by Faulkner's craftsmanship, yet repelled by the racial myths perpetuated in his fiction. Thus they are wedded in an "engaging disengagement" with Faulkner. Indeed, the mimicry associated with some jazz musicians also distinguishes Toni Morrison's fiction. Ralph Ellison in his essay "On Bird, Bird-Watching, and Jazz," as contained in the collection *Shadow and Act*, describes the mocking style of jazz saxophonist Charlie Parker as consonant with his nickname "Bird": "Further, [Bird] was as expert as issuing his improvisations from the dense brush as from the extreme treetops of the harmonic landscape, and there was, without doubt, as irrepressible a mockery in his personal conduct as in his music" (223)

Further evidence of Morrison's mimicry is contained in the novel *Song of Solomon*. Therein Morrison subverts the myth of the loyal black retainer, such as Clytie of Faulkner's *Absalom, Absalom!* , who destroys the Sutpen mansion and incinerates both herself and her half-brother Henry Sutpen in order to protect the secrets of Sutpen Hundred and to save Henry from criminal prosecution for the murder of Charles Bon. Similar to Clytie, Circe of *Song of Solomon* outlives her slave owners, the Butlers, but contrary to Clytie, Circe's longevity is motivated by revenge rather than a fidelity to memory, as Circe utilizes the Weimaraners bred by Mrs. Butler to desecrate Lincoln's Heaven (236) for which the Butlers had "stole for, lied for, killed for" (249). She corrects Milkman who confuses her presence there with attachment:

"Ha! And I want to see it all go, make sure it does go, and that no-body fixes it up. I brought the dogs in to make sure. They keep strangers out too. Folks tried to get in here to steal things after she [Mrs. Butler] died. I set the dogs on them. Then I just brought them all right in here with me. You ought to see what they did to her bed-room. Her walls didn't have wallpaper. No. Silk brocade that took some Belgian women six years to make. She loved it—oh, how much she loved it. Took thirty Weimaraners one day to rip it off the walls." (249-50)

Circe of *Song of Solomon* is a response to Clytie of *Absalom, Absalom!* She may also be considered a response to the loyal retainer Raby of "Evangeline," on whom Clytie is predicated.

Finally, another example of Morrison's signification on Faulkner is the identification of the unshod foot in the novel *Paradise* with contrition rather than poverty, as evidenced in *Light in August*. King David, as a sign of contrition, goes barefoot after he lives to see the prophecy of the Lord fulfilled, namely, "the sword shall never depart from thine house" (Samuel II: 12; 10). Deacon Morgan, in a similar sign of contrition, after the wanton destruction by the men of the Convent and the orphaned women who have resided there, walks the streets of Ruby fully attired, but without shoes:

[Deacon Morgan] wore his hat, business suit, vest and a clean white shirt. No shoes. No socks. He entered St. John Street, where he had planted trees fifty feet apart, so great was his optimism twenty years earlier. He turned right on Central. It had been at least a decade since the soles of his shoes, let alone his bare feet, had touched that much concrete. (300)

The upshot is that Beaver's characterization of Ernest Gaines' fiction may be said to be descriptive in part of Morrison's fiction as well in that the racial myths surrounding the loyal black retainer, in addition to the brogan, or man shoes, become subverted in Morrison's fiction into signs of female power, and race consciousness, respectively:

The African American novelist (and especially those born in the South) is invariably locked in an "engaging disengagement" with Faulkner; attracted to his power of description and mastery of lan-guage, but repelled by his perpetuation of racial myth. One finds this is most certainly the case for Ernest Gaines, especially since he has alluded to Faulkner's influence over "every Southern writer" who has followed him. (qtd. In Barthelemy 194-95)

The inversion associated with the fiction of Toni Morrison, which is analogous to that found in the Black musical tradition, extends itself to the hip-hop, or rap, music of the urban generation. Michael Eric Dyson argues in the article "The Culture of Hip-Hop" that one antecedent to rap is blues singer Bessie Smith and her "rapping to the beat in some of her tunes" (401). In both genres, *machismo* is glorified and pain given voice: "The blues functioned for another generation of blacks much as rap functions for young blacks today: as a source of racial identity, permitting forms of boasting and asserting machismo for devalued black men suffering from social degradation, allowing commentary on social and personal conditions, [. . .] and fostering the ability to transform hurt and anguish into art and commerce" (405). Moreover, the genres, blues and hip-hop, are similar in that the artists appropriate disparate musical forms to produce a provocative new sound, a "musical hybrid of fiery lyricism and potent critique" (403). More to the point, the inversion associated with hip-hop, or rap, music extends to urban gear as well, as the high-topped shoe, aka the Timberland boot, and the prison-inspired fashion, such as beltless, baggy pants, become transformed into urban chic. Hence the function of the African American artist, to some extent, as subversive becomes inseparable from the larger African American tradition of overcoming by transforming.

Chapter 2

Wedded Imagery in Fitzgerald's *Tender Is the Night,* Faulkner's *Absalom, Absalom!* and Toni Morrison's *Paradise* and *Love*

In *Love,* by Toni Morrison, hotel owner Bill Cosey dies suddenly without having finalized his will. However, L, chef at the hotel resort owned by Cosey, has located scribbled notes on a menu purported to contain his last wishes. Among the heirs, the survivor identified only as "sweet Cosey child" could reference Heed Cosey, who refers to him as Papa (79), or it could reference the granddaughter Christine and Cosey's only biological living relative. Heed, through marriage, is Christine's grandmother although Christine is eight months older than Heed (131). The fifty-two-year-old widower had married the eleven-year-old Heed, following the loss of his son Billy Boy, in a desperate attempt to have children: "Word was he [Cosey] wanted children, lots of children, to fill the mirror for him the way Billy Boy used to. For motherhood only an unused girl would do" (104). The implication, though, is that Cosey's marriage to Heed had come with a price tag, as money had changed hands with Heed's parents Wilbur and Surrey Johnson: *"So why not let their youngest girl marry a fifty-two-year-old man for who knew how much money changed hands"* (138). The incestuous union between Heed and Cosey is replicated in Christine's prostitution of herself with a man who resembles her grandfather: "[Fruit] would have mourned again if he knew what she had settled for: kept woman to a mimeographed copy of her bourgeois grandfather" (167). The leitmotif of incest becomes the lens through which Toni Morrison in *Love* examines the victimization of women. To be sure, the leitmotif incest is a unifying element in fiction by F. Scott Fitzgerald and William Faulkner as well, two authors whose fiction also is linked herein.

In *Some Sort of Epic Grandeur: The Life of F. Scott Fitzgerald*, Matthew Bruccoli writes that Faulkner and Fitzgerald not only had in common the literary agent Harold Ober, identified by Bruccoli as Fitzgerald's editor and banker as well (287), but their career paths also followed a similar trajectory, as both Faulkner and Fitzgerald were employed at one point in their careers as Hollywood studio writers (426n). Bruccoli notes too in *Some Sort of Epic Grandeur* that alcohol addiction was to plague not only Faulkner and Fitzgerald, but was to become the bane of a number of American authors: "The studies of literary alcoholism are inconclusive. Many of the best American writers of the twentieth century have had alcohol problems: Fitzgerald, Faulkner, O'Neill, O'Hara, Lardner, Hemingway, Lewis, Chandler, Hammett. There is evidently a connection between alcoholism and the creative personality" (187). Frederick Robert Karl echoes Bruccoli's critical observation on the connection between alcoholism and creative performance in the biography *William Faulkner: American Writer*:

> One of the most telling statistics is that, of the eight Americans who have won the Nobel Prize in literature, five were alcoholics or excessive drinkers: Faulkner, Eugene O'Neill, and Sinclair Lewis, with John Steinbeck and Ernest Hemingway not far behind. Among those who might have been competitive for the Nobel Prize are F. Scott Fitzgerald, Thomas Wolfe, Theodore Dreiser, Jack London, John Cheever, Robert Lowell, John Berryman, Wallace Stevens [. . .], Edmund Wilson, Thornton Wilder, and others. Careers have been curtailed or destroyed by drinking. (130)

In addition to observations on the writers' battle with alcoholism, Frederick Karl records that both Faulkner and Fitzgerald transmuted their personal experiences into art and identifies Estelle Oldham and Zelda Sayre, respectively, as the inspiration for much of Faulkner's and Fitzgerald's fiction:

> Faulkner found the means to transmute most personal problems into fiction. Rejection becomes one of his themes and subtexts. Estelle herself becomes transformed into many of his fictional portraits, as Fitzgerald used and reused Zelda. His growing family responsibilities become interwoven into his novels, which despite their often sensational scenes are deeply moralistic and ethical. His own sense of personal inadequacy becomes submerged in characters like Quentin and Darl, sensitive figures for whom life is too much. In nearly every respect, Faulkner found the means to use personal pressures as part of his professional life and, in the act, transform them into creative materials. (348-49)

The influence of Zelda Sayre and Estelle Oldham on Fitzgerald and Faulkner, respectively, extended to collaboration, as the writers had a collaborative literary history with their wives. Estelle's short story "Selvage," for instance, was revised and published by Faulkner in *Story* magazine (350-51 Karl). By the same token, a number of Zelda Sayre's magazine articles appeared under a joint by-line since magazine editors insisted upon it, deeming the pieces only marketable under Fitzgerald's name:

> [I]n 1927 [Sayre] sold three articles: "The Changing Beauty of Park Avenue" to *Harper's Bazaar*, "Looking Back Eight Years" to *College Humor*, and "Editorial on Youth" to *Photoplay* (published as "Paint and Powder" by the *Smart Set* in 1929 under Fitzgerald's by-line). Most of her work was published under the joint byline "F. Scott and Zelda Fitzgerald" because the magazines insisted on using his name. At first Zelda seemed amused that her writing was salable only with her husband's name on it; but as their marriage became openly competitive, Zelda resented the arrangement. (Bruccoli 260)

As literary contemporaries, Faulkner and Fitzgerald were undoubtedly acquainted with one another's work. Karl reports that Faulkner, when asked in 1955 about African American authors, likened the talent of Richard Wright and Ralph Ellison to that of both Hemingway and Fitzgerald as young men: "He says those two [Ellison and Wright] have the talent that both Hemingway and Fitzgerald had as young men" (919).

A shared literary agent, battles with alcoholism, careers in Hollywood are some of the biographical links between the two authors William Faulkner and F. Scott Fitzgerald. Likewise, their literary works may be linked thematically as well as imagistically. One thematic parallel between the authors has been adumbrated in part by Frederick Karl in his biographical work *William Faulkner:*

> This inversion of values, in which the man of faith is deemed a grotesque by a society reversing truth and falsehood, accommodated Faulkner's growing sense of irony, his own use of "grotesques" to carry his sense of society reversal of values. In this, progress is retrograde, success is failure, advancement an aspect of decline, and high position a sign of bad faith. Such ideas are commonplace now, but in the first quarter of the century, though while not new, they were still fresh, and they were the stuff of fiction, as also seen in Hemingway, Dreiser, and parts of Fitzgerald. (194-95)

Encapsulating the theme, i.e., an inversion of values, is the motif of bankruptcy that permeates the fiction of both Fitzgerald and Faulkner. On the theme of emotional bankruptcy, Matthew Bruccoli in his biographical work on Fitzgerald has written: "The concept of emotional bankruptcy became a key idea for

Fitzgerald. He believed that people have a fixed amount of emotional capital; reckless expenditure results in early bankruptcy, which leaves the person unable to respond to the events that require true emotion. Appropriately, Fitzgerald developed a theory of character in terms of a financial metaphor" (292). In the three-part series "The Crack-Up" that appeared in *Esquire* magazine, Fitzgerald referred to himself, aged 39 (70) as "a cracked plate" (75), having expended prematurely his emotional capital, as a result of hard living, to the extent that he felt "like a man overdrawing at his bank" (77): "I was living hard, too, but 'Up to forty-nine it'll be all right,' I said. 'I can count on that. For a man who's lived as I have, that's all you could ask'" (70). Accordingly, both Fitzgerald and Faulkner use the motif of bankruptcy as a barometer of character and, as can be gathered from Fitzgerald's comments in "The Crack-Up," of the ravages of time. On the latter, Faulkner considers Thomas Sutpen of *Absalom, Absalom!*, aged sixty (179), an existential victim of time whose moral accounts, similar to the Biblical Abraham, must be reconciled by his sons Henry Sutpen and Charles Bon:

> Maybe he knew then that whatever the old man had done, whether he meant well or ill by it, it wasn't going to be the old man who would have to pay the check; and now that the old man was bankrupt with the incompetence of age, who should do the paying if not his sons, his get, because wasn't it done that way in the old days? the old Abraham full of years and weak and incapable now of further harm, caught at last and the captains and the collectors saying, 'Praise the Lord, I have raised about me sons to bear the burden of mine iniquities and persecutions;' (325)

The short story "Babylon Revisited," by F. Scott Fitzgerald, is identified as a work that anticipates *Tender is the Night* in its calculation of time in moral terms (Lehan 144-45). In "Babylon Revisited," Charles Wales returns to Paris from Prague to re-claim his daughter Honoria, who is under the legal guardianship of her maternal aunt. Charlie has recovered from his alcoholism and has recovered too, after one and a half years, his fortune lost during "the crash" (633). However, the sister of Charlie's late wife, Marion, is reluctant to relinquish guardianship of her niece since she blames Charlie for the premature death of her sister Helen, whom he had drunkenly locked out of their home in 1929 prior to a snowstorm, thus precipitating the pneumonia that caused her death. Marion also fears Charlie's inevitable relapse, particularly as "ghosts out of the past" (622) arrive unexpectedly at the Peters home. Richard D. Lehan observes that the scene of Lincoln's "'swinging Honoria back and forth like a pendulum from side to side' (631) is an obvious symbol of time; Charles is the victim of his past; and 'Babylon Revisited' reveals--as much as any other story—that Fitzgerald believed that time is given to us in trust. The past lies about Charles Wales like ashes, and, because he is no longer 'young,' he has no dreams to buoy up the future" (145-46). The Great Crash, too, according to Lehan, finds an equation in Charlie's moral bankruptcy: "As the financial recklessness of the twenties led to the Great Crash, so did Charlie's reckless living lead to his physical and emotional breakdown, the loss of Honoria (his honor), and his feeling of regret and guilt about his misspent past" (145).

Indeed, the self-destructiveness of Charlie Wales finds an echo in both Abe North and Dick Diver of *Tender Is the Night*, by F. Scott Fitzgerald. Abe North, once a devoted musician, now leads a life of dissipation, which, in turn, leads to imbroglios with foreign police and strangers. Abe North is characterized in Book One as suicidal in nature: "All of them were conscious of the solemn dignity that flowed from him, of his achievement, fragmentary, suggestive and surpassed. But they were frightened at his survivant will, once a will to live, now become a will to die" (82-83). Unsurprisingly, his life ends violently, as it is reported by Tommy Barban that North "was beaten to death in a speakeasy in New York" (199). The harrowing fate of Abe North becomes iconic of the payment exacted as well by Dick Diver for his recklessness that stems from alcoholism, "Of course we make him pay afterward for his moment of superiority, his moment of impressiveness" (108). Diver's professional casualties are further evidence of decline; Dick Diver deteriorates from a brilliant psychologist to one whose patients can no longer be entrusted to his care. The parents of an Australian patient, Von Cohn Morris, being treated for alcoholism, remove him from the premises after the son had disclosed to them that Dr. Diver himself has a drinking problem (253):

> "Not once, but twice Von Cohn says he has smelt liquor on your breath. I and my lady have never touched a drop of it in our lives. We hand Von Cohn to you to be cured, and within a month he twice smells liquor on your breath! What kind of cure is that there?"

To be sure, Dick Diver's problems with alcohol are autobiographical, as Bruccoli notes in *Some Sort of Epic Grandeur* that not only did Fitzgerald have "the reputation of being one of the heaviest drinkers among American writers" (185), but "his preferred tipple was straight gin, which gave him the quickest lift and which he thought was difficult to detect on his breath" (185). In *Tender is the Night,* following the removal of the patient by his parents, Dick Diver concedes that in "[tippling] with gin in the afternoon," he had provoked the current crisis:

> But what absorbed Dick after the disappearance of the caravan was the question as to what extent he had provoked this. He drank claret with each meal, took a nightcap, generally in the form of hot rum, and sometimes he tippled with gin in the afternoon—gin was the most difficult to detect on the breath. He was averaging a half-pint of alcohol a day, too much for his system to burn up. (254)

Fitzgerald's own inertia following publication of *The Great Gatsby* may be attributed to dissipation caused by the Fitzgeralds' riotous lifestyle (Donaldson 136): "What really worried him was the remarkable output of 1919-1924: three novels including *Gatsby,* about fifty stories, a play, and numerous articles. That spirit, he feared, 'might have taken all [he] had to say too early,' especially considering that he and Zelda were then 'living at top speed in the gayest worlds [they] could find.'"

Inertia, caused by sloth rather than the dissipation characteristic of Americans during the twenties, as described by Fitzgerald in *Tender,* has precipitated the moral bankruptcy of the minister Gail Hightower in William Faulkner's *Light in August.* Entrapped in an ancestral past of Confederate glory and defeat, "the dogma he was supposed to preach all full of galloping cavalry and defeat and glory just as when he tried to tell them on the street about the galloping horses, it in turn would get all mixed up with absolution and choirs. . ." (57), Hightower, as a result of his romanticized delusions, forsakes his wife and ministry. His indifference leads indirectly to the suicide of his wife, which creates a public scandal and forces Hightower's removal from the church and exclusion from the community. His persecution at the hands of the community Hightower considers the debt paid for immunity, as he resists the attempts of his friend Byron Bunch to involve him in the affairs of Lena Grove, a twenty-year-old female who has traveled from Alabama to Jefferson in search of Lucas Burch, the father of her unborn child: "'I wont. I wont. I have bought immunity.' It was like words spoken aloud now: reiterative, patient, justificative: 'I paid for it. I didn't quibble about the price, No man can say that. I just wanted peace; I paid them their price without quibbling'" (293).

Characters that populate Faulkner's universe are often plagued by an inertia that renders them psychologically impotent. Testimony to their inertia is their depiction as voyeurs, or spectators. Robert Dale Parker writes in *Faulkner and the Novelistic Imagination* that the novel *Sanctuary* concerns watchers and the watchers being watched:

> The novel even begins in voyeurism, with an incomprehensible scene of unprovoked terror, as Popeye simply watches Horace for two hours. Temple is introduced as the incessant object of other people's watching at the university, and when she and Gowan crash into the tree, Popeye and Tommy step out of the bushes, watching (28-29, 38). Tommy watches Temple innocently, with no sense of the terror his peeping provokes [. . .].Popeye watches Goodwin and Tommy watch Temple; then, when Goodwin sends Tommy as emissary to Temple, she converts him to her guardian and has him watch Goodwin. (72)

Faulkner suggests that the inertia of Hightower, as well as that of the community, in *Light in August* is indicative of a moral collapse, made evident by the twin murders of Joanna Burden and Joe Christmas that are sanctioned by the apathy of the community. Hightower's obesity is the outward symbol of Hightower's inertia. He is described as "in his shirt sleeves, tall, with thin blackclad legs and spare, gaunt arms and shoulders, and with that flabby and obese stomach like some monstrous pregnancy" (291). Lena Grove's presence in the novel provides minor characters such as Gail Hightower and the Hineses a Second Chance of redemption for their moral failures. In the words of Lyall H. Powers: "Lena Grove and her 'Joey' have given these people the chance to demonstrate their capacity to love. Indeed, they are really thus given their Second Chance, for it is a chance to compensate for their collective failure to accord true charity to Joe Christmas and hence the chance to gain something very like redemption for themselves" (99).

Frederick Karl has identified in the biography *William Faulkner* the thematic link between Fitzgerald and Faulkner, namely, the inversion of moral values; however, that inversion, inasmuch as it represents a divorce from established logical principles, may be considered evidentiary as well of the absurd, as described by Albert Camus in *The Myth of Sisyphus* (29-30). In other words, the face of reality is the obverse of expectations, as in the proffer of a recyclable Folgers Classic Roast coffee tin for bid at a garage sale in the hope of a $.50 net sum or, in a more profound sense, the trampling of individual rights under the guise of a protection of animal rights or other interests.

Paradigmatic of the moral bankruptcy of characters, as portrayed by Fitzgerald, Morrison, and Faulkner, is not only the inertia of some of the characters, but the practice of incest. An antinomy, provided its breach of a given set of assumptions, namely, the parent as protector, incest may also be considered evidentiary of the absurd, as defined by Camus. The nervous collapse of Nicole Warren is caused by the act of incest committed by Devereux Warren, following her mother's death. Linda C. Pelzer identifies the act of incest as symptomatic of the inversion of civilized values:

> Fitzgerald uses the motif of incest to make clear the destructive power of the violence and sexual disorder he depicts. Devereux Warren's incestuous act of selfish possession of his daughter Nicole victimizes the vulnerable and innocent, mocking the very notion of parental love and protection, one of the most sacred trusts of virtually every civilization. Warren then compounds his crime first by refusing to accept responsibility for his actions, thereby hindering Nicole's treatment, and then by using his vast fortune to avoid punishment. Because Warren can afford the expense of Swiss sanitoriums and brilliant psychiatrists who care only about their patient's recovery, he can even purchase a certain measure of self-absolution. He has, after

all, provided Nicole with the best care to heal her wounded psyche.
(120)

By comparison, the psychological decline, or nervous collapse, of May in
Love, by Toni Morrison, coincides with Cosey's second marriage:"Events begun
in 1942 with her father-in-law's second marriage heaped up quickly throughout
the war and long after until, disoriented by her struggle against a certain element
in her house and beyond it, she became comic" (96). Indicative of her decline is
her paranoia that drives her to bury the deed of Cosey's Hotel and Resort as she
fears that Cosey's alliance with the sheriff will deem him a traitor to the movement: "She is frantic with worry that the hotel and everybody in it are in immedi-
ate danger. That city blacks have already invaded Up Beach, carrying lighter
fluid, matches, Molotov cocktails; shouting, urging the locals to burn Cosey's
Hotel and Resort to the ground and put the Uncle Toms, the sheriff's pal, the
race traitor out of business" (80). Throughout May's loyalty has been to Cosey
rather than her daughter Christine. Thus when Cosey proposes that Christine be
sent to boarding school in order to defuse the volatile situation in the household,
May does not object. The perceived betrayal creates a rift between the two
friends Heed and Christine as well as between mother and daughter: "[May's]
whole life was making sure those Cosey men had what they wanted. The father
more than her own daughter" (102).

Particular to the literature by Faulkner and Fitzgerald is the perspective that
dysfunction frequently cannot be separated from caste. In both *The Great Gatsby*
and *Tender is the Night,* Fitzgerald makes the point that money sanitizes and
serves to absolve the wealthy from responsibility. Daisy Buchanan, after the hit-
and-run accident in Gatsby's car that fatally wounded Myrtle Wilson, remains
silent and indirectly implicates Gatsby in the murder of Myrtle, as it was Daisy,
not Gatsby, who was driving Gatsby's car. Thus she is no different from, among
others, the "Leeches" (65) who attend Gatsby's lavish parties and take advantage
of Gatsby's largesse. In the same vein, Nicole Diver in *Tender is the Night* ra-
tionalizes her affair with Tommy Barban as innocent and thus unlikely to result
in repercussions: "All summer she had been stimulated by watching people do
exactly what they were tempted to do and pay no penalty for it—moreover, in
spite of her intention of no longer lying to herself, she preferred to consider that
she was merely feeling her way and that at any moment she could withdraw"
(291-92). Dick Diver, in his marriage to Nicole Warren, has become an instrument of the wealthy and, subsequently, has begun to adopt the credo of absolution provided by wealth. Witness Dick Diver's illegal removal of the body of
Jules Peterson from Rosemary's room in order to avoid public scandal and to
protect the innocent image of Rosemary. Diver's servitude to the wealthy is
made implicit in Fitzgerald's alliance of servitude and exquisite manners. On
Abe North, the fictional double of Diver, Fitzgerald writes: "A little later, with the
exquisite manners of the alcoholic that are like the manners of a prisoner or a family ser-

vant, he said good-by to an acquaintance, and turning around discovered that the bar's great moment was over as precipitately as it had begun" (103). Warren identifies as a symptom of Nicole's psychosis the accusation of a valet, or servant, as her molester. The social and ethical breach signified by the link presages that represented in the relationship between Dick Diver, who has been aligned with the valet via his servanthood to the wealthy, namely, the Warrens via his role as psychiatrist to Nicole.

Dick Diver's affair with Rosemary Hoyt, similar to his relationship with Nicole, is of pathological origin. Rosemary is described as "almost eighteen, nearly complete, but the dew was still on her" (4). Importantly, she has starred in the movie "Daddy's Girl" and, in conversation with Dick Diver, identifies her father, similar to Dick Diver, as a doctor (63). Contained in the name symbolism of "Rosemary" is the coinage of youth, as the shrub rosemary is valued for its mint, the latter made synonymous in *Tender Is the Night* with infancy. In a veiled reference to Rosemary, Dick disavows her because of her youth: "I don't like ickle durls. They smell of castile soap and peppermint. When I dance with them, I feel as if I'm pushing a baby carriage" (172). Richard D. Lehan notes further that at the time of Dick's affair with Rosemary, one he identifies as "symbolic incest" (132), Dick is "already used up, and this scene reveals how completely he has abandoned his self-discipline, a discipline that has obviously been open to attack from the beginning" (131). Similarly, Linda C. Pelzer has argued the dysfunctional nature of Dick Diver's marriage to Nicole Warren, as well as his relationship with Rosemary Hoyt, another "Daddy's girl," namely, that both are demonstrative of the Oedipus/Electra Complex to the extent that they represent, respectively, a betrayal of professional ethics and youthful idealism: "When Dick, following his release from the Roman prison, wants 'to explain to these people how I raped a five-year-old girl' (235), he reveals his perception of the criminal nature of his affair with Rosemary and even, perhaps, of his marriage to Nicole. It is as incestuous as Devereux Warren's and thus makes him Warren's moral equivalent" (128). The writer would contend further that evidentiary of the pathological relationship between Dick and Nicole and Devereux Warren is the self-same response that the two elicit from Nicole. She accuses both Dick and family members of perpetuating the delusions that have hampered rather than improved her mental health: "It's always a delusion when I see what you don't want me to see" (190; 123)

Interwoven in Faulkner's novel *Sanctuary* is also the theme of the Oedipal/Electra Complex. Popeye, "the embodiment of crawling, sleazy evil" (Minter 372), murders Tommy, who sought to protect Temple Drake from the advances of Lee Goodwin, and both rapes and kidnaps her. The eighteen-year-old Drake, the daughter of a judge, however, identifies with that evil and, in an act of transference, similar to the transference of Nicole's affection for her father onto Dick (*Tender* 139), expresses her ambiguous feelings of love and hatred for her father whom Popeye, referred to as "Daddy," comes to represent. Critics have identified the Oedipal/Electra dynamic at work in terms of Temple Drake's relationship with her father. Frederick R. Karl in his work *William Faulkner: American Writer* argues that

> In a kind of inversion of the Freudian family romance, [Temple Drake] has repudiated her high birth and sought out a lower, more satisfactory one; and Popeye becomes the father-lover replacement, with a vengeance. In this respect, he satisfies her desires for revenge on a family and background which, evidently, provided little sustenance, or failed to perceive who and what she was growing into. Only in Popeye's hands, . . . does she find her center—however perversely, they fill her emptiness, and once more we are returned to the idea of a sanctuary which serves none of its moral functions. (367)

Characteristic of the Oedipal/Electra Complex in *Love,* by Toni Morrison, is Junior's obsession with Bill Cosey, one that parallels that of the Cosey women. The neglect by Junior's mother and abandonment by the GI father Ethan Payne, Jr. only exacerbated Junior's desire for a father. Thus when she answered a newspaper ad in the local newspaper, placed by Heed, for a personal assistant, Billy Cosey, referred to as "her Good Man" (117), became a substitute father onto whom she transferred her childhood fantasies:

> This was the right place and there he was, letting her know in every way it had been waiting for her all along. As soon as she saw the stranger's portrait she knew she was home. She had dreamed him the first night, had ridden his shoulders through an orchard of green Granny apples heavy and thick with boughs. (60)

In keeping with this theme of inversion, e.g., "inversion of the Freudian family romance" (Karl 367), the convoluted, or incestuous, relations of Thomas Sutpen of *Absalom, Absalom!* may be cited as one of the reasons, in Rosa Coldfield's estimation, *"God let us lose the War: that only through the blood of our men and the tears of our women could He stay this demon and efface his name and lineage from the earth"* (11). Widowed by the death of Ellen Coldfield, Thomas Sutpen proposes marriage to Rosa Coldfield, a marriage that, if consummated, would have made Ellen and Judith Sutpen both aunt/stepmother and niece/stepdaughter. Thus incest is attributable in *Absalom, Absalom!* to Sutpen's fiendish pursuit of class. That is, the choice of a union with the Coldfields was driven by Sutpen's desire for the respectability denied him when, as an eleven-year-old, he had sought to deliver a message to the planter from his father and was denied entry to the planter's home by a servant. To achieve that respectability, Sutpen had compromised himself dearly, putting aside his first octoroon wife and Charles Bon, the offspring of that union, and making the indecent proposal at the age of 59 to the twenty-year-old Rosa Coldfield after Charles Bon, in a vain attempt to claim his birthright, had proposed marriage to Judith Sutpen, his sister, thus setting in motion the destructive cycle of events that was to lead to the destruction of the design. Faulkner makes the point throughout *Absalom, Absalom!* that Sutpen's tragedy has stemmed from the failure to recognize that his design has been built on "the shifting sands of opportunism and moral brigandage" (260) and hence destined to implode:

> [I]t was that innocence again, that innocence which believed that the
> ingredients of morality were like the ingredients of pie or cake and
> once you had measured them and balanced them and mixed them and
> put them into the oven it was all finished and nothing but pie or cake
> could come out. (263)

Apparent is Morrison's signification on *Absalom, Absalom!*. Parody, as defined by Henry Louis Gates, Jr. in *The Signifying Monkey,* "[distorts], with the minimum of verbal or literal change, to convey a new sense, often incongruous with the form" (107). Congruent with *Absalom, Absalom!* is the following. Both Sutpen and Cosey have lost a son; one through disavowal; the other, death. The loss becomes the catalyst for another attempt at progeny. The difference is that Heed proves to be barren. Thus Morrison pursues *reductio ad absurdum* Sutpen's marriage proposal to Rosa Coldfield, which amounts to a trade: marriage in return for a son. The marriage between Cosey and Heed likewise is tantamount to a trade, as Cosey assumes the role of guardian/father/owner. The language, as used by Heed in conversation with Christine, is telling:

> You know May wasn't much of a mother to me.
> At least she didn't sell you.
> She gave me away. (184)

The in breeding integral to caste in Faulkner, Fitzgerald, and Morrison may be viewed as indicative of the narcissism associated not only with class but also with race. In *Tender,* a patient at the well-appointed clinic in Zurich, now afflicted with eczema, is described in terms of a glamour that is in-bred: "The frontiers that artists must explore were not for her, ever. She was fine-spun, inbred—eventually she might find rest in some quiet mysticism. Exploration was for those with a measure of peasant blood, those with big thighs and thick ankles who could take punishment as they took bread and salt, on every inch of flesh and spirit" (185). The eczema patient was inspired by Zelda Sayre who likewise suffered from eczema, a condition Fitzgerald had diagnosed as the result of a defective immune system. In a January 1931 letter to Dr. Ford, Fitzgerald had written: "Mrs. Fitzgerald *encourages* her nervous system to absorb the continually distilled poison. Then the exterior world, represented by your personal influence, by the stock of Eglantine, by the sight of her daughter causes *an effort of the will toward reality, she is able to force this poison out of her nerve cells* and the process of elimination is taken over again by her skin" (Bruccoli 311). The correlation of the two females betokens an infirmity, read moral pollution, whose source is deep-rooted. In Faulkner's *Absalom, Absalom!* the disintegration of the Sutpen dynasty, a microcosm of the South, becomes interwoven with Sutpen's refusal to acknowledge Charles Bon as his son, a refusal emblematic of the South's refusal to acknowledge the fraternity of the black man. In the words of Ilse Dusoir Lind: "The Sutpen tragedy is the means of conveying the larger social tragedy. In its broader outlines, the Sutpen tragedy is in many ways analogous to the social. Sutpen had two sons: one white, the other Negro; fratricide resulted. The Civil War, too, was a fratricidal conflict caused by denial of the Negro" (293). In correspondent fashion, the adoption of white standards by Bill Cosey's progenitor, David Robert Cosey, links father and son to an exploitative slave past that reduces individuals to commodities. Vida Gibbons speaks glowingly of Bill Cosey since he, in her view, rescued her from the "plantation" by hiring her as a clerk at Cosey's Hotel and Resort (*Love* 18; 33). Bill Cosey's incestuous union with Heed, a female from Up Beach, becomes synonymous therefore to the social dysfunction mirrored in *Absalom, Absalom!*.

The character Quentin Compson, who serves as a narrator in *Absalom, Absalom!*, re-enacts in his relation to Candace Henry Sutpen's narcissistic obsession with Judith. The character Henry murders his half-brother Bon to prevent the marriage between Bon and Judith, Bon's half-sister. Irwin contends, though, that the murder of Bon by Henry is tantamount to suicide since the act symbolizes the attempted exorcism by Henry of his own demons or incestuous impulses. The genesis of the doubling motif Irwin locates in the myth of Narcissus that destroys all that is inimical to the idealized self: "In this case the ego's towering self-love and consequent overestimation of its own worth lead to the guilty rejection of all instincts and desires that don't fit its ideal image of itself. The rejected instincts and desires are cast out of the self, repressed internally only to return externally personified in the double, where they can be at once vicariously satisfied and punished" (33). Quentin's eventual suicide John T. Irwin also relates in *Doubling and Incest/Repetition and Revenge: A Speculative Reading of Faulkner* to Quentin's sense of failure to rescue Caddy from a doomed marriage to Herbert Head; likewise, to assume the masculine role expected of him by society:

> In Quentin's world young men lose their virginity as soon as possible, but their sisters keep their virginity until they are married. The reversal of this situation in the case of Quentin and Candace makes Quentin feel that his sister has assumed the masculine role and that he has assumed the feminine role. Quentin's obsessive concern with Candace's loss of virginity is a displaced concern with his own in-

ability to lose his virginity, for, as both novels clearly imply, Quentin's virginity is psychological impotence. Approaching manhood,
Quentin finds himself unable to assume the role of a man. (38)

The psychological impotence of Quentin in *The Sound and the Fury* and in
Absalom, Absalom! is conveyed imagistically through another fictional double
Benjy of *The Sound and the Fury* whose obsession with Candace parallels Quentin's own obsession: "Quentin's brother Benjy is in certain respects a double of
Quentin—in his arrested, infantile state, in his obsessive attachment to Candace,
in his efforts to keep Candace from becoming involved with anyone outside the
family, Benjy is a copy of Quentin, and when their brother Jason has Benjy
gelded for attempting to molest a little girl, Benjy's physical condition doubles
Quentin's psychological impotence. . ." (Irwin 51-52).

Rooted in the obsessiveness of the characters Quentin and Benjy, respectively, is a proprietary claim to the body of the female that obtains its full expression in "The Bear" of *Go Down, Moses,* by William Faulkner. The grandson of
Carothers McCaslin, Ike McCaslin, inspects archaic family ledgers and discovers
buried therein the truth of the family's miscegenated and incestuous blood lines:
Carothers had fathered a daughter Tomasina with the slave Eunice and had fathered also a son, Terrel, or Tomey's Terrel, with his daughter Tomasina, thus
becoming both slaveholder-grandfather-father to Tomasina who had died giving
birth to Tomey's Terrel. Evidentiary of Terrel's miscegenated parentage is the
one thousand dollars that Carothers bequeaths to Terrel and his progeny in a
futile attempt to balance accounts: "[Carothers] made no effort to punctuate or
construct whatever, just as he made no effort either to explain or obfuscate the
thousand-dollar legacy to the son of an unmarried slave-girl, to be paid only at
the child's coming-of-age" (269). In order to escape "old Carothers' doomed and
fatal blood" (293), Ike repudiates the legacy to which he is entitled "on the accident of [his] own paternity" (269). The upshot is that incest in literature by
Faulkner, interpreted within the context of American history and the institution
of slavery, becomes intertwined with narcissistic claims to power and domina-
tion. According to Thadious M. Davis:

> Carothers exercises absolute power in an incestuous narcissistic vio-
> lation. As his property, Tomasina must surrender her will in obedi-
> ence to his. Her body is thus marked incest victim and is re-marked a
> second time as doubly the property of the father, though this specific
> incest narrative is generally left out of the critical discourse on
> Faulkner's usage of incest in his fiction. (92-93)

Gerrie Reaves argues in her article "The Slip in the Ballet Slipper: Illusion
and the Naked Foot" that the dancer's foot is a synecdoche for the dancer's body
(252). The ideal is the "lotus-like" foot that in x-ray images resembles the bound

foot of the Chinese female that for centuries became a measure of beauty and desirability: "Chinese women, primarily Han Chinese women, underwent this unspeakably brutal procedure to create the invaluable asset, the lotus foot, which would endow a woman with beauty, and therefore status and a marriage of material security" (254). According to Reaves, ballerinas have confessed to subjecting themselves to plastic surgery in order to possess the lotus foot: "[D]ancers go so far as to have plastic surgery to break the arch of the foot and realign the bones in a more perfect arch and pointe, a measure that parallels the tortures of foot binding" (256). The slipper, which forms a second skin for the dancer, conceals the mutilation wrought to the body in order to achieve perfection; simultaneously, it conceals the oppressive practices associated with its origin: "The revealing intrusive-obtrusive ballet shoe is a unifier, a guarantee of coherence and a diffuser of the threat of castration or loss of power" (254).

Importantly, Temple Drake of Faulkner's *Sanctuary* is described as wearing "slippers" (68). Given the circumstances surrounding her depiction, the footwear may be construed as "high-heeled slippers." She had been described as the date of Gowan Stevens who was to escort her to a dance at the University she attended. Gowen's intoxication en route, however, had led to an accident while the two were headed to a baseball game in Starkville. The inutility of the "slipper" also helps to define it: "'Putty hard walkin, aint it?' [the man in overalls] said. 'Ef she'll take off them high heel shoes, she'll get along better'" (39). Reaves identifies the correlation between the high-heeled shoe and the slipper in her article "The Slip in the Ballet Slipper: Illusion and the Naked Foot." In her view, the "teetering" gait of the high-heeled wearer simulates that of the ballerina, or the "lotus gait":

> The "wobbling" or "quivering," "tottering" or "teetering" seen in the gait of someone in very high or slender heels not only resembles the "willow walk," the "golden lotus limp," or the "lotus gait," but mimics some ballet steps that fetishize the foot and emphasize its vulnerability. (257)

In light of the significance equated to the "lotus foot," and, by extension, the "lotus gait," Rosemary of Fitzgerald's *Tender Is the Night* might be seen in a new light. Her beauty is attributable to her carriage, which is evocative of a ballerina: "When she walked she carried herself like a ballet-dancer, not slumped down on her hips but held up in the small of her back" (4). The quest for perfection explains, in part, the vulnerability of dancers to the condition anorexia nervosa. According to Reaves: "Given the struggle [. . .] in the professional ballet world, it is no surprise that ballet dancers are especially vulnerable to anorexia nervosa, a 'tempestuous warfare against [their bodies]'" (262). Consequently, the "slipper" becomes a metonym for that vulnerability (256).

To be sure, the vulnerability of Nicole in *Tender Is the Night* is clear, as she, at the age of 11, had been grief-stricken following the loss of her mother. Her emotional fragility, ironically, had led instead to her violation at the hands of her father Devereux Warren. He had confessed to Doctor Dohmler, the psychiatrist to whom he had gone for the treatment of his daughter: "'After her mother died when she was little she used to come into my bed every morning, sometimes she'd sleep in my bed. I was sorry for the little thing. Oh, after that, whenever we went places in an automobile or a train we used to hold hands'" (129).

The correlation between vulnerability and rape is apparent in *Love* as well. Christine had split with Comrade Fruit following the conspiracy of silence over the rape of a student volunteer by one of the group's members. Inasmuch as the raped was white and the raper black, the offense was not among the list of Unacceptable Behavior deserving of expulsion or reprimand, particularly as a history of past offenses became a license for present behavior. In a deft stroke, Morrison not only reveals the double standards of some organizations that agitate for freedom yet ignore women's rights but likewise questions the ethics of those who pursue policies that subordinate women to political efficacy (166-67):

> This assault against a girl of seventeen was not even a hastily added
> footnote to his [Fruit's] list of Unacceptable Behavior since the raped
> one did not belong to him. Christine did the racial equation: the rapee
> is black and the raper white; both are black; both are white. Which
> combination influenced Fruit's decision?

The narcissism associated with color caste, as opposed to race and gender, figures prominently in the novel *Paradise,* by Toni Morrison, one rich with Faulknerian cadences, according to one reviewer: "The opening chapter, 'Ruby,' contains wonderful writing. Faulknerian, with rich, evocative and descriptive passages, it is a haunting introduction to the repressed individuality that stalks 'so clean and bless a mission'" (377). "Eight-rock" is the designation given to the nine founding families of the all-black town Ruby. Banished from settling in Fairly, Oklahoma (188), due to their dark features, their darkness was to become in Haven, later renamed Ruby in memory of the twins' late sister, a badge of pride. Witness the community's ostracism of Patricia Best and her father Roger Best whose marriage to "a wife with no last name, a wife without people, a wife of sunlight skin, a wife who could pass for white" (197) was the first violation of the blood rule that forbade marriage outside the color line. At the annual Christmas pageant that re-enacts the turning away of Mary and Joseph at the inn and, concomitantly, the turning away of the nine families, commonly referred to as the "Disallowing," schoolteacher Patricia Best notices the exclusion of two of the nine founding families, possibly among them the Cato line, deemed of mixed origin. In an interview Morrison had observed that Paradise, predicated on color caste, was marked by its exclusivity:

> The isolation, the separateness, is always a part of any utopia. And it
> [the novel] was my meditation . . . and interrogation of the whole
> idea of paradise, the safe place, the place full of bounty, where no
> one can harm you. But, in addition to that, it's based on the notion of
> exclusivity. All paradises, all utopias are designed by who is not
> there, by the people who are not allowed in. (qtd. in Reames 21)

The narcissism practiced by the eight-rock families results not only in their intolerance of outsiders, but leads as well to their own extirpation, as the in-breeding among the eight-rock families leads to their diminution (217): "All those generations of 8-rocks kept going, just to end up narrow as bale wire?"

Incest in *The Bluest Eye*, by Toni Morrison, not only becomes symbolic of the narcissism associated with class and gender that subsequently produces insipidity, as gathered from Fitzgerald's description in *Tender Is the Night* of the eczema patient, but also of the moral collapse associated with the absurd. J. Brooks Bouson has written:

> *The Bluest Eye* has been described as a work that can make readers
> feel 'helpless and afraid' and also 'ache for remedy'. . . or as a work
> that offers readers 'no refuge from Morrison's anger'. . . or that uses
> 'obscenity' to shock the readers' 'sensibilities' and also urges readers
> to see the 'destructive absurdity' of American life and to recognize
> that 'the real horrors are still loose in the world.' (26-27)

A third generation progeny of a British nobleman, Sir Whitcomb, the mulatto Elihue Micah Whitcomb, a.k.a. Soaphead Church, may be described as one of those perceived as having "a weakening of faculties and a disposition toward eccentricity" (133) alleged to be the result of incestuous unions (133): "They blamed the flaw on intermarriage with the family; however, not on the original genes of the decaying lord. In any case, there were flukes." Soaphead Church, a charlatan who is also a child molester, tricks Pecola, who had come to him with the request for blue eyes, into believing that the sacrifice of the landlady's aged dog is needed in order to grant her wish. Thus the exploitation by Soaphead Church for his evil purposes confirms further Pecola's victimhood as she becomes the vehicle through which the community exorcises its shame and self-hatred.

An antithesis to Soaphead Church and similar characters in the literature is the creature identified by Faulkner as "a fyce" whose mongrelism, reflective of the Negro, ironically, renders it the most adaptable to its environment: "The fyce represents the creature who has coped with environment and is still on top of it, you might say. That he has—instead of sticking to his breeding and becoming a decadent degenerate creature, he has mixed himself up with the good stock where he picked and chose" (*Faulkner in the University* 37). Indeed, the dog produced "to stop Old Ben and hold him" (219) in "The Bear" is the mongrel Lion, "part mastiff, something of Airedale and something of a dozen other strains probably" (218), belonging to Sam Fathers, born of "a negro slave and a Chickasaw chief" (206), one whose endurance is comparable to the bear, or Old Ben, he has been trained to hunt: "Lion inferred not only courage and all else that went to make up the will and desire to pursue and kill, but endurance, the will and desire to endure beyond all imaginable limits of flesh in order to undertake and slay" (237). The mongrel Lion of *Go Down, Moses* is mirrored by Morrison in the Settlement dogs of *Love*. A motley assortment of mixed breeds, the Settlement dogs are "brilliant" hunters (55). Collectively, in both works, mongrelism becomes a motif for miscegenation.

Verily, the motif of incest in selected fiction by F. Scott Fitzgerald, William Faulkner, and Toni Morrison becomes paradigmatic not only of the narcissism associated with class, gender, color caste, and race consciousness, but likewise of the absurd illuminated by Faulkner, Fitzgerald, and Morrison, respectively, in the following: Devereux Warren and Dick Diver of Fitzgerald's *Tender Is the Night;* Thomas Sutpen of Faulkner's *Absalom, Absalom!;* Quentin Compson of *The Sound and the Fury;* Carothers McCaslin of *Go Down, Moses;* Bill Cosey of Morrison's *Love;* and Cholly Breedlove of *The Bluest Eye,* individuals who ignore sacred tenets and thus are rendered spiritually denuded.

Chapter 3

What's in a Name? The Custom Among African-Americans of Name Bestowal In Selected Fiction by Morrison, Hurston, and Angelou

The ten-year-old Maya in Angelou's *I Know Why the Caged Bird Sings* works in the kitchen of Mrs. Viola Cullinan assisting the cook that Mrs. Cullinan has re-named "Glory." Upon the advice of lady friends, "I'd call her Mary if I was you" (104), Mrs. Cullinan, having first mis-pronounced Marguerite's name, calling Maya "Margaret," gives up entirely and begins addressing Maya as "Mary" (105). Aware that she would not be allowed by Grandma Henderson to quit her job without justification, Maya confides in her brother Bailey who convinces her of a way to earn her dismissal with impunity, to destroy one of Mrs. Cullinan's favorite heirlooms, "Her favorite piece was a casserole shaped like a fish and the green glass coffee cups" (107). Maya's motivation has been anger for Mrs. Cullinan's refusal to acknowledge her humanity, or selfhood, by renaming her. Angelou describes in *I Know Why the Caged Bird Sings* the aversion by African Americans to being called "out of [their] name[s]":

> Every person I knew had a hellish horror of being "called out of his name." It was a dangerous practice to call a Negro anything that could be loosely construed as insulting because of the centuries of their having been called . . . jigs, . . . blackbirds, crows, boots and spooks. (106)

To name is to take possession of the named, to fix the identity of the named as Other and hence different (Benston 3). Thus African Americans, given the names of slaveholders, had bestowed upon them marks of enslavement. For African Americans, naming then becomes interwoven with self-creation and a reconstruction of a fragmented past, or, as Kimberly W. Benston has argued, "Naming is inevitably genealogical revisionism. All of Afro-American literature may be seen as one vast genealogical poem that attempts to restore continuity to the ruptures or discontinuities imposed by the history of black presence in America" (3). In *The Autobiography of Miss Jane Pittman,* by Ernest Gaines, "Ticey" changes her slave name to "Jane," an act that finds correspondence later in Ned's adoption of the name "Douglass" in honor of the abolitionist Frederick Douglass. The choice by Ned, Jane's adopted son, identifies him with the history of Black resistance, as invoked by the name. As Benston has written in the article "'I Yam What I Am': Naming and Unnaming in Afro-American Literature": "[T]he association with tropes of American heroism ('Lincoln,' 'Sherman,' etc.) was also an act of *naming,* a staging of self in relation to a specific context of revolutionary affirmation" (3) The reconstitution of a fragmented past is signaled as well by the choice of Biblical names that affirms an identity of oppression.

Unique to the fiction of Toni Morrison, as well as that of other African American authors such as Zora Neale Hurston, James Baldwin, and August Wilson, among others, is the bestowal of Biblical names upon characters, a practice in keeping with African American folk custom. Two popular Biblical names in Morrison's and Hurston's fiction, respectively, are those of the Hebrew prophets Zechariah and Ezekiel. The popularity of Hebrew names, such as Zechariah and Ezekiel in African American fiction, testifies not only to the spirituality of African Americans, but also to their identification with the Israelites who likewise were an orphaned and oppressed people.

The text of John Buddy's sermon in *Jonah's Gourd Vine* is the prophesy from the Lord of hosts to Zechariah of the restoration of the Israelites to Jerusalem after their purification by fire (Zechariah 13:9). Prior to their salvation, however, would be a two-part extinction with false prophets among the damned. Ironically, John Buddy, likewise heralded "a False Pretender" (200), preaches a sermon that takes as its text a chapter from Zechariah condemning false prophets (13: 4-5), thus calling into question his social being; the text that is supposed to exonerate him instead exposes him as the shaman he is, one who "wear[s] a rough garment to deceive."

The implicit parallel of the plight of African Americans to that of the Israelites is inscribed too in the popularity of names accorded the twelve disciples of Christ. John Buddy of *Jonah's Gourd Vine* is named "John" after one of the twelve disciples; so too is John of *Go Tell It on the Mountain,* by James Baldwin. Inasmuch as John Buddy of *Jonah's Gourd Vine* and John of *Go Tell It* relish the adulation that the disciple John eschews, the appellation is ironic. The irony is underscored as John Buddy confesses to being "a False Pretender" prior to his fatal car crash. To underscore the humility of the prophets, Christ, the Son of God, had accentuated the message over the messenger (John 8: 50). Given too that John of *Go Tell It* uses his "sainthood" as a weapon against his stepfather, rather than for the deliverance of the community, his "sainthood" is deemed likewise illusory.

The novel *Paradise* similarly echoes the story of the Israelites and their Exodus from Egypt. The extinction prophesied in the Bible becomes in Steward's ratiocination a call to sacrifice. The murmurings of the Israelites against their liberation eventuated in their disinheritance, as they and their descendants were deemed unworthy of the Covenant made with the nation of Israel. Subsequently, they were made to wander forty years in the Wilderness; only those of the third and fourth generations would reach the land of Canaan (Numbers 14: 12). The twin Steward, in accordance with Scripture, considers that K.D., his nephew, is among the generation marked for levying: "He wondered if that generation—Misner's and K.D.'s—would have to be sacrificed to get to the next one" (94). That adherence to prophecy thus becomes the pretext for the carnage at the end of the novel. The five Convent women, Mavis, Gigi, Pallas, Seneca, and Consolata, referred to as "detritus" (4), are eliminated by a band of nine men, led by Deek and Steward, who consider their presence in the town of nine founding families an abomination. The motto "Beware the Furrow of His Brow" enshrined on the Oven that popularly is believed to refer to their "Disallowing" (189), their banishment from the settlement in Fairly, Oklahoma, because of their black skin, instead becomes a veiled threat to those who commit the cardinal sins of race tampering or "whoredom" (Numbers 14: 33), as did Roger Best who married Delia, "a wife of sunlight skin" (197), and Consolata, a woman of "sundown skin" (223) who had an affair with the twin Deacon (217):

> It was clear as water. The generations had to be not only racially untampered with but free of adultery too. "God bless the pure and holy" indeed. That was the deal Zechariah had made during the humming prayer. It wasn't God's brow to be feared. It was his own, their own.

The Oven has become a memorial to the sacrifices of the founding families of Ruby, namely, "Big Daddy," or Rector Morgan, the twins' father, and "Big Papa," Zechariah Morgan, the twins' grandfather, who are described by the twin Deacon in terms that recall the Hebrews' peculiar bondage of constructing cities from the mortar made from straw with their own hands. Thus any change in the motto on the Oven, "Beware the Furrow of His Brow" (86), as the young agitate to do, is viewed as blasphemous:

> Deek looked steadily at Roy. "They dug the clay—not you. They carried the hod—not you." He turned his head to include Destry, Hurston and Caline Poole, Lorcas and Linda Sands. "They mixed the

mortar—not a one of you. They made good strong brick for that oven
when their own shelter was sticks and sod. You understand what I'm
telling you? And we respected what they had gone through to do it.
Nothing was handled more gently than the bricks those men—men,
hear me? Not slaves, ex or otherwise—the bricks those men made.
(85).

The twins' grandfather, "Big Papa," also Zechariah, as remembered by Steward,
summoned his son, Rector Morgan, also, "Big Daddy," into the forest where
they communed with the Lord and experienced a visitation from "a small man,
seemlike, too small for the sound of his steps" (97) who guided the wanderers
from Fairly, Oklahoma, to Ruby, their land of Caanan, a journey that recalls the
Lord of hosts' leadership of the Hebrews "in a pillar of cloud by day" and "in a
pillar of fire" by night (Exodus 13: 21). Furthermore, allusions are made in
Paradise by Morrison to the manna from Heaven, "morning bread" and "evening flesh" to sustain the hungry pilgrims, as recorded in the Old Testament
(Exodus 16: 8):

> Even as they watched, the man began to fade. When he was com-
> pletely dissolved, they heard the footsteps again, pounding in a direc-
> tion they could not determine: in back, to the left, now to the right. Or
> was it overhead? Then suddenly, it was quiet. Rector crept forward;
> Big Papa was crawling too, to see what the walker had left behind.
> Before they had gone three yards they heard a thrashing in the grass.
> There in the trap, bait and pull string undisturbed, was a guinea fowl.
> Male, with plumage to beat the band. (98)

The Old Testament prophet Zechariah also had the visions of a scattering of
nations as well as their unification. Thus the vision of the Biblical Zechariah and
the fictional one in Toni Morrison's *Paradise* coincides, namely, the one of the
Diaspora:

> Zacharias, father of John the Baptist? Or the Zechariah who had vi-
> sions? The one who saw scrolls of curses and women in baskets; the
> one who saw Joshua's filthy clothes changed into rich ones; who saw
> the result of disobedience. The punishment for not showing mercy or
> compassion was a scattering among all nations, and pleasant land
> made desolate. (192)

The "scattering," as referred to in *Paradise,* takes on both a literal and figurative
meaning connoting the pilgrimage of the founding families, their loss of children
(only four of Rector's children survived), as well as a diminution of fertility:
"Zechariah would have hated that. Moving would have been 'scattering' to him.
And he was right, for sure enough, from then on the fertility shriveled, even
while the bounty multiplied. The more money, the fewer children; the fewer
children, the more money to give the fewer children" (193).

Likewise, in Hurston's *Jonah's Gourd Vine*, the orphanage of John Buddy which renders him homeless calls to mind the dispersion of the Jews in the Old Testament, "And he answered me, These are the horns which have scattered Judah, Israel, and Jerusalem" (Zechariah 1:19). John Buddy is evicted at the age of 16 from the family home by his stepfather Ned Crittenden under the pretext of necessity (6), "Aw, Ah reckon we kin make it heah all right, when us don't have so many moufs in de meal barrel we kin come out ahead." Consequently, John Buddy, upon the advice of his mother Amy Crittenden, finds work with Alf Pearson of Notasulga (11), Amy's former slave master and the unacknowledged father of John Buddy. John Buddy returns from across the creek after landowner Shelby's refusal to take on the family as sharecroppers without John Buddy (40). After another falling out with stepfather Ned Crittenden, caused by John Buddy's insubordination, John Buddy returns over the creek to Alf Pearson's plantation (47). His movement, or odyssey, after his return from over the creek is the following: to Opelika and the tie camp (57) after a dispute with Duke over Exie (56); a return to Notasulga where he marries Lucy Potts (65); from Notasulga to Sanford (103) after Bud Potts, John Buddy's brother-in-law, swears out a warrant for his arrest following Potts' assault by John Buddy for Potts' confiscation of Lucy's marital bed as payment for a $3.00 debt (90); from Sanford to Eatonville (108); and from Eatonville to Plant City following his expulsion from Zion Hope by members of his congregation (186) as a result of the scandal created following his marriage to Hattie Tyson three months after the death of Lucy and the couple's recent divorce on the grounds of John Buddy's infidelity.

Interwoven with the vagabondage of the Jews, as replicated by Hurston in her fiction, was their bondage. Exemplary of the bondage of the Biblical Hebrews is their charge to make bricks but without the essential straw (Exodus 5: 10-11). The Israelites had been deemed a threat by the new king of Egypt due to their prolix nature. Consequently, the Egyptians felt threatened by engulfment (Exodus 1: 9-10) and dealt accordingly with the Israelites lest they join forces against them with their enemies.

The fates of the sharecroppers Amy and Ned Crittenden of Zora Neale Hurston's *Jonah's Gourd Vine* are similar. Amy and Ned Crittenden toil ceaselessly for no recompense as Rush Beasley cheats them out of their share, the worth of sixteen bales (6), after calculation of wages against expenditures. As the former slave owner of Amy says, "Those backwoods . . . folks over the creek make their living by swindling" (21). As a result of the swindle, Ned has to poach a yearling belonging to Beasley in order to feed his family. By all accounts, Ned and other family members have to hunt animals of the wild in order to survive (45). The mule becomes a symbol in Hurston's *Their Eyes Were Watching God* not only of African American bondage, but also of female bondage. Nanny tells Janie (29): "De . . . woman is de mule uh de world so far as Ah can see. Ah been prayin' fuh it tuh be different wid you." Subsequently, Killicks, Janie's first husband, aims to secure a second mule "gentled up so even uh woman kin handle him" (46) in an attempt to break Janie's spirit. Of Joe Starks, Janie's second husband, Janie has this to say: that he, in effect, attempted to "[squeeze] and [crowd out] mah own mind . . . tuh make room for yours in me" (133). The analogy of the mule to oppression is evidenced in its liberation from the abuse and deprivation to which it has been subjected by the largesse of Joe Starks (91-92).

   In the article "The Harlem Ghetto," James Baldwin recognized the following affinity between Blacks and Jews. As Leeming reports in his biography on Baldwin: "Jews and blacks, he wrote, have a natural alliance based on racial oppression. The black church has traditionally expressed its longing for freedom in the metaphors of the Old Testament Jews. Yet the realities of racial discrimination—applied to both Jews and blacks—mean that for the child growing up in Harlem, the Jew is often the landlord demanding his payment" (51).

   Parallels between the historical African American bondage and the Biblical Hebrew bondage are contained as well in James Baldwin's *Go Tell It on the Mountain.* Florence identifies the story of the Hebrews and their suffrage as one that held significance to the long-suffering Blacks, such as her mother, who had grown up during slavery and who had considered their deliverance imminent; the periodic slave uprisings were interpreted therefore as precursors to their ultimate liberation:

> "slaves done ris," was whispered in the cabin and at the masters' gates: slaves in another country had fired the masters' houses and fields and dashed their children to death against the stones. "Another slave in Hell," Bathesheba might say one morning, shoving the pickaninnies away from the great porch: a slave had killed his master, or his overseer, and had gone down to Hell to pay for it. "I ain't got long to stay here," someone crooned beside her in the fields, someone who had gone by morning on his journey north. All these signs, like the plagues with which the Lord had afflicted Egypt, only hardened the hearts of these people against the Lord. (71)

   In another parallel to the Israelites, Gabriel Grimes, an evangelical minister in James Baldwin's *Go Tell It on the Mountain,* relates the sinfulness of the unfaithful to the darkness of the wilderness that engulfed the Hebrews during their forty years of wandering in the Wilderness of Sin prior to reaching the land of Canaan (Exodus 16:35). The irony, though, is that Gabriel, similar to the minister John Buddy in Hurston's *Jonah's Gourd Vine,* is among the wicked inasmuch as he persecutes his stepson John Grimes for his illegitimacy albeit he has likewise sired with Esther an illegitimate son Royal:

> Behind them was the darkness, nothing but the darkness, and all around them destruction, and before them nothing but the fire—a

bastard people, far from God, singing and crying in the wilderness! (137)

Further evidence of Baldwin's re-creation of the Biblical story of the Jews is the portraiture of John Grimes in *Go Tell It on the Mountain* as Moses. He is the fourteen-year-old in whom family members hold their aspirations. For example, as Elizabeth Grimes gives to her son John the coins to celebrate his birthday, she tells him (32), "You going to be a mighty fine man, you know that? Your mama's counting on you." As an exceptional student in school, John had been singled out also by school administrators as a future race leader: "He might become a Great Leader of His people. John was not much interested in his people and still less in leading them anywhere, but the phrase so often repeated rose in his mind like a great brass gate, opening outward for him on a world where people did not live in the darkness of his father's house" (19). The imagery that surrounds John, namely, Baldwin's reference to the divine, or supernatural, rod of Moses also suggests a link between the two (196):

> [John] thought of the mountaintop, where he longed to be, where the sun would cover him like a cloth of gold, would cover his head like a crown of fire, and in his hands he would hold a *living rod*. But this was no mountain where John lay, here, no crown. And the *living rod* was uplifted in other hands. (emphasis added)

Not only is John aligned with the Hebrew leader Moses, but a central metaphor—Jacob's wrestling with an angel—encapsulates the internal conflict among a number of the characters between the carnal and the spiritual, or the body and the soul; likewise, the bid by John, an archetype of the African American, for his natural birthright. Jacob, son of Issac, who was son of Abraham, had falsely laid claim to his older twin Esau's birthright. To escape the wrath of Esau, Jacob had fled to Laban (Genesis 27: 43). He was renamed Israel after having successfully wrestled with the Lord's angel. In *Go Tell It on the Mountain,* John is the elder of two sons; however, due to his illegitimacy, he is not favored by Gabriel. Instead, the incorrigible Roy is the "apple of his eye" while the elder son John is used as a scapegoat by Gabriel for his own guilt. Witness Gabriel's explosion against John after Roy has been knifed by some white boys with whom he has gotten into a scrape. According to Gabriel's logic, the race John had favored had betrayed him by violence against his brother: "'You see?' came now from his father. 'It was white folks, some of them white folks *you* like so much that tried to cut your brother's throat'" (45). To some extent, *Go Tell It on the Mountain* can be read as an unrequited love story, as the illegitimate son John will forever seek his father's love, or birthright, and will forever be denied it given that Gabriel views him as an unnatural heir to his birthright in the same manner that Esau was robbed of his legitimate birthright. As recompense to

Esau, however, Abraham prophesied dominion over his tormentors (Genesis 27:40).

The ultimate dominion of John is foretold in *Go Tell It on the Mountain*. The fourteen-year-old John Grimes experiences a religious conversion on his birthday. On the one hand, his becoming one of the "saints" represents his bid for the affection denied him by Gabriel. On the other, his becoming one of the "saints" represents his attempt to thwart Gabriel's dominance by becoming himself one of the elect. At the very least, his conversion successfully puts Gabriel in checkmate as it renders John, by his magnetism as a young prophet, capable of eclipsing the fifty-six-year-old Gabriel who has become "a kind of fill-in speaker, a holy handyman" (51). The symbol of "the rod" identifiable with the supernatural power of Moses, indeed, underscores the rivalry between the two (197). Michel Fabre in the article "Fathers and Sons in Baldwin's *Go Tell It on the Mountain*" comments on the instrumentality of religion in the hands of John: "Religion furnishes the adolescent a means of disqualifying his father before dominating him: he becomes the son of God in order to count Him an ally" (126).

Given the role of the Biblical Moses as divine leader of dual heritage, one can understand the popularity of the name among African Americans, as it embodies their condition of orphanage. Witness John of *Go Tell It* who, as stepson of Gabriel, is made to feel himself the interloper, a condition that becomes an archetype for that of African Americans in their adopted homeland. John Buddy of *Jonah's Gourd Vine* refers to himself as "big Moose" (113), read Moses. Indeed, the analogy of John Buddy to a hoodoo doctor who has charmed his congregation links him to Moses who is identified in *Jonah's Gourd Vine* as "de greatest hoodoo man dat God ever made" (147). The dislocation of the Hebrew leader would explain in part the popularity of his name. The Egyptian Pharaoh had ordered the murder of all male babies born to Hebrew women. To forestall the murder of her son, Jochebed, Moses' mother, had placed the young Moses in a basket lined with goose feathers and set it afloat on the Nile River where the basket containing Moses was discovered by the Princess of Pharaoh and brought to live in Pharaoh palace as an Egyptian. Thus Moses, born a Hebrew but adopted as an Egyptian, may be said to symbolize the dispossession of the African Americans of their birthright as Africans. That the hybridity representative of Moses stands as a synecdoche for Blacks can be seen in Joe Starks of Hurston's *Their Eyes Were Watching God* who personifies that betweenity (76): "It was bad enough for white people, but when one of your own color could be so different it put you on a wonder. It was like seeing your sister turn into a 'gator. A *familiar* strangeness. You keep seeing your sister in the 'gator and the 'gator in your sister, and you'd rather not."

Hurston's fascination with the Biblical story of Moses is omnipresent in the author's literature beginning with the first novel *Jonah's Gourd Vine* and ending with the last novel entitled *Moses, Man of the Mountain*. Witness the following. The name of Isis, given to the second daughter of John Buddy and Lucy of *Jonah's Gourd Vine,* may be traced to the Biblical story of Moses. To obtain the secrets of the book guarded by the deathless snake on the river of Koptos, Moses had made a burnt offering and a drink offering to the Egyptian god Isis. Hurston has written in *Moses, Man of the Mountain:* "[Moses] had gone into the temple of Isis at Koptos and brought an ox and a goose and some wine and made a burnt offering and a drink offering before Isis of Koptos" (118-19). As a result of this supplication to the Egyptian god Isis, the reader is led to believe that Moses was aided in his neutralization of the deathless snake and his obtainment of the book that contained within it knowledge of both Life and Death: "Then Moses took the box out of the golden box that was closed in all the other boxes. And when he went with the book Light went before him and Darkness after. He knew the ways and the meaning of Light and he heard the voice of Darkness and knew its thoughts" (119). Moreover, a son of Emmeline and Richard Potts, Lucy's parents, is given the name of Aaron in honor of the Hebrew priest who was appointed as the mouthpiece of Moses after Moses received the command from the Lord of Hosts to liberate the Hebrews from their Egyptian bondage (*Moses* 130). Finally, John Buddy pastors the church named Pilgrim's Rest following his marriage to Sally Lovelace, his third wife.

The name "Pilgrim's Rest" is evocative of the Exodus of the Hebrews from Egypt; more specifically, their punishment following their Exodus designed to transform a dispirited people into a unified nation of believers. Those not possessed of that essence were doomed to death in the wilderness. Moses prophesizes in *Moses, Man of the Mountain:*

> "Their carcasses shall rot in this wilderness. I am not talking about Joshua and Caleb, Lord. I am talking about those others. I can make something out of their children, but not out of them. They have the essence of greatness in them and I shall fight them and fight myself and the word and even God for them. They shall not refuse their destiny. In this wilderness shall they be consumed, and here they shall die." (259)

The newly freed slaves in *The Autobiography of Miss Jane Pittman,* who begin their journey North following Emancipation, re-name themselves "Lincoln" and "Moses" (18) to demarcate a new beginning. Indicative of the new beginning, as noted in the chapter "Heading North," is an abstention from previous vices that have defined their being. Big Laura challenges the men to "go'n act like free men. If you want act like you did on that plantation, turn around now and go on back to that plantation" (20). Also indicative of the new beginning is the determination of the freed slaves to chart their own course, however suspect, as Jane is determined to make it to Ohio in search of Corporeal Brown who has re-named her, despite the folly of her pursuit (30): "Oh, Lord, child," the white lady said . . . . "You going to Ohio looking for a Yankee soldier called

Brown? A Yankee soldier who might 'a been killed the day after he spoke to you?" Indicative too of the new beginning of the freed slaves is the determination to preserve a stolen, or lost, legacy, as signified by the flint and the iron that Ned carries with him in memory of his mother, Big Laura, and his sister who were murdered by the patrollers as the group attempted to flee North following Emancipation. Upon Ned's return to the South to educate the Black youth of the Bayonne, he instructs them not to forfeit their inheritance of the land: "[D]on't let no man tell you the best is for him and you take the scrap. No, your people plowed this earth, your people chopped down the trees, your people built the roads and built the levees. These same people is now buried in this earth, and their bones's fertilizing this earth" (113).

In August Wilson's play *Joe Turner's Come and Gone,* Seth, a fifty-year-old carpenter or craftsman who operates, along with his wife Bertha, a boardinghouse, identifies a previous boarder as named Moses Houser: "Man went crazy and jumped off the Brady Street Bridge" (38). The name "Moses," introduced as it is here, signals the historical condition of dispossession associated not only with Moses but also with Blacks. For example, Herald Loomis (15) who was conscripted for prison labor for five years—from 1901 to 1908—has spent approximately four years in search of his wife. He tells the conjurer Bynum:

> LOOMIS. I just wanna see her face so I can get me a starting place in the world. The world got to start somewhere. That's what I been looking for. (72)

The twenty-five-year-old union of Seth and Bertha sets in sharp relief the mobility of the boarders who patronize their establishment. Even the names of the characters are indicative of a perambulatory nature. The conjurer is named "Bynum Walker," and as Seth explains, before Bynum reached the age of maturity, he was never one to remain stationary:

> SETH. He's one of them fellows could never stay in one place. He was wandering all around the country till he got old and settled here. The only thing different about Bynum is he bring all this heebie-geebie stuff with him. (35)

The Exodus North at the turn of the nineteenth century, as referenced in *Joe Turner,* is another example of a migratory, or Diasporic peoples. Seth explains that the Blacks (6) "keep on coming. Walking . . . riding . . . carrying their Bibles." In effect, their perambulatory nature, or vagabondage, may be seen as symptomatic of their disenfranchisement. As Mary L. Bogumil, author of *Understanding August Wilson,* has written:

That disfranchisement is further illustrated in some of the key male characters' need to wander or to turn away from that which is familiar—hence, causing the "Joe Turner syndrome," a cultural idiom that refers both to the convict-lease system devised as a post-Reconstruction socio economic advantage allowing white southern landowners to further exploit black labor as well as the institution of slavery. (62-63)

Further evidence of a perambulatory nature that echoes the Biblical Exodus in *Joe Turner's Come and Gone* is Jeremy Furlow. The name "Furlow," which seems a corruption of "furlough," is suggestive of a condition of temporariness, as in a furlough of workers, or a temporary lay-off of workers. Furlow, newly-arrived from North Carolina, leaves Mattie Campbell, the woman with whom he has recently taken up, in order to place his lot with another boarder Molly:

> JEREMY. We can make it better together. I got my guitar and I can play. Won me another dollar last night playing guitar. We can go around and I can play at the dances and we can just enjoy life. (65)

Mattie's Campbell's husband is also someone who has been afflicted with the "walking blues," a legacy of slavery. Former slaves bound over from master/mistress to master/mistress seemingly found it difficult to grow roots. For instance, Mattie's husband "just started walking. Didn't look back" (23). One critic has noted that Mattie Campbell and Molly Cunningham are related to the extent that their initials are similar and they offer different responses to their condition of abandonment. Peter Wolfe, author of *August Wilson*, has written:

> Mattie is one of two women of 26 who move into the boardinghouse soon after Loomis's arrival there with Zonia, the other being Molly Cunningham. Being the same age and having the same initials makes them, if not alter egos, then possible directions for one another, a presumption given force by their nearly simultaneous arrival at the home of a couple who have been married 27 years and who could thus be their parents. Finally, although both Mattie and Molly have suffered for love, they try to overcome heartache differently. Molly doesn't want to put down roots. She makes both Seth and Bynum repeat their names after being introduced to them because she's thinking of the next place her wanderlust will take her. By contrast, Mattie, who wants to settle in permanently with one man, has the nesting instinct. (88)

In the same way that the nomadic existence of John Buddy in *Jonah's Gourd Vine* is a motif for the dispossession of Blacks, so too is the perambulatory nature of the characters in Wilson's *Joe Turner's Come and Gone* a sign of their dis-ease. Both *Jonah's Gourd Vine* and *Joe Turner's Come and Gone* are set around the turn of the century. Both are descriptive therefore of the Great

Migration North comparable to the Biblical Exodus of the Jews. Hurston has written in *Jonah's Gourd Vine:*

> Whereas in Egypt the coming of the locust made desolation, in the farming South the departure of the Negro laid waste the agricultural industry—crops rotted, houses careened crazily in streets. On to the North! The land of promise. (151)

Conscriptive prison labor, as evidenced by Loomis in Wilson's play *Joe Turner's Come and Gone*, was one of a number of strategies following Emancipation in 1865 designed by whites to keep Blacks servile. Another was terrorism intended to enforce the subjugation the "Black Codes" had legislated. Milton D. Morris writes in his article "Democratic Politics and Black Subordination":

> The "Black Codes," a harsh series of laws passed immediately after the Civil War, virtually reimposed total slavery and were employed to maintain full control over the black population. Partly as a result of these laws, Congress intervened to restrain white Southerners in these excesses and to alleviate the hardship on blacks. Later terroristic activities by whites, a series of laws and constitutional changes, and the economic vulnerability of blacks combined to ensure their continued subordination. (584)

A protection of economic interests was the primary reason for the "Black Codes." Another was fear of engulfment, another correlation to the Jews. As revealed in the Book of Exodus, the King of the Egyptians had forewarned of their engulfment by the Israelites who were "fruitful and increased abundantly" (1:7). Consequently, their persecution was based in part on Egyptian fears of extirpation. Morris identifies a similar rationalization for the persecution of Blacks:

> A second and equally potent factor in seeking new rationalizations for the oppression and enslavement of blacks was fear. White Americans had always been fearful of the seething black slave population and the prospect that it might one day rise up and destroy its oppressor. This fear lay behind many of the stringent rules affecting the slave as well as the black nonslave populations of many states. (588)

The pervasiveness of terroristic activity is seen in Hurston's *Jonah's Gourd Vine*. Nightriders, referred to as "patteroles," were perceived by Lucy as the principal threat to John Buddy upon his flight to Sanford from the custody of Judge Pearson after his arrest for the assault of Bud Potts. Pheemy attempts to allay Lucy's fears by remarking the protection offered John Buddy by the office of Judge Pearson (100): "Dey ain't gwine set foot on Judge Alf Pearson's place, if dey run on 'im outside dey'd grab 'im. Dey might go in some folks' quarters, but 'tain't never no patter roller set foot on dis place. Dey know big wood from brush."

"The little Negro village" of Eatonville (107) becomes therefore a haven from terrorism. Indeed, the lushness of Eatonville makes it a virtual Paradise: "The warmth, the foliage, the fruits all seemed right and as God meant her [Lucy] to be surrounded" (109). Importantly, Lucy sees Eatonville as a place free from the prejudice that could warp the spirit and undermine the potential for growth (109): "John, dis is uh fine place tuh bring up our chillun. Dey won't be seein' no other kind uh folks actin' top-superior over 'em and dat'll give 'em spunk tuh be bell cows theyselves." Thus it comes as no surprise that Zeke would follow John Buddy, whom he idolized, to Eatonville, where "uh man kin be sumpin 'thout folks tramplin' all over [him]" (107):

> [John] began to see a good deal of Zeke who had moved with his
> family to Florida, a year or two before Lucy died. He loved seeing
> Zeke because he was just as great a hero in his brother's eyes as he
> had been when he was the biggest Negro Baptist in the State and
> when Zion Hope had nine hundred members instead of the six hun-
> dred now on its roll. Zeke talked but always spared him. (142)

Zeke is one of two stepbrothers named, respectively, Zeke and Zack, or Ezekiel and Zechariah, in honor of the two Old Testament Hebrew prophets. Ezekiel is the prophet identified as a watchman sent by the Lord of hosts to warn the Hebrews of their impending doom by sounding the trumpet and harkening them from their iniquity (Ezekiel 33: 7). In Hurston's *Jonah's Gourd Vine*, Ezekiel, a messenger for John Buddy and Lucy during their separation, functions in the same capacity as the prophet Ezekiel who is sent by the Lord of hosts to the children of Israel to prophesy the message of damnation for their transgressions absent repentance (Ezekiel 2: 3-4). To the extent that Ezekiel serves as liaison for John Buddy and Lucy, he safeguards their relationship. Thus his function is comparable to that of the Biblical Ezekiel who functions as both messenger and guardian. When John Buddy goes to the tie camp in Opelika after leaving Pearson's plantation, he places Ezekiel on watch over Lucy (57): "Naw, you stay 'round heah and watch out for Lucy. Git word tuh me iffen any ole mullet-head tries tuh cut me out. Ahm gointer write tuh you and you way-lay her and git her tuh read it fuh yuh."

Ralph Ellison contends in the piece "Hidden Name and Complex Fate: A Writer's Experience in the United States," as included in *Shadow and Act,* that "a concern with names and naming was very much a part of that special area of American culture from which I came" (149). Given the import of names among African Americans, the verisimilitude of an author's craft, as it pertains to African American culture, may be gauged to a degree by the names of the fictional characters. Peculiar to Faulkner's *Sanctuary* is the nickname "Popeye," as given to one of the characters; however, the correlation between name and being is never established although it could signal for the reader, as noted earlier, the character's impotence in his identification as voyeur. To be sure, at least in

Sanctuary, names are not accorded the same significance as they are in the literature by African American authors. The correlation between name and being is seen clearly, however, in Faulkner's character Anse of *As I Lay Dying* who is named for the African trickster Ananse, thus underscoring Faulkner's familiarity with African and African American folklore, as will be argued in the subsequent chapter. On the other hand, the correlation between name and being in the respective works by Morrison and Hurston is clear.

In *Their Eyes Were Watching God,* by Zora Neale Hurston, the character "Motor Boat" is given the nickname as the result of his buoyancy, his ability to ride out a hurricane while asleep in a hilltop house in the Everglades while others perished (256-57). The names "Deacon" and "Steward" in Morrison's *Paradise* affirm their guardianship of both history and memory: "His grandfather had named his twins Deacon and Steward for a reason. And their family had not built two towns, fought white law, Colored Creek, bandits and bad weather, to see ranches and houses and a bank with mortgages on a feed store, a drugstore and a furniture store end up in Arnold Fleetwood's pocket" (55). Deek's surveillance of the Oven, a symbol of the past, is paradigmatic of the twins' role as keepers of the flame (113).

Not only do the names of Hurston's and Morrison's characters provide cultural cues, but also the settings in their novels are similar. *Paradise* is set in the all-black town Ruby. *Jonah's Gourd Vine* and *Their Eyes Were Watching God* are set in the Negro hamlet Eatonville. However, whereas Eatonville is depicted as a sanctuary from terrorism and race prejudice, Haven and Ruby are viewed as a "prison calling itself a town" (308) rather than a Paradise. Connie tells Mavis, "Scary things not always outside. Most scary things is inside" (39). Morrison considers the exclusivity of class, internecine battles, zealotry, and unbridled male power as responsible in part for the purgatory that is, ironically, Haven. Nonetheless, in the hands of Hurston and Morrison, the Biblical legend contained in their works becomes a vehicle for an examination of historical and cultural values. For example, the names of African Americans are not only revelatory of "sovereignty over one's self" (King 116), but also of historical and cultural legacy. In an interview with Anne Koenen, Toni Morrison has spoken specifically of the practice among African Americans of selecting names from the Bible (218): "My mother's name is Ramah, which was chosen that way. That's a city, and she would fuss and say, 'The least they could have done was choose a person instead of a city.' For me, it was that gesture of getting something holy, but at the same time, you don't really look to choose a person." In her novel *Paradise,* Zechariah Morgan, born Coffee Morgan, a misspelling of "Kofi," renames himself Zechariah, a practice among former slaves symbolic of their affinity with the dispersed Jews (192): "All of that would fit nicely for Zechariah Morgan: the curse, the women stuffed into a basket with a lid of lead and hidden away in a house, but especially the scattering. The scattering would have frightened him" (192). Sigrid King has argued in the article "Naming and Power in Zora Neale Hurston's *Their Eyes Were Watching God,*" the import of names among African Americans (115): "Naming has always been an important issue in the Afro-American tradition because of its link to the exercise of power. From their earliest experience in America, Afro-Americans have been aware that those who name also control, and those who are named are subjugated."

On a personal note the bestowal of Biblical names upon offspring has been practiced within the author's own family. For example, a schoolmate in the author's home state of Georgia was given the Hebrew name Zebedee (Zebedee was father of the disciples James and John); a propertied neighbor was named for the disciple Thaddeus, while a cousin was named Moses. The author herself was named for her father and paternal grandfather, Thomas Jackson, Jr. and Thomas Jackson, Sr., respectively, as well as for her maternal grandfather, Lee Clarke. The name "Thomas" has Biblical derivation, as Thomas was one of the twelve disciples; the other eleven, as identified in Matthew 10: 2, were Peter, Andrew, James, John, Philip, Bartholomew, Matthew, James, the son of Alphaeus, Thaddeus, Simon, and Judas. Therefore, the name "Tommie," a female version of Thomas, in a manner described by Ellison, has properties that may be deemed prophetic.

In his reflections upon his experiences as a writer in America, Ralph Ellison is the speech "Hidden Name and Complex Fate" delivered before the Library of Congress, described his career as a writer as fortuitous. Tar Baby, the character from folk culture, which stood for the world and its variety of human commerce, held him transfixed as though under a spell. What began as play, however, resulted in labor that exacted its own price—an attempt to master the craft of fiction. Ellison considered that a precondition to the mastery of the craft of fiction was ownership of his name Ralph Waldo, which had been the gift of his father who admired Emerson and who projected his desires and hopes onto his son: "For it is through our names that we first place ourselves in the world. Our names, being the gift of others, must be made our own" (147). The name therefore became a burden as well as a charge as it challenged him to broaden the literature; concomitantly, preserve the literary standards of his namesake and other literary predecessors, such as Herman Melville, Mark Twain, Ernest Hemingway, Richard Wright, and William Faulkner: "If all this sounds a bit heady, remember that I did not destroy that troublesome middle name of mine, I only suppressed it. Sometimes it reminds me of my obligations to the man who named me" (166).

Chapter 4

The Influence of African American Folktales on Selected Literature by William Faulkner and Toni Morrison

In the West African folktale "Anansi and Anene Go Fishing," the trickster Anansi uses misdirection to get his way. The very ploy used by Anansi to discourage Anene instead encourages him. Thus Anansi advises Anene to rest while the former weaves traps; to follow rather than carry the traps to the river; to stand idly by while Anansi goes into the river to lay the traps; to take the small fish after they have been gathered from the traps while he, Anansi, awaits the larger ones. The upshot is that Anansi not only fails to expend himself but also enjoys the harvest gathered daily while Anene holds out futilely for a larger harvest. Once Anene discovers Anansi's deceit, he attempts to even the score by selling the traps, but Anansi foils him by volunteering to sell the traps himself. The traps, falsely advertised by Anansi as "rotten," do not sell, an outcome that has been Anansi's goal all along, but Anansi is beaten for his umbrage, an outcome unanticipated by the trickster Anansi. The Ashanti version of the Haitian variant of the tale "Bouki and Ti Malice Go Fishing" has been published in the 1976 edition of *A Treasury of Afro-American Folklore*, as collected by Harold Courlander:

> The chief said, "you with the rotten fish traps, what do you take the people for? Are you yourself a fool, or do you consider this to be a town of fools? No man wants a rotten trap. But you, vendor of rotten traps, you persist in insulting us." The chief called his guards. He

instructed them. They took Anansi to the gates of the town. They
whipped him and sent him away. (585)

In Caribbean and African American communities, the trickster may be
known as Nancy, Aunt Nancy, and Sis' Nancy (Courlander 135); the name of
the character "Anse" in Faulkner's *As I Lay Dying* therefore seems a truncation
both of the name "Ananse" and Aunt Nancy. Unmistakable, however, are the
characteristics, namely, parasitism, associated with Ananse.

Similar to the Ashanti trickster in the folktale "Anansi and Anene Go Fishing," Anse seeks to profit without exertion. Darl narrates in *As I Lay Dying* that
Anse has not exerted himself since he was twenty-two years old when he
worked in the fields and took ill. Since then, he has adjured work, explaining
that, "If he ever sweats, he will die" (17). The reader is unsure whether this reported incident is true or fabricated by Anse; also, whether Anse believes his
own theory. Nonetheless, the daughter Dewey Dell cites Anse's disability as the
cause for the generosity of neighbors (25): "Pa dassent sweat because he will
catch his death from the sickness so everybody that comes to help us." Vernon
Tull is one neighbor who displays a generosity in keeping with the concept of
"noblisse oblige," as he volunteers his assistance with the Bundrens' corn crop
following a visit to the dying Addie Bundren: "'About that corn,' I say. I tell
him again I will help him out if he gets into a tight, with her sick and all. Like
most folks around here, I done holp him so much already I can't quit now'"
(32). Upon hearing of the collapse of the bridge due to a flood, neighbors sur-
mise that the Lord will come to Anse's aid for the same reason they've assisted
him over the years: "'I reckon He's like everybody else around here,' Uncle
Billy says. 'He's done it so long now He can't quit'" (84). Another neighbor,
Armstid, is prepared to part with his mules upon the realization that Anse has
nothing to mortgage for a replacement team after losing his team in the flood
waters while attempting to cross the bridgeless ford (179). The physician Pea-
body who has treated Cash's broken leg provides Cash with funds needed to pay
hotel expenses in Jefferson, undoubtedly the result of pity for the injury done to
Cash by Anse's attempt to stabilize the limb by encasing it in cement: "'Pea-
body just give me enough to pay the hotel with'" (249). The responsiveness of
individuals to Anse is conjectured to be the result of Anse's conjure. For example, Jewel's decision to swap the spotted horse for a replacement team of mules
is believed to be caused by Anse's use of conjure: "'And if it hadn't a been
Jewel, I reckon it'd a been me; I owe him that much, myself. I be durn if Anse
don't conjure a man, some way. I be durn if he ain't a sight'" (184).

In a review of the criticism of the novel, surprisingly, no critic has identified the name symbolism of Anse and its relationship to character albeit Daniel
J. Singal has identified the name as emblematic of a lower life form, an ant, a
condition which underscores man's diminutiveness in the face of forces beyond
his control: "[Anse's] very name, echoing the word 'ants,' suggests that he belongs among the lower forms of life" (146). In the section that features Addie's

narration, Addie confesses her disappointment in marriage since it did not end her existential loneliness. Consequently, she had sought revenge by attempting to secure a promise from Anse to return her remains to Jefferson for burial in the family plot. The irony, though, is that Addie's scheme of revenge backfires as Anse and other family members use the journey to Jefferson for their own selfish purposes: Anse to purchase a set of dentures and thereby secure a new wife. In other words, Anse, in peculiar trickster fashion, neutralizes Addie's plot to subject him to the movement he loathes: "But then I realized that I had been tricked by words older than Anse or love, and that the same word had tricked Anse too, and that my revenge would be that he would never know I was taking revenge" (164). The image of Anse, as provided by Darl, is symbolic of the incongruity associated by Faulkner with Anse. Faulkner portrays imagistically the obverse impact of Anse's attempts to console:

> He touches the quilt as he saw Dewey Dell do, trying to smooth it up
> to the chin, but disarranging it instead. He tries to smooth it again,
> clumsily, his hand awkward as a claw, smoothing at the wrinkles
> which he made and which continue to emerge beneath his hand with
> perverse ubiquity, so that at last he desists, his hand falling to his side
> and stroking again, palm and back, on his thigh. (51)

Faulknerian critics such as John Pilkington acknowledge the deceit of Anse but fail to recognize the clue provided by Faulkner in the name derivative of the Ashanti trickster Anansi. Pilkington observes that Anse's assertion of a promise made to Addie is suspect, given Anse's moral lassitude: "Doubts about Anse's commitment to Addie are further increased by the fact that in her last moments he violates his promise to keep 'the team here [at home] and ready' in order to make three dollars for one more load. Nowhere in the novel does Anse appear to be a man of strict adherence to ethical principles" (97). Thadious M. Davis contends in her work *Games of Property: Law, Race, Gender, and Faulkner's* Go Down, Moses that the works *As I Lay Dying, The Hamlet, The Town,* and *The Mansion* are "the most racialized of Faulkner's work—those with no visible black presence at all" (254). To the contrary, the name "Anse" reveals Faulkner's familiarity with African American folklore that he must have acquired from the individual affectionately known as "Mama Callie" who helped shape Faulkner's sense of loyalty (Karl 632) as well as his imagination. Frederick R. Karl has written in the biography *William Faulkner: American Writer:*

> These occasions [camping trips] afforded William a rich vein
> of storytelling, whether from the mouth of Mammy Callie, with her
> tales of the Civil War and Reconstruction, or the tales of the men, of
> hunting bear and deer; the setting later became so absorbed into
> Faulkner's imagination that he wrote about woods as if, like Sam Fa-
> thers, he had been born into them. (65)

African American folktales that have evolved from those of the Ashanti spider Anansi are those that feature Brer Rabbit. According to Richard M. Dorson, "folklorist, Martha Warren Beckwith, assembled a whole volume of Anansi the spider stories in Jamaica, but Anansi fails to set foot in the United States, bowing out to Brer Rabbit" (17). Brer Rabbit tales have more than entertainment value as they enabled Blacks to identify vicariously with the exploits of Brer Rabbit against his larger opponents. In the words of J. Mason Brewer, "The rabbit actually symbolized the slave himself. Whenever the rabbit succeeded in proving himself smarter than another animal the slave rejoiced secretly, imagining himself smarter than his master" (3-4).

"Sheer Crops" is a tale that depicts excellently the shrewdness of Brer Rabbit who is purported in one tale to be the 'mos' cunnin' man dat go on fo' legs" (Brewer 7). Brer Rabbit consistently profits from a sharecropping arrangement designed to swindle him of his earnings as a tenant farmer. If Brer Bear demands the top crop as his share, Brer Rabbit plants potatoes, so that Bear yields vines; bottom, Rabbit plants oats, so that Bear yields straw; top and bottom, Rabbit plants corn in order to "git de middles" (15). On the allegorical meaning of the Brer Rabbit tales, Missy Dehn Kubitschek has argued in *Toni Morrison: A Critical Companion* that the tales represent a form of black resistance against white hegemony (109):

> In the dramatically racialized society of the United States, the tar baby tale becomes a racial allegory . . . In this reading, the white farmer represents the white world's power to enslave blacks, and Brer Rabbit stands for African Americans. Directly struggling against this power merely leads to disaster (Brer Rabbit stuck to the tar). Instead, blacks must learn to fool the white masters by wearing a mask—playing the part that the whites expect (in this case, the frightened, stupid captive). Using what they know of the master (in this case his desire to be as cruel as possible) ultimately leads to freedom (the briar patch).

In the fourth novel by Toni Morrison, *Tar Baby,* the character Son, in his chameleon-like attributes, shares characteristics of Brer Rabbit. The novel was inspired by the folktale of Tar Baby, essentially a papier-mâché, which the fox concocts in order to trap Brer Rabbit. The character Jadine serves as the "Tar Baby" for the fugitive Son, also allegorical double for the son of the retired American couple, Valerian and Margaret Street. Identical as well to Brer Rabbit is Son's capacity for deception, or the "art of hiding" via distraction, as when he offers to serenade Jadine in order to deflect rage directed at him for the hysteria created by his discovery in L'Arbe de la Croix: "She saw planes and angles and missed character. Like the vision in yellow—and now this man with savannas in his eyes was distracting her from the original insult" (158).

Deception is defined by David Nyberg in the following manner in *The Varnished Truth:* "Deception is the shrewd and sober art of 'showing and hiding' which is meant to control what is and is not perceived, assumed or understood" (67). From this definition, Nyberg divides the 'art of showing' into the sub-categories of mimicking, counterfeiting, and misdirecting; the 'art of hiding' into the sub-categories of disappearing, disguising, and distracting. From the sub-categories that comprise the 'art of showing,' Brer Rabbit appears most often an exemplar of the strategy of misdirection; that is, he "emphasizes an alternative to [his] real interest" (73), for example, roasting, or hanging rather than being thrown in the briar patch. Also, to the extent that Brer Rabbit often escapes the punishment intended for him by supplying others as scapegoats, as seen in the folktale "Who Ate Up the Butter?" he utilizes as well, from the sub-category of the 'art of hiding,' the strategy of distraction, identified by Nyberg as subterfuge designed "to escape notice by uncertainty in the perceiver" (64).

In the folktale "Who Ate Up the Butter?" the Bear becomes a scapegoat for the gluttonous Brer Rabbit who devises a test that Bear is destined to fail: "Now Brother Rabbit told them, 'We'll make a big log heap and set fire to it, and run and jump, and the one that falls in it, he ate the butter'" (70). Accordingly, the test becomes a smokescreen that focuses attention away from Rabbit's own thieving onto the gullible Bear. Hence, it is tantamount to legerdemain, or a magician's trick that "[focuses] our attention on his right hand while his left hand slips a card up his sleeve" (Nyberg 69). In a similar sleight of hand, Anse in *As I Lay Dying* camouflages his own deviousness by the series of crisis that he creates around him: Cash's broken leg that resulted from an attempt to rescue Addie's coffin from the river; the loss of a team of mules while trying to cross a bridgeless ford immediately following a flood. The mishaps occurred following Anse's decision to journey to Jefferson when circumstances dictated otherwise, one that appears to defy both the gods and common sense: "Anansi not only aims to defy creatures and man, but the deities as well" (Courlander 135). Cora, the wife of the neighbor Tull, notes with irony the manipulative nature of Anse that is paradigmatic of the trickster who puts others at risk while he remains unscathed: "And you're one of the folks that says Darl is the queer one, the one that ain't bright, and him the only one of them that had sense enough to get off that wagon. I notice Anse was too smart to been on it a-tall" (145).

Further evidence of the "art of hiding" is Anse's decision to send Darl to Jackson in order to avoid potential liability for the destruction of Gillespie's barn and the subsequent endangerment of his stock after Darl had set fire to the barn in order to incinerate the deteriorating body of Addie "dead eight days" (193). Cash identifies the link between Anse's survival and Darl's incarceration: "It wasn't nothing else to do. It was either send him to Jackson, or have Gillespie sue us, because he knowed some way that Darl set fire to it" (222). Finally, Anse's strategy of deception in the form of distraction, a sub-category of the "art of hiding," may be said to be the dentures that he expects to purchase in Jefferson. In fact, the journey to Jefferson for the burial of Addie provides Anse and family members a disguise for their own self-interest. Vardaman wishes to see the toy train on display in a shop window; Cash aims to purchase a radio; Dewey Dell hopes to acquire a purgative in order to rid herself of an unwanted pregnancy; and Anse hopes to secure a second wife. Inasmuch as the characters utilize a red herring as a tool to distract, they are correspondent to Wambui of *A Grain of Wheat* who, in prototypical trickster fashion, makes modesty an issue while her objective, as gunrunner for the Mau Mau revolutionaries, remains shrouded (20). To be sure, Faulkner, in related trickster fashion, misleads the reader to expect the purchase of dentures as Anse's crowning achievement, given the many references to Anse's sacrifice. The pronouncement of his willingness to give up money saved for the purchase of dentures induces Jewel to trade his prized horse for a span of mules:

> "I ain't had a tooth in my head," he says. "God knows it. He knows in fifteen years I ain't et the victuals He aimed for man to eat to keep his strength up, and me saving a nickel here and a nickel there so my family wouldn't suffer it, to buy them teeth so I could eat God's appointed food. I give that money. I thought that if I could do without eating, my sons could do without riding." (181-82)

Jeanne Campbell Reesman, in the Introduction to *Trickster Lives: Culture and Myth in American Fiction,* lists some trickster characters that appear in American literature and identifies their Native American, Asian American, African American and African equivalents:

> The most characteristic appearances of trickster in American literature are those that originate in the traditions of Native American Indian and African American literatures, and to a somewhat lesser degree Asian American and Latino writing—such figures as Wakdjunkaga, Ikotomi, Coyote, Raven, Esu, Legba, Damballah, Brer Rabbit, John the Slave, Fu Mu Lan, Monkey King, and La Malinche, for example. (xi)

William G. Doty adds to the characterization of the trickster in his article "Native American Tricksters: Literary Figures of Community Transformers." He defines him as a liminal figure that crosses boundaries and becomes, in so doing, a figure of inversion: "They often violate taboos . . . or proscriptions. . . , becoming figures of inversion" (6). The trickster figure becomes as well in the literature a trope for survival. Jeanne Rosier Smith has asserted in her work *Writing Tricksters: Mythic Gambols in American Ethnic Literature:*

> As liminal beings, tricksters dwell at crossroads and thresholds and are endlessly multifaceted and ambiguous. Tricksters are uninhibited by social constraints, free to dissolve boundaries and break taboos.

> Perpetual wanderers, tricksters can escape virtually any situation, and
> they possess a boundless ability to survive. It is these last two quali-
> ties that make the trickster not simply a figure to laugh at but also a
> hero. Even while transgressing all boundaries, trickster always con-
> firms a human and cultural will to survive. (7-8)

To be sure, Anse, as well as his creator, is linked to the land, as signified
by the brogans that each owns: "Beside his chair his brogans sit. They look as
though they had been hacked with a blunt axe out of pig-iron" (11). The inter-
viewer Simon Claxton remarks the disparity between the appearance of Faulkner
and his creative genius, as Faulkner, attired in brogans, or "dirty old farm boots"
at Rowan Oak (*Lion in the Garden* 273) mirrors to some extent the characters he
has created, namely, Anse Bundren and Lena Grove of *As I Lay Dying* and *Light
in August* respectively. In addition to the brogans, their link to the land is adumbrated in their respective personas as farmers. Their union with the land, similar
to that of Alexandra in Willa Cather's novel *O Pioneers!*, takes on a religious, or
divine mien. Thus readers are not surprised to learn that Willa Cather is among
the contemporaries Faulkner loves to read (*Lion in the Garden* 67-68) inasmuch
as she depicts in her works the lives of peasants closely bound to the soil. Indeed, one critic, namely Walter Brylowski, considers that Anse's marriage at the
close of *As I Lay Dying*, in addition to Dewey Dell's pregnancy, represents the
novel's affirmation of life forces, an interpretation corroborative of the trickster
as a motif of survival:

> The Bundren family has rid itself of the corpse of Addie and the
> penetrating insights of Darl who could not survive the tests of the
> journey. Anse has his new truth and a new wife and Dewey Dell re-
> mains pregnant. Somehow through all of this blundering, the stasis of
> death and the malignant powers of nature have been overcome and
> the forces of life have reasserted themselves. (96)

In interviews, Faulkner has observed that professional satisfaction has
come from making old ideas appear new: "People write about the same stories
because there're so few to write about, but to take one—human beings in the old
familiar dilemma and predicament—and by the imagination and the hard work
to show them in some new, interesting, tragic, or comical instance of the struggle within the dilemma, that to me is fun" (*Faulkner in the University* 258).

Faulkner, after being asked whether he consciously or unconsciously
sought to parallel his novel *As I Lay Dying* after Nathaniel Hawthorne's *The
Scarlet Letter,* responded that he took "whatever I needed wherever I could find it,
without any compunction and with no sense of violating any ethics or hurting anyone's
feelings because any writer feels that anyone after him is perfectly welcome to take any
trick he has earned or any plot he has used" (*Faulkner in the University* 115). Given the
deference that Faulkner has accorded writers such as Homer, Charles Dickens,
Leo Tolstoy, those who have stood the test of time, it is clear that they have be-

come for him writers who have left their mark, who have asserted through their literature that "Kilroy was here." Such a mark, Faulkner has affirmed, is the measure of any writer:

> I think that a writer wants to make something that he knows that a hundred or two hundred or five hundred, a thousand years later will make people feel what they feel when they read Homer, or read Dickens or Balzac, Tolstoy, that that's probably his goal. (*Faulkner in the University* 61)

Not only has a writer such as Homer become a measure of literary excellence; Faulkner's novel *As I Lay Dying* is evocative of Homer's *The Odyssey* in its depiction of the carpenter Cash Bundren.

　　Cash is reported as having fallen "twenty eight foot, four and a half inches" (85) from a church roof and having suffered a broken leg. Thus his joints are sensitive to climatic changes. While Cash's accident was the result of unsure footing caused by "wet planks" (85), the accident of the warrior Elpenor in Homer's *The Odyssey* was the result of dulled senses caused by drink. The Greek hero Odysseus, having angered Poseidon, the Earth-Shaker, by blinding the giant Cyclops, son of Poseidon, was fated to wander for twenty years before returning to Ithaca from the city of Troy. Odysseus' fate had been foretold by the seer Teiresias upon a voyage to Hades, as directed by the Goddess Circe. Circe had concealed a potent poison in the drink of Odysseus' men and had transformed them into swine. With the assistance of the Goddess Athene, as well as Hermes, the Wayfinder, Odysseus was able to deliver his men from Circe's spell and to continue his quest. Prior to the crew's departure to Hades, however, Elpenor, suffering the effects of feast and drink, had plunged to his death from the roof of Circe's house (Book 10; lines 598-604). The fall of Cash from a church roof and of Elpenor from the roof of Circe's dwelling in, respectively, *As I Lay Dying* and *The Odyssey* casts the two men as ill fated; also, their congruence underscores Faulkner's acknowledged "kleptomania," as he has identified in interviews (*Faulkner in the University* 203).

　　By the same token, Toni Morrison has related in an interview that the origin of her fiction is often "the cliché because the experience expressed in it is important: a young man seeks his fortune; a pair of friends, one good, one bad; the perfectly innocent victim. We know thousands of these in literature. I like to dust off these clichés, dust off the language, make them mean whatever they may have meant originally" (LeClair 121).

　　In the previous chapter "What's In a Name?" the argument was made that *Paradise,* by Toni Morrison, is a re-visitation of the Biblical story of the Exodus; the novel *Tar Baby* is a re-fashioning of the folktale "Tar Baby" that often begs the question of the identity of the "tar baby," given its paradoxical features, as described by Morrison in her interview with Thomas LeClair:

> In the book I've just completed, *Tar Baby,* I use that old story because, despite its funny, happy ending, it used to frighten me. The story has a tar baby in it, which is used by a white man to catch a rabbit. "Tar baby" is also a name. . . that white people call black children, black girls, as I recall. Tar seemed to me to be an odd thing to be in a Western story, and I found that there is a tar lady in African mythology. I started thinking about tar. At one time, a tar pit was a holy place, at least an important place, because tar was used to build things. It came naturally out of the earth; it held together things like Moses's little boat and the pyramids. For me, the tar baby came to mean the black woman who can hold things together. The story was a point of departure to history and prophecy. That's what I mean by dusting off the myth, looking closely at it to see what it might conceal. (122)

Missy Dehn Kubitschek in *Toni Morrison: A Critical Companion* notes that Jadine assumes characteristics of both the Tar Baby and Brer Rabbit. She is the object of allure designed to attract Brer Rabbit, or Son, yet Morrison's description of her mired in quicksand calls to mind Brer Rabbit:

> A reading of Jadine as the tar baby oversimplifies. *Tar Baby* itself might seem to confirm that interpretation because when Jadine falls into the swamp, she emerges covered with tar. That text can be read another way, however. After his escape, Brer Rabbit sits in the brier patch and licks tar from his fur. Jadine may, then, be Brer Rabbit. Son is certainly Brer Rabbit because in the final scene the narrator describes him as moving with the same sound as the Brer Rabbit of the fable, "lickety split." (112)

The allure of Jadine, similar to the papier-mâché that ensnares Brer Rabbit, is iterated throughout the novel. The washerwoman Thérèse intuits the presence of Son, purportedly one of the 100 legendary horsemen for whom Isle des Chevaliers (9) is named, as directly related to Jadine (107): "I told you! He's a horseman come down here to get her. He was just skulking around waiting for his chance." Son's continued presence on L'Arbe de la Croix (10), even following Valerian's offer to secure for him a return visa to the United States, is due wholly to his fixation with Jadine. Morrison writes in *Tar Baby:*

> So the first time he entered her room he stayed only a few seconds, watching her sleep. Anybody could have told him it was only the beginning. Considering the piano and Cheyenne and this sleeping woman he was bound to extend his stay until he was literally spending the night with her gratified beyond belief to be sitting on the floor, his back against the wall, his shirt full of fruit. . ., in the company of a woman asleep. (138)

Kubitschek in *Toni Morrison: A Critical Companion* argues that the respective values that Son and Jadine represent likewise constitute "a tar baby" that creates for the couple irreconcilable differences: "To each, the other's values make up a tar baby, a white-designed trap. Son claims to embody authentic black culture and more than once implies that no matter what Jadine's skin color, she is essentially European. Jadine sees Son's refusal to consider usual kinds of employment as effectively choosing poverty and ignorance, and then calling the result true blackness. Unable to live together or even agree on a place to try, Jadine and Son part." (94). In an interview, Morrison has noted that the skeleton of the Tar Baby story was used to convey the cul-de sac that both characters face: whether to move forward (Son) or continue to deny their past (Jadine): "The choice is irrevocable, and there is no longer any time to mistake the metaphor. It seemed to me the most contemporary situation in the world. We are in a critical place where we would either cut off the future entirely and stay right where we are—which means, in an imaginative sense, annihilate ourselves totally and extend ourselves out into the stars, or the earth, or sea, or nothing—or we pretend there was no past, and just go blindly on, craving the single thing that we think is happiness" (Ruas 112).

Morrison's use of folklore and mysticism in *Tar Baby,* according to Hudson-Weems and Samuels, imbues the work with "an element of the African continuum" that is characteristic of Morrison's novels:

> Whereas the boundaries between myth and reality were muddled before, in *Tar Baby* they seem to disappear completely. Here Morrison does more than merely make allusions to myth and folklore, here the genre provides the novel's title and its central theme. In addition, she continues to weave into her discourse elements of mysticism—conjuration, superstitions, and spiritual visitations. Throughout the interaction between the physical and the spiritual worlds, an element of the African continuum—which has become a dominant characteristic of her writings—is made evident. (88)

To be sure, an equivalent to the Tar Baby folktale is the Ashanti folktale "Anansi Plays Dead," as recorded in the 1996 edition of *A Treasury of African Folklore,* by Harold Courlander. Fearful of starvation during a famine, Anansi had imparted to his wife the instruction, allegedly received from a diviner, relative to Anansi's death: to supply his grave with a pestle and mortar, dishes, spoons, and cooking pots so that he may care for himself in the Other World. Following Ananse's "death," a grave had been outfitted by Aso, Ananse's wife, as the diviner, purportedly, had ordained. Nightly, Ananse had stolen out of his grave to pilfer his own crops until the family, suspicious of theft, constructed a figure from sticky gum that resembled a man. Ananse was discovered as the thief, as his attempts to remove himself from the gum figure only served to bind him more tightly to it (151). His shame, upon discovery, had driven him into the forest. The story therefore serves as an explanation of the spider's, or Ananse's, habitat (151): "From that day until now, Anansi had not wanted to face people because of their scoffing and jeering, and that is why he is often found hiding in dark corners" (Courlander 151).

Langston Hughes in *The Book of Negro Folklore* comments on the omnipresence of Afro-American folklore in works by American writers such as Ralph Ellison, Mark Twain, and William Faulkner: "A carry-over from Negro folktales into the American writing by and about Negroes, from Mark Twain to William Faulkner and Ralph Ellison, is also conspicuous" (vii). In fact, the tricksterism of the writers is often inseparable from the characters they create. Ralph Ellison has asserted in the essay "Change the Joke and Slip the Yoke," as contained in *Shadow and Act,* that masking is part of the American grain: "Hemingway poses as a non-literary sportsman, Faulkner as a farmer; Abe Lincoln allowed himself to be taken for a simple country lawyer—until the chips were down [. . .]. America is a land of masking jokers" (55). William Faulkner, in a letter to Joan Williams, a student at Bard College with whom he collaborated on the play *Requiem for a Nun,* wrote the following: "I wonder if you have ever had that thought about the work and the country man whom you know as Bill Faulkner—what little connection there seems to be between them" (*Selected Correspondence* 348). Thus the duality and double-voicedness of the narrative methods are common to the authors studied here. As Jeanne Rosier Smith has affirmed in her work *Writing Tricksters,* tricksterism, in the hands of the authors, becomes part of a rhetorical strategy: "Tricksters are not only characters, they are rhetorical agents. They infuse narrative structure with energy, humor, and polyvalence, producing a politically radical subtext in the narrative form itself" (2). The list of writers whose works are influenced by trickster tales may be extended to include, among others, writers such as Toni Morrison, Zora Neale Hurston, and Charles Chesnutt; trickster authors who disrupt boundaries "between self and other, between male and female, between the real and the fantastic, and even between story and audience" (Smith 21). John Lowe, author of *"Jump at the Sun": Zora Neale Hurston's Cosmic Comedy,* describes Hurston in a matter congruent with the characters she has created:

> Dismissing her and her characters as simple or romantic, [many of Hurston's critics] underread and undervalue a profoundly serious, experimental, subversive, and therefore unsettling artist who found the complex humorous traditions of her culture worthy of presentation in their own right, but also useful in furthering her preferred method of writing by indirection. (2)

In a number of her works, Hurston describes characters whose subversive power transforms a weakness into a source of strength, as shown in one of the animal tales included in the collection *Every Tongue Got to Confess: Negro Folk-tales from the Gulf States,* by Zora Neale Hurston (251-52). A variation of the tale also appears in the collection *American Negro Folktales* (Dorson) under the title "Mr. Rabbit and Mr. Frog Make Mr. Fox and Mr. Bear Their Riding-Horses" (89-90). Albeit the principals are the same, the number of principals differs; however, the tales both illustrate the misdirection, or "the art of showing," typical of the Brer Rabbit tales.

Brer Rabbit denies interest in the object of desire, the female for whom he competes with Brer Bear. To thwart Bear and Fox, Rabbit proposes additional interests for him and Frog rather than compete for the hearts of the two females alongside Brer Bear and Brer Fox. The concession is itself a disguise. To impress the female that both Rabbit and Fox were dating, Rabbit had identified Fox as his riding horse. By feigning illness and disarming his opponent, thus eliciting a ride, Rabbit emerges the victor inasmuch as his dismount is made virtually impossible, given that he had equipped himself beforehand with the saddle, whip, and spurs necessary to sustain the illusion:

> So they started to the girl's house—they ran and ran and ran. When Brother Fox saw the house about fifty feet away, he said: "Get off now," but Brother Rabbit put the spurs to him and away he ran right up to the house. Brother Rabbit jumped down and ran into the house and said: "I told you Brother Fox was my riding horse, I told you Brother Fox was my riding horse, I told you. Ha! Ha!" (252)

John Lowe considers in his work *"Jump at the Sun": Zora Neale Hurston's Cosmic Comedy* that the image contained in the eulogy of Sam Watson of Matt Bonner's mule, namely, a "mule heaven" wherein mules ride people, makes it analogous to the one in the tale that features a rabbit riding a fox:

> Sam Watson's speculations about "mule heaven" parody the folktales about blacks flying around Heaven, utilizing the absurd image of mule angels: "miles of green corn and cool water, a pasture of pure bran with a river of molasses. . . and . . . *no* Matt Bonner. Mule-angels would have people to ride on" (95). This particular image recalls folktales about the trickster rabbit conniving the fox to ride on his back. These comic reversals are ubiquitous in black folktales that offer basic images of social inversion. (172)

The inversion of weakness into strength characterizes too the Tar Baby folktale on which Morrison's novel has been based; however, as Smith has averred, Morrison's approach to the tale has been revisionist: "The trickster's power in the tar baby tale lies in manipulating the farmer's control over him, in inverting his powerlessness into subversion. By questioning the tar baby's motives [his complicity with the farmer], and emphasizing the positive as well as the negative qualities of tar, Morrison undercuts or subverts any monologic message in the tale" (132-33).

The transformation of weakness into a source of strength characterizes as well the trickster character of Uncle Julius in Charles Chesnutt's *The Conjure Woman*. Indeed, Uncle Julius practices the art of surrender, as described by Robert Greene in *Power:* "Learn his ways, insinuate yourself with him slowly, outwardly conform to his customs, but inwardly maintain your own culture. Eventually you will emerge victorious, for while he considers you weak and inferior, and takes no precautions against you, you are using the time to catch up and surpass him. This soft, permeable form of invasion is often the best, for the enemy has nothing to react against, prepare for, or resist" (168). To be sure, Chesnutt not only depicts a character that uses craftiness, but the author himself has used the "soft, permeable form of invasion" as a weapon against racial bias. He has written in his journal on his aims as an author:

> The object of my writings would be not so much the elevation of the whites—for I consider the unjust spirit of caste which is so insidious as to pervade a whole nation, and so powerful as to subject a whole race and all connected with it to scorn and social ostracism—I consider this a barrier to the moral progress of the American people; and I would be one of the first to head a determined, organized crusade against it. Not a fierce indiscriminate onset, not an appeal to force, for this is something that force can but slightly affect, but a moral revolution which must be brought about in a different manner. The subtle almost indefinable feeling of repulsion toward the Negro, which is common to most Americans—cannot be stormed and taken by assault; the garrison will not capitulate, so their position must be mined, and we will find ourselves in their midst before they think it. (H.M. Chesnutt 21).

The limited edition of *A Conjure Woman* features a picture of Uncle Julius spliced between two rabbits on a red background, a coverleaf that betokens a link between the character and Brer Rabbit *(Charles Waddell Chesnutt* 107). According to Henry Louis Gates, Jr., characteristic of the Signifying Monkey, another trickster figure in black vernacular tales, is "to imply, goad, beg, boast, by *indirect* verbal or gestural means" (54).

Signifying, also known as "capping" and "sounding" (Gates 94), is identified by Henry Louis Gates, Jr. in *The Signifying Monkey: A Theory of Afro-American Literary Criticism* as having eight characteristics, among them indirection, humor, rhythmic fluency, puns, and the unexpected (94-96). The most salient feature of signifying, according to Gates, is indirection (103): "[L]inguists stress indirection as the most salient feature of this strategy."

This rhetorical strategy of indirection links Uncle Julius of *The Conjure Woman* to the trickster character Brer Rabbit in black vernacular tales. A former slave hired as coachman by the Northern couple John and Annie, Uncle Julius McAdoo, spins yarns of plantation life ostensibly to entertain but with the surreptitious motive to profit: the use of the one-room schoolhouse as a church in

"Po' Sandy" and funds to purchase a suit of store-bought clothing in "The Conjurer's Revenge" from John's purchase of a horse. More to the point, the story of Sandy's misfortune prevents use of wood from the schoolhouse to construct a new kitchen for Annie; John's purchase of a horse rather than a mule, upon Julius' recommendation in "The Conjurer's Revenge," enables Julius, or so reasons the narrator John, to profit from the sale of the horse. His use of misdirection, the 'art of showing,' is similar to that practiced by the conjure woman in "Mars Jeems's Nightmare" who relieves the suffering of the slaves at the hands of the overseer Ole Nick by the provision of a new target, presumably the slave master himself who has been transformed into a slave. Indeed, Chesnut in his collection provides sufficient clues to justify the claim that Uncle Julius uses the strategy of disguise to "hide and show" (Nyberg 67).

Robert Greene distinguishes between the red herring and the smoke screen in *The 48 Laws of Power*. Albeit both devices serve, respectively, to misdirect and distract, the smoke screen is more illusory than real: "In the decoy and red herring devices [. . .], you actively distract people; in the smoke screen, you lull your victims, drawing them into your web. Because it is so hypnotic, this is the best way of concealing intentions" (28). Greene gives an example of the Ethiopian leader Haile Selassie, whose guise of obsequiousness disarmed his opponent Dejazmach Balcha Sidamo and rendered the warrior who dared to dethrone him gullible to entrapment; the banquet hosted by Selassie became the means to neuter his opponent. Greene writes in *The 48 Laws of Power*:

> Knowing that Balcha would have heard a noisy battle and hurried back with his 600-man bodyguard, Selassie had armed his own troops with baskets of gold and cash. They had surrounded Balcha's army and proceeded to purchase every last one of their weapons. Those who refused were easily intimidated. Within a few hours, Balcha's entire force had been disarmed and scattered in all directions. (26-27)

The upshot is that Selassie lasted longer than most Ethiopian leaders because, according to Greene, "he lured his victims with sweet smiles, lulling them with charm and obsequiousness before he attacked" (27).

Masking tales, as narrated by acquaintances Just Black, Cool Clyde, Tight Coat and Red Leg, are recounted by Maya Angelou in her autobiography *I Know Why the Caged Bird Sings*. The tales aim to instruct her against victimization and to illuminate the Principle of Reverse (215): "Anything that works against you can work for you."

In one tale the bias of the mark, or victim, is exploited, as he is swindled out of $40,000. A rumor is floated that a Black man is the owner of valuable real estate and is, at the same time, being courted by a Northern prospective buyer. Thus interest by the mark in the property is directly proportional to his contempt for his Northern competitor, an antipathy that blinds him to the motives of the con artists, one of whom plays the fool in order to separate the mark from his money: "The mark told me no Negro was safe with that kind of money [fifty thousand dollars]. I said I knew it but I had to have at least forty thousand dollars. He agreed. We shook hands" (217). Through use of the familiar, namely, the stereotype, the mark is distracted in a manner described by Greene:

> The familiar, inconspicuous front is the perfect smokescreen. Approach your mark with an idea that seems ordinary enough—a business deal, financial intrigue. The sucker's mind is distracted, his suspicions allayed. That is when you gently guide him onto the second path, the slippery slope down which he slides helplessly into your trap. (25)

The *noble gesture* is identified by Greene as another effective smokescreen: "An adaptable concept, the smoke screen can be practiced on a number of levels, all playing on the psychological principles of distractions and misdirection [. . .]. People want to believe apparently noble gestures are genuine, for the belief is pleasant. They rarely notice how deceptive these gestures can be" (28). In Hurston's *Seraph of the Suwanee,* Bradford Cary II, governor of the state of Florida, is a skillful practitioner of the *noble gesture* in order to realize his political aspirations. A Southern aristocrat, Cary had capitalized upon the friendship that his son had developed with Kenny Meserve while the two were students at the University of Florida by cultivating in turn a friendship with Maria Henson, Kenny Meserve's grandmother. Upon Maria Henson's death, Cary seized upon the opportunity to shoulder the expenses for her funeral, thus becoming the family's benefactor. In so doing, his political motives were shrouded as he was thrust in the role of politician that he had coveted all along. On the other hand, Joe Clarke, through his use of ambiguous signals, illuminates another principle of distraction and misdirection, namely, the red herring, in the short story "The Bone of Contention."

In the short story "The Bone of Contention," by Zora Neale Hurston, the mayor, postmaster, and storekeeper Joe Clarke uses a decoy to disguise his real intentions of discouraging potential rivals to his post as mayor in the town of Eatonville, Florida, which he has founded. Aware that a newcomer to the town, Reverend Simms, a Methodist preacher, has aspirations to become mayor, Joe Clarke, himself a Methodist (214), sides with the Baptists who wish to drive Jim Weston, a Methodist, from town for thievery and assault upon Dave Carter, a Baptist, with a mule bone. Not only does Reverend Simms rally to the cause of the accused, that is, he is foiled by the decoy, but he has been served notice by Joe Clarke who, in a show of power, wrests control of the court proceedings held in a Baptist church, that he is unwelcome in Eatonville: "'By ziggity, dat ol' mule been dead three years an' still kickin'! An' he done kicked more'n one person outa whack today.' And he gave Simms one of his most personal looks" (220). Thus Joe Clarke, in his alliance with a rival group, has used skillfully the tactic described by Robert Greene (21): "A tactic that is often effective in setting up a red herring is to appear to support an idea or cause that is actually contrary to your own sentiments."

Popularized by Joel Chandler Harris, variations of the trickster tales were those of characters, such as John or Jack, who utilized wit effectively to disarm their opponents. In the animal tale, "John and the Lion," John declares himself "de King of de World," dispensing with the grizzly bear and with his other challenger the lion by demonstrating his mastery with weapons, including his tongue. He subdues the lion with both his rifle and his tongue: "Yeah, Ah'm de King. Don't you like it, don't you take it. Here's mah collar, come and shake it! (Hughes 17).

The folk hero, High John de Conquer, analogous to the aforementioned Son of *Tar Baby,* by Toni Morrison, and Uncle Julius of *The Conjure Woman,* by Charles Chesnutt, is identified as a chameleon with a number of disguises. In "High John De Conquer," Hurston equates him with Brer Rabbit in folktales who is able to make "a way out of no-way" (141):

> He was traveling, and touristing around the plantations as the laugh-provoking Brer Rabbit. So Old Massa and Old Miss and their young ones laughed with and at Brer Rabbit and wished him well. And all the time, there was High John de Conquer playing his tricks of making a way out of no-way. Hitting a straight lick with a crooked stick. Winning the jack pot with no other stake but a laugh.

In *Mules and Men,* a collection of folklore by Zora Neale Hurston, the story is told of John who won every dare against his master. After allegations that John had beaten the master's horse but had spared his own, John had warned the master against the prescribed punishment, killing his horse, lest "Ah'll beatcher makin' money" (42); killing his grandmother for purportedly taking her riding in the master's buggy; drowning him, lest "Ah'll beatcher makin' money" (45). With each victory, the fortune of the fortune-telling John multiplied to the extent that the master, in pursuit of material gain, sought the fate—death—he had reserved for John.

High John de Conquer is associated not only with laughter, but also with wisdom and guile: "Old John, High John could beat the unbeatable. He was top-superior to the whole mess of sorrow" (140). His power is found in the High John de Conquer root, commonly used by conjurers (142): "Only possess that root, and he can be summoned at any time." Importantly, he represents a psychological freedom that rejects physical shackles (141): "He who carries his heart in his sword must perish. So says the ultimate law. High John de Conquer knew a lot of things like that. He who wins from within is in the 'Be' class. *Be* here when the ruthless man comes and *be* here when he is gone." On the significance of John de Conquer, Henry Louis Gates, Jr. and Sieglinde Lemke have written in the Introduction to *The Complete Stories,* by Zora Neale Hurston:

> John is the figure of courage and faith. He embodies joy over misery
> and he is the hero who shows that all that counts is in the soul and in
> the imagination. Those who are deprived of material wealth discover
> that their principal asset is spiritual wealth, rhythm, and laughter. (xx)

The beginnings of African American folklore were the Southern planta-
tions during the slavery era (Dorson 12). Given the lack of schooling, the storytelling tradition remained significantly an oral one. The fables were popularized
by the publication *Uncle Remus: His Songs and His Sayings* of Joel Chandler
Harris, a journalist for the *Atlanta Constitution* (Dorson 13); however, the belief
that stories of talking animals harkened back to an African ancestral past was
confirmed by Melville J. Herskovits in his work, *The Myth of the Negro Past*
(1941): "When American anthropologists such as Melville J. Herskovits and his
students turned their attention to Africa, they reinforced the thesis of African
origins with the best scholarly credentials" (Dorson 13). The harvest of tales
from the Southern region of the United States establishes the African American
storytelling tradition of an African ancestry. J. Mason Brewer collected tales
from North and South Carolina and the Brazos bottoms of East Texas; Zora
Neale Hurston gathered tales from Middle Georgia (Dorson 14) and all of Florida. Carla Kaplan writes in the Introduction to *Every Tongue Got to Confess,* by
Zora Neale Hurston, published posthumously in 2002, that "[Hurston] had a
small ($1,400) grant from Carter Woodson's Association for the Study of Negro
Life and History, and the intellectual support of Columbia University's re-
nowned anthropologist Franz Boas. Over the next two years she traveled to Florida, Alabama, Georgia, New Orleans, and the Bahamas, collecting material she
would draw on for the rest of her life, recycling it often and in various forms
into her work, and attempting, in spite of constant resistance, to bring authentic
black folklore to mainstream, popular audiences" (xxi-xxii). Richard M.
Dorson's own collection, published in 1956, stems from fieldwork conducted in
Michigan in "Negro communities" formed by those who had come from Mississippi, Alabama, Louisiana, Georgia, Tennessee, North Carolina, Missouri, Arkansas, West Virginia, and Texas (15).
   Toni Morrison's parents were among the transplanted African Americans
during the first migration North. Her mother, Rahmah Willis Wofford, was one
of seven children born to sharecroppers in Alabama. Toni Morrison's maternal
grandmother had traveled North with her seven children because she feared for
their safety in the South. Morrison's father, George Wofford, hailed from Georgia where the racial climate was similar to that in Alabama. Unsurprisingly,
Morrison speaks often of the storytelling that she grew up surrounded by that
has influenced her own art: "Morrison remembers her father as the best storyteller of a talented family, terrifying and delighting them every night with ghost
stories. In this way, the Wofford home typifies the centrality of storytelling to
African culture" (Kubitschek 3). Hence, the work of Toni Morrison is not only a
part of the American, African American tradition (Kubitschek 6), but likewise of

the Southern tradition of storytelling, associated with the slave era, that influenced writers such as, among others, Charles W. Chesnutt, Zora Neale Hurston, William Faulkner and Toni Morrison. Helen M. Chesnutt in *Charles Waddell Chesnutt: Pioneer of the Color Line* provides an account of evenings spent by Charles W. Chesnutt with his three daughters:

> [Chesnutt] read to them as they sat around the fireplace in the sitting room. He read *Mother Goose, Alice in Wonderland, Gulliver's Travels, The Swiss Family Robinson, Tom Brown's School Days, Little Women, The Nonsense Book, David Copperfield, Uncle Remus, The Arabian Nights, Pilgrim's Progress, Nicholas Nickeby, Old Curiosity Shop, Oliver Twist, Aesop's Fables, Grimm's Fairy Tales,* and scores of other classics became the literary background of the children. (48)

Daniel J. Singal has noted in his work *William Faulkner: The Making of a Modernist* that Faulkner's preparation as a writer began with his omnivorous reading under the tutelage of his mother and maternal grandmother who introduced him to such classics as Grimm's fairy tales, *Robinson Crusoe,* Stevenson's *Treasure Island,* and *Uncle Remus.* That tutelage was buttressed by the treasure trove of folklore acquired from Callie Barr, Faulkner's surrogate mother, alongside the stories and gossip accumulated from his post on the village square (40-41).

Faulkner's familiarity with *Uncle Remus* is indicated by the fashioning of a character in *The Reivers* loosely based on the trickster. Ned McCaslin is a family retainer of McCaslin-Edmonds-Priest described as possessing uncanny abilities with a horse. On a road trip, as stowaway, to a Memphis brothel with eleven-year-old Lucius Priest and Boon Hogganbeck in the stolen Winton Flyer belonging to "Boss" Priest, Lucius' grandfather, Ned, in an attempt to rescue a relative Bobo Beauchamp from gambling debts, trades the Winton Flyer for the horse Lightning stolen by Bobo from his employer Mr. Van Tosch. The intention has been all along to settle Bobo's gambling debts with earnings from a successful race and re-trade the horse for the Winton Flyer. Albeit the revelation by Lucius, who relates the story of his escapade to his own grandson, that the trick by Ned to get Lightning to run was the promise of a "sour dean" (286), the mysterious potion that produced the phenomenon of Ned's mule (123) also produced the phenomenon of Lightening, as the unlikely horse was able to win two of the three heats, thus bestowing upon Ned the manipulative powers of a conjurer evocative of his characterization as Uncle Remus (182). Lest the reader take seriously this parodic tale of thievery, as reflected in the title, Faulkner makes allusions to a mockingbird as Ned recounts his tale to the men seated in the library of Colonel Linscomb, a friend of "Boss" Priest:

> There were. . . pictures of horses and jockeys on the walls . . . and a bronze figure of Manassas. . . on the mantel, . . . and a French win-

dow that opened onto the gallery above the rose garden so that you could smell the roses even in the house, and honeysuckle too and a mockingbird somewhere outside. (284)

On the other hand, Morrison's parents, part of the Great Migration North at the turn of the century, carried with them to their new northern homes traditions with which they had grown up in the South, thereby imparting the storytelling tradition to subsequent generations. Importantly, Morrison's describes her first trip to the South as similar to "going home" inasmuch as "Black culture survives everywhere pretty much the same way" (Wilson 136). Morrison deems the folklore of the past of inestimable worth for its instructional value; also, for its authentic measure of African Americans for the unique individuals that they are:

> I don't want to disregard that mythology because it does not meet the credentials of this particular decade or century. I want to take it head on and look at it. It was useful for two thousand years. We also say "primitive," meaning something terrible. Some primitive instincts are terrible and uninformed, some of them not. The problem is to distinguish between those elements in ourselves as human beings, as individuals, and as a culture, that are ancient and pure or primitive—that are there because they're valuable and ought to be there—and those that are primitive because they're ignorant and unfocused. (Ruas 113)

Thus the folklore, as used by both Morrison and Hurston, in contrast with its use by Faulkner in *As I Lay Dying,* obtains a transcendent value not merely a literary one ascribed to characterization. Flannery O'Connor, another Southern author, uses the trickster character in some of her fiction that illustrates as well the popularity of the genre. Witness the short stories "Good Country People" and "The Life You Save May Be Your Own" wherein the Bible salesman in "Good Country People" and the one-arm tramp, Mr. Shiftlet, in "The Life You Save May Be Your Own," are deemed harmless via virtue of stereotype, "I'm just a country boy" (270), and disability. In both instances, the con artists turn the tables on their victims securing a car from Lucynell Crater ("The Life You Save May Be Your Own") and the wooden leg of Joy/Hulga ("Good Country People") that renders the latter immobile. On the other hand, Hurston associated folklore with "a people's artistry and sensibility, their humor, their grievances, their worldview" (Kaplan xxi). Albeit Morrison admits to not having read Hurston until the completion of *The Bluest Eye* and *Sula,* the extent to which critics have been able to link their works makes the correlation all the more "binding" since it underscores a sensibility associated with Black women authors and, more generally, with African American and Southern authors. In an interview with Gloria Naylor, Morrison stated:

> [I]f I had read [Hurston], then you could say I consciously was following in the footsteps of her, but the fact that I never read her and

still there may be whatever they're finding, similarities and dissimilarities, whatever such critics do, makes the cheese more binding, not less, because it means that the world as perceived by black women at certain times does exist. (214)

Chapter 5

Snopeism as a Form of Tricksterism

As was seen in the folktale "Anansi and Anene Go Fishing," denial of the desired object by the subject only enhances its allure to the one being denied its possession, as Anansi is compelled by Anene to accept that which he has voluntarily relinquished—the fish. In similar fashion, the Texan in William Faulkner's *The Hamlet* refuses to make a sale of one of the wild horses to Henry Armstid and thereby ensures Armstid's determination to ascertain the elusive object, despite his lack of means. The sale of the spotted horses by Snopes with the Texas agent, the sale and re-sale of Ike Snopes' $10.00 note for profit, and the exposure by Flem Snopes of Eula's eighteen-year-long affair with Manfred Spain, respectively, become indicators of the crass materialism known as Snopeism in the trilogy *The Hamlet, The Town,* and *The Mansion.* Inasmuch as Snopeism is inseparable from moral degeneracy, Snopes represents the *reductio ad adsurdum* of those roguish qualities found in Anse of *As I Lay Dying* and becomes iconic of the new order of the South. It befalls R.V. Ratliff, the itinerant sewing-machine agent, the lawyer Gavin Stevens, who collectively form the moral nucleus of the trilogy, the insuperable task of attempting to neutralize the character Flem Snopes in the "science and pastime of skullduggery" (82).

Subsequent to Snopes' arranged marriage to Eula Varner, following her impregnation by Hoake McCarron, Snopes returns to Frenchman's Bend accompanied by a Texan named Buck Hipps and a number of wild spotted horses that they aim to trade. Symbols of raw masculine energy, the horses prove irresistible to the more than fifty men (*The Hamlet* 271) gathered outside the lot where they have been corralled to await the auction of the horses which they suspect belong to Flem Snopes but cannot get Eck Snopes, the blacksmith, to confirm. One of the prospective buyers is Henry Armstid who arrives at the auction in time for the Texan's announcement that he will give to Eck Snopes one of the horses on the condition he starts the bidding process. Faulkner's description of the surrey belonging to Armstid is an indicator that Armstid is the least able to afford a horse at the asking price of $15.00 each:

> Another wagon had come up the lane. It was battered and paintless. One wheel had been repaired by crossed planks bound to the spokes with baling wire and the two underfed mules wore a battered harness patched with bits of cotton rope; the reins were ordinary cotton plowlines, not new. It contained a woman in a shapeless gray garment and a faded sunbonnet, and a man in faded and patched though clean overalls. There was not room for the wagon to draw out of the lane so the man left it standing where it was and got down and came forward—a thin man, not large, with something about his eyes, something strained and washed-out, at once vague and intense, who shoved into the crowd at the rear. (276)

Nonetheless, it is his deprived state that makes his bid on one of the horses all the more poignant as it expresses Armstid's psychological need for precisely that which he cannot afford. The objection by Mrs. Armstid to any who would listen that (277) "He ain't no more despair than to buy one of them things . . . and us not but five dollars away from the poorhouse" goes unheeded, particularly by Armstid who is intent on asserting his capacity to bid precisely on that which he can ill afford. Meanwhile Buck Hipps is not reluctant to accept Armstid's bid, despite Mrs. Armstid's curse (279). It is only after Armstid strikes his wife with a coiled rope for her failure to corner the horse, which he must now capture following the purchase, that the Texan voids the sale, instructing Mrs. Armstid, to whom he had returned the banknote, "Get him into the wagon and get him on home" (282). True to form, the Texan's refusal to make the sale only steels Armstid's resolve to purchase the horse, as Armstid retrieves the banknote from Mrs. Armstid and gives it to Flem Snopes, arguing, "It's my horse. I bought it. These fellows saw me. It's my horse" (282).

The trickster ploy of withholding in order to increase longing, as exhibited by the Texan in *The Hamlet,* is characteristic of Brer Rabbit in African American folklore. The story is told in the folktale "Why Br' Gator's Hide is So Horny" the origin of the alligator's horny exterior. Self-satisfied and contemptuous of land creatures, the alligator is fancied in the tale as not "so smart" as he accepts literally Br' Rabbit's comment, "We [land creatures] sho' is been seein' a heap o' trouble!" (Hughes 24). Incredulous at Br' Gator's confession, "I nebber yeddy 'bout him, needer seen him" (24), Br' Rabbit coyly demurs at an introduction he has insinuated he is able to arrange. True to form, the more hesitant Br' Rabbit is to arrange a meeting, the more insistent is Brer Gator's demands: "An' Br' Alligator 'suade an' beg, an' beg an' 'suade, till at last' Br' Rabbit 'gree to show him Trouble" (25). The day of the meeting, Br' Alligator and his family meet Br' Rabbit at the appointed place, a rice field. From there the party is led by Br' Rabbit to a field so thick in broom-grass and briar that "you hardly kin' see roun in it an' tis dry as tinder, an' yaller like de pure gol' (27). On the pretense of being summoned by a voice that only he can hear, Br' Rabbit escapes and torches the field from a distance, announcing as the alligators steadfastly make their way through the thicket, "Br' Alligator! I reckon you is seen Trouble now!" (29). The skulking return of the alligators to their lair following the baptism by fire is said to have produced their horny hide (29-30).

The folktale "Why Br' Gator's Hide is so Horny" demonstrates the effectiveness of indifference to enhance allure; another, "Who Ate Up the Butter?" illuminates the effective use of the decoy. Brer Rabbit deflects suspicion onto Brer Bear although Bear is the one creature immune from culpability since he, among the others, never visited the site of the theft. In similar fashion Flem deflects suspicion away from himself and onto the Texan. Not only does he escape liability for the injury suffered by Armstid who attempted to capture the horse he had purchased, but it is the Texan, not Snopes, who is implicated for fraud. The absurd comedy is played out in the court proceedings of Armstid vs. Snopes and Tull pl. vs. Eckrum.

The runaway horse given to Eck Snopes by the Texan injured Tull; the horse collided with his team as it made its way across the bridge headed in the opposite direction. Since ownership cannot be established absent the legal transfer of property from one hand to another, punitive damages against either the Texan or Flem Snopes cannot be pursued. The only recourse for the plaintiffs is to seize possession of the very animals they have been unable to capture. As the Justice narrates the dispensation due the plaintiffs Tull pl. vs. Eckrum:

> "Your damages are fixed by statute. The law says that when a suit for damages is brought against the owner of an animal which has committed damage or injury, if the owner of the animal either cant or wont assume liability, the injured or damaged party shall find recompense in the body of the animal. And since Eck Snopes never owned that horse at all, and since you just heard a case here this morning that failed to prove that Flem Snopes had any equity in any of them, that horse still belongs to that Texas man. Or did belong. Because now that horse that made your team run away and snatch your husband out of the wagon, belongs to you and to Mr. Tull" (315-16)

James Gray Watson, author of *The Snopes Dilemma: Faulkner's Trilogy*, has enumerated the absurdist elements in the "spotted horses" episode: "Moreover, since Armstid versus Snopes failed to establish Flem's ownership of the horses, the horse that injured Tull still belongs to the Texan. Nonetheless, having been injured by the horse, the injured or damaged party shall find recompense in the body of the animal" (69).

To be sure, Faulkner transmuted his memories into art. Faulkner was chauffeur for his uncle John Faulkner who had been appointed to District Court to fill the vacancy left by the death of Judge W.A. Roane. In the fall 1924, he had waged his own campaign to fill the office to which he had been appointed.

On a trip to Calhoun County, Faulkner had witnessed from a boardinghouse the arrival of wild ponies, their auction, and their escape from the lot before their owners could take possession of them. Joseph Blotner maintains in *Faulkner: A Biography:* "Faulkner was now embellishing whatever he and his uncle John had seen from that boardinghouse veranda in Calhoun County four years ago. Under the minute strokes of his pen the Snopes proliferated" (193).

Another trickster in the trilogy is Egglestone Snopes. A member of the state legislature representing the interests of the citizens of Yoknapatawpha County, Senator C. Egglestone Snopes of *The Mansion* now has aspirations to become United States Congressman for the district, but is thwarted by Ratliff who forces his withdrawal from the race by subjecting him to public scorn. Prior to the incident with the canines, fooled into mistaking Clarence's pants leg for a waystation, Clarence Snopes had demonstrated his effrontery not only by using his opponent's platform to his advantage and the opponent's disadvantage, but had proven his worthiness as a trickster by refusing to participate in the forthcoming election, thus ensuring his electability by being drafted into service as a staunch segregationist opposed to the progressive views of the war veteran Colonel Devries. In the words of Gavin Stevens, "You can't beat him" (957):

> Clarence was already elected, the county and the district would not even need to spend the money to have the ballots cast and counted; that Medal of Honor which the government had awarded Devries for risking death to defend the principles on which the government was founded and by which it existed, had destroyed forever his chance to serve in the Congress which had accoladed him.

By all accounts, Jody Varner, son of Will Varner, had underestimated the threat posed by Snopeism. Flem Snopes had been given a job as clerk in the store on the condition that his father Ab Snopes is prevented from setting fire to Varner's barn. Jody Varner had intended to blackmail Snopes and cheat him out of his crops; a hint of Varner's knowledge of Ab Snopes' prior history would compel Snopes, Varner believed, to put distance between them for fear of reprisals. What Jody Varner had not counted on was himself being displaced, particularly given Flem's perceived innocence: "It was as though its wearer, entering though he had into a new life and milieu already channeled to compulsions and customs fixed long before his advent, had nevertheless established in it even on that first day his own particular soiling groove" (52). The clerk Lump Snopes, who replaces Flem, subsequent to the latter's marriage to Eula Varner, expresses well the sentiment, one of condescension, toward the newcomers, the Snopes, who are largely viewed as interlopers ripe for plucking: "'Has Flem ever said they [horses] was [his]?' he [Lump] said. 'But you town fellows are smarter than us country folks. Likely you done already read Flem's mind'" (295).

The character Heed of *Love,* by Toni Morrison, is underestimated as well. She is dismissed because of her semi-illiteracy; she "knew some block letters but not script" (75). Yet she is characterized as a Brer Rabbit because as an interloper, she is a formidable opponent. When Junior is hired as a personal secretary, Heed playacts the role as a helpless widow. She misleads Junior into thinking she is ripe for the plucking. Meanwhile, Heed assesses the vulnerability of the thief-smarts Junior in order to induce her loyalty, a trait needed given Heed's design: forgery of a "will" that, readers later learn, is itself fraudulent. According to Heed, her gamesmanship has resulted in the losses of others, namely, an entire town, given *her* selection as Billy Cosey's wife, despite her seeming unsuitability:

> Knowing she had no schooling, no abilities, no proper raising, [Papa] chose her anyway while everybody else thought she could be run over. But here she was and where were they? May in the ground, Christine penniless in the kitchen, L haunting Up Beach. Where they belonged. She had fought them all, won, and was still winning. Her bank account was fatter than ever. (72-73)

Heed's ascension is marked in part by a residence on Monarch Street in Silk. On the other hand, Faulkner marks Flem's ascension within the community through Flem's dress: a gray cloth cap and gray trousers, a white shirt, and the latest addition, a black bow tie worn in the fashion of Will Varner whose son Jody Varner Flem has supplanted; rather than underscore a correspondence with the Varners, however, the bow tie accentuates Flem's difference:

> It was not two inches long and with the exception of the one which Will Varner himself wore to church it was the only tie in the whole Frenchman's Bend country, and from that Sunday morning until the day he died he wore it or one just like it—a tiny viciously depthless cryptically balanced splash like an enigmatic punctuation symbol against the expanse of white shirt which gave him Jody Varner's look of ceremonial heterodoxy raised to its tenth power and which postulated to those who had been present on that day that quality of outrageous overstatement of physical displacement which the sound of his father's stiff foot made on the gallery of the store that afternoon in the spring. (58-59)

Some critics, namely, Richard Gray, has identified the anti-Snopesism in *The Hamlet* as symbolic of anti-Semitism since Flem Snopes is attacked for an economic system that he did not create, but instead exploited. Gray writes in *The Life of William Faulkner*:

> Some readers have been tempted to interpret *The Hamlet* as the tale of a peaceful and bucolic community disrupted by an agent of capitalism, in the cool, quiet shape of Flem Snopes. More recent commentators, turning that interpretation on its head, have found a kind of structural anti-Semitism at work in the narrative: by which Flem Snopes becomes the scapegoat, the object of blame for the callous in-

difference of an economic system that he did not introduce, and still less controls, because it was already in place when he arrived. (254-55)

Similarly, Edmond L. Volpe has observed that the anti-Snopesism prevalent in *The Hamlet* represents the prejudice that has been directed against the various immigrant groups to America:

> In many ways, this anti-Snopesism reflects a feeling that is identical with the feeling every new immigrant group in the United States has engendered in the entrenched social group. Before individuals have emerged, the new group is collectively considered immoral, unsanitary, excessively prolific, socially obnoxious, and economically unscrupulous and pushing—in short, a menace to the community. These are the very characteristics of Snopesism. (308-9)

Furthermore, Lyall H. Powers in his work *Faulkner's Yoknapatawpha Comedy* has asserted that Flem Snopes merely mirrors the malignant cancer fostered, it may be added, by the mercantilism already existent within the community:

> The evil that Snopeses do is always to a considerable extent the responsibility of the rest of society. Snopeses somehow realize (by a kind of reductio ad absurdum) the evil already potentially or latently present in society. As they take advantage of the moral decay already begun, they are the sign perhaps even more than the agent of evil and corruption—the scab on the moral sore, or (in Faulkner's own terms) the mold on the cheese. (157)

Will Varner and Ratliff represent the alliance between Snopesism and the community they inhabit. Will Varner is the single largest landowner in Frenchman's Bend, an area populated by the descendants of the foreigner said to have been French, but could have been otherwise, Welsh or Scottish. He is also "beat supervisor in one county and Justice of Peace in the next and election commissioner in both." In a word, he is both maker of the law and executor of the law albeit he seems impervious to the law he has been sworn to uphold. Indicators are that he has become the largest landowner by foreclosures on properties to which he held mortgages. At the very least, there is the hint of double-dealing; Ab Snopes moves his family into a cabin to work the land recently foreclosed by Varner. He is often seen by the townspeople seated in a makeshift chair his blacksmith has constructed by sawing a flour barrel in half, pondering, it is believed, his next foreclosure. At the very least, foreclosure on properties to which he holds liens smacks of conflict of interest. Varner considers his greatest mistake the inability to sell the Old Frenchman's homesite. Over the years, vandals have looted it for kindling; however, as he tells Ratliff, he is reluctant to demolish it as it is a reminder of his "one mistake" (*The Hamlet* 10). Flem's ability to sell the property to Boatwright, Armstid, and Ratliff is testimony to Flem's matchless duplicity.

By design V.K. Ratliff had encouraged Flem Snopes to make a preemptive strike and purchase fifty head of goats from Ben Quick (77) by circulating his intention among the men gathered before Varner's store to purchase the goats for re-sale to a goat rancher, a Northerner, who had recently established a goat ranch in the county. Ratliff had been assured of a profit from the spread between the sub-contract, which he had purchased from the original contract holder, and the original contract. Ratliff had counted on the notes, courtesy of Mink Snopes, kinsman of Flem, to make impregnable his negotiations with Flem, namely, his trade of the goats at $.75 per head for the cancellation of the note belonging to Mink. What Ratliff had not counted on, as he sought to cancel Mink's note to Ike, was the identification of Ike Snopes as an idiot; Flem, his guardian. Thus, cancellation of the note by Flem would result only in its re-sale. To thwart the possibility of inevitable parasitism, Ratliff burns the note at a loss of profit from the transaction and gives to Mrs. Littlejohn, Ike's caregiver, the value of the note plus interest for expenditure in accordance with Ike's needs. In that way, Ratliff achieves at least a Pyrrhic victory over Flem.

In light of the sagacity accorded Ratliff throughout the trilogy, his purchase, alongside Boatwright and Armstid, of the old Frenchman's Bend place from Flem is unbelievable; however, if one relates Ratliff to the horse trader Ab Snopes who equated the successful horse trade with the honor of the community, Ratliff's involvement makes sense. In fact, it would appear to have been telegraphed, as was Ab Snopes' involvement with the legendary horse trader Pat Stamper and the Negro hostler; Ab Snopes' involvement is likened to quicksand: "[Ab] was realizing now he had got in deeper than he aimed to and that he would either have to shut his eyes and bust on through, or back out and quit, get back in the wagon and go on before Beasley's horse even give up to the fish hook" (38-39).

The clerk Lump had remarked in astonishment following the sale of horses for which Flem had denied ownership, "You can't beat him" (302). The same may be said of the horse trader Stamper who trafficked in the fraudulent sale and re-sale of horses to their previous owners. Indeed, his practice is startlingly similar to that of Flem Snopes who, as his nephew's guardian, sells and re-sells Isaac Snopes' note to the possessor of the note for profit. In like manner, Pat Stamper had traded Beasley Kemp's horse to Ab Snopes; Snopes had attempted to trade the same horse to Stamper, but Stamper, upon possession of the horse, had inflated the hide of the horse with a bicycle pump and had re-sold the same horse to Snopes in return for the separator.

The loss for Ab Snopes has been cattle, which his wife had to redeem for the return of the separator; for Armstid, the indemnity and possible loss of his farm; for Ratliff, the trade of earnest money for fool's gold as Armstid, Boatwright, and Ratliff fall for the age-old con of the salted mine; gold is planted for discovery by the miners, at a value far short of the amount paid by the prospectors for the deed to the property. Indeed the cultivation of illusion, for instance, Will Varner's transmogrification of scrawny cattle into full-bred Herefords, a magician's trick analogous to Stamper's, is part and parcel of the legerdemain associated with illusion:

> He [Stamper] was a legend, even though still alive, not only in that country but in all North Mississippi and West Tennessee—a heavy man with a stomach and a broad pale expensive Stetson hat and eyes the color of a new axe blade, who travelled about the country with a wagon carrying camping equipment and played horses against horses as a gambler plays cards against cards, for the pleasure of beating a worthy opponent as much as for gain, assisted by a Negro hostler who was an artist as a sculptor is an artist, who could take any piece of horseflesh which still had life in it and retire to whatever closed building or shed was empty and handy and then, with a quality of actual legerdemain, reappear with something which the beast's own dam would not recognize, let alone its recent owner. (32-33)

In the following aspects—the use of the decoy to distract the mark, the use of the salted mine to separate the mark from his money, but, more importantly, the characterization of Flem Snopes as a nondescript interloper—Snopes and Stamper fit the paradigm of the trickster, or the confidence man, associated with African American folklore. The horse trader Stamper is described as an outsider: "It was the fact that Pat Stamper, a stranger, had come in and got actual Yoknapatawpha County cash dollars to rattling around loose that way. When a man swaps horse for a horse, that's one thing and let the devil protect him if the devil can. But when cash money starts changing hands, that's something else. And for a stranger to come in and start that cash money to changing and jumping from one fellow to another, it's like when a burglar breaks into your house and flings your things ever which way even if he don't take nothing" (37). Daniel Joseph Singal has noted that Faulkner's preparation as a writer began with his omnivorous reading under the tutelage of his mother and maternal grandmother who introduced him to such classics as Grimm's fairy tales, *Robinson Crusoe*, Stevenson's *Treasure Island, Uncle Remus,* and in time the novels of Dickens and Cooper (40). That tutelage was buttressed by the treasure trove of folklore acquired from Callie Barr, alongside the stories and gossip accumulated by Faulkner from his post on the village square (40).

"The trouble with us is, we don't never estimate Flem Snopes right. At first we made the mistake of not estimating him a-tall. Then we made the mistake of overestimating him. Now we're fixing to make the mistake of underestimating him again" (501). These are the words of Ratliff following Flem's substitution of whiskey for developer in Montgomery Ward's studio in *The Mansion* in order to induce the socially sanctioned charge of bootlegging rather than the reviled one of pornography. The Snopes watchers, having witnessed Flem's failure to come to the rescue of Mink Snopes following his murder of Houston, had assumed incorrectly a similar indifference toward a kinsman's fate. What they had failed to calculate was Flem's avid pursuit of respectability, which was signaled by his marriage to Eula Varner and which allied him increasingly against his own kin.

A similar miscalculation pertained to the response of Flem respecting the eighteen-year-long affair between Manfred De Spain and Eula Varner. A cuckolded husband, the townspeople had misinterpreted Flem's lack of intervention for ignorance. As revealed in *The Town,* however, Flem Snopes had simply bided his time until an opportunity arose to exploit the adulterous affair. His ascendancy to bank president was achieved by exposure of the affair indirectly to Will Varner, Eula's father. Rather than risk the disgrace to Eula, Linda, his granddaughter, and the Varner clan, through a threatened divorce, Will Varner had tendered to Flem Snopes his daughter's inheritance, which the granddaughter had then forfeited to Flem in exchange for his agreement to her matriculation at a state university, a forfeiture which established him as a majority stakeholder in one of two Jefferson County banks and assured his ascent to presidency; Manfred De Spain had relinquished his shares in a bill of sale to Flem Snopes in exchange for Eula, who is obliged now to sunder all ties with Flem. She tells lawyer Gavin Stevens:

> "If I don't go with him [Manfred], he'll have to fight. He may go down fighting and wreck everything and everybody else, but he'll have to fight. Because he's a man. I mean, he's a man first. I mean, he's got to be a man first. He can swap Flem Snopes his bank for Flem Snopes's wife, but he cant just stand there and let Flem Snopes take the bank away from him." (*The Town* 635)

The reward of the superintendent's job for unfettered access to Eula and for Flem's silence was the bargain struck earlier by De Spain with Flem. The townspeople, cognizant of the affair, had considered themselves co-conspirators in the adulterous affair since they had sanctioned it through their silence. But as Ratliff had opined, Flem had only feigned ignorance of the affair until the time was ripe for him to benefit from its exposure: "Not catching his wife with Manfred de Spain yet is like that twenty-dollar gold piece pinned to your undershirt on your first maiden trip to what you hope is going to be a Memphis whorehouse. He dont need to unpin it yet" (*The Town* 375).

Not only does Flem become bank President by virtue of being the majority stakeholder, but also he takes possession of Manfred de Spain's residence, or mansion, and bests Will Varner by the use of de Spain as decoy. According to James Gray Watson, author of *The Snopes Dilemma: Faulkner's Trilogy,* such is Flem's ability to exploit human frailties:

> Flem is, in fact, a Baptist deacon, and to Mrs. Varner, Linda's will is yet another instance of Flem's making a profit from his original condonation of sin. Flem leaves it to her to tell her husband about the will, trusting that her aroused Puritan righteousness will heighten

Varner's outrage at again being duped. When Varner arrives in Jefferson, Flem directs the old man's anger against Manfred by the simple expedient of telling Varner that Manfred is Eula's lover. He thereby forces Varner to join with him in ousting De Spain from the bank presidency. With De Spain removed, Flem uses his half interest in Varner's estate to vote himself president, replacing Manfred and duping Varner yet again. (134)

A similar underestimation occurs relating to Linda Snopes, the daughter of Eula Varner Snopes. Widowed in *The Mansion,* she has returned to Jefferson to reside with Flem in the mansion that previously belonged to De Spain. Her husband Barton Kohl is a casualty of the Spanish civil war; she too is a war casualty, as she has been rendered deaf from a shell explosion during her participation in the war effort as an ambulance driver. Her association both during and following the war betokened her Communist ties. Thus unsurprising was the graffiti scrawled on the pavement outside the mansion believed to have been a deterrent to dissuade Linda from her campaign to educate Blacks. The townspeople, suspecting that the scrawled words were a portent of disaster, were hoodwinked again when evidence revealed that Flem Snopes himself not only sought to use Linda's Communist card against her, but that he must have scrawled the words on the pavement himself in order to deflect attention from his malevolent purpose and to garner public sympathy. The narrator Chick Mallison reacts following accounts by his Uncle Gavin:

> He [Flem] will use it to destroy her. It was he himself probably who scrawled Jew Communist Kohl on his own sidewalk at midnight to bank a reserve of Jefferson sympathy against the day when he would be compelled to commit his only child to the insane asylum. (The Mansion 893)

The third installment in the trilogy, *The Mansion,* has been criticized for its redundancies, or summaries of accounts from the previous installments. Edmond L. Volpe has written in *A Reader's Guide to William Faulkner:*

> Despite the profundity of Faulkner's theme in this novel and the masterful way in which it is handled and developed, *The Mansion* has too many weaknesses to rank among Faulkner's great works. For one thing, it shares *The Town's* weakness in being too obviously a finale to the County novels. Too much effort is devoted to tying up loose ends, to re-telling stories that are not essential to the theme and development of the novel. (341)

Others, namely, Lyall H. Powers, have responded more positively to the novel. Powers sees *The Mansion* as a dramatization of the theme—the Saving Remnant—inasmuch as Linda Snopes sets in motion the series of events that lead to the destruction of Flem Snopes and, in so doing, avenges, through Mink as agent, both her mother and Manfred De Spain, the two individuals Flem has destroyed:

> Of course [Mink] has help, and mainly from Linda, Eula's daughter. And in the union of Linda and Mink for the purpose of exterminating Flem, we have the conjunction of two of Faulkner's major dominant themes. To the theme of the Self-Destructiveness of Evil is now added the theme of the Second Chance (the Quo Vadis theme, which we have already seen stated briefly in the story of the Reverend J.C. Goodyhay). (238)

By the same token, the novel *The Town* has been identified as flawed not only because of the reduction of Eula Varner, "a mythic figure of the female principle" (Powers 221), to the commonplace, but also because of the inconsistent characterization of Will Varner who shifts from moral indifference to Eula Varner's pregnancy by Hoake McCarron in *The Hamlet* to outrage at Eula's infidelity with Manfred De Spain in *The Mansion.* This vacillation, according to Volpe, is difficult for the reader to accept, especially from a character who himself is described as morally challenged:

> Will Varner's role in the crisis is difficult to accept, also. In *The Hamlet,* he is a likeable character despite his immoral financial and sexual activities. He is certainly no moralist. Jody is outraged when Eula announces that she is pregnant, but Will is calm. . . . In *The Town,* we are hardly prepared for Will's role as moralist by Gavin's repetition of information he received from Ratliff: that Will had three mulatto concubines "By whom he now had grandchildren." (327)

The blurred characterization associated with Will Varner also defines Eula. In the second installment of the Snopes trilogy, for instance, Eula is related to by Gavin Stevens, one of the three narrators in *The Town,* as an Earth Goddess: "The fact is, though, that all the narrators share the tendency to translate Eula into an earth goddess, and to see her in terms of desire and absence: to identify her, in short, with a familiar Faulknerian vocabulary that spells out the legendary name, 'Woman'" (Gray 340). However, in the subsequent depiction of her as a suicide determined to salvage respectability for her daughter Linda, she is diminished to the commonplace. The fissure in her characterization, according to Gray, testifies to Faulkner's uncertainty of purpose:

> The two versions of Eula, Lilith and Bovary, the 'incandescent shape' 'too much . . . for any one human female package to contain' and the pathetic victim of the boredom of provincial life: these do not go together, any more than the narrative idioms to which they belong do. We are left, as a result, with a character who is neither clear nor clearly represented as an enigma: someone about whom the author

seems to have changed his mind, in the course of writing the book. (341)

For his part, Faulkner was aware of discrepancies that resulted in part from his transcription of tales, many of which had been published separately as short stories, over a span of years. In a 10 February letter to his agent Albert Erskine, Faulkner had enumerated some of the discrepancies in the trilogy, one of which had to do with the age of Clarence Snopes, which varied from 20-25 in *Sanctuary* to 19 and 28, respectively, in *The Town* and *The Mansion,* albeit the date— 1928—was unchanged. Faulkner had qualified these discrepancies by noting that "the essential truth of these people and their doings, is the thing; the facts are not so important" (*Selected Letters* 422).

Unchanged, however, in *The Hamlet, The Town,* and *The Mansion* is the portraiture of Eula Varner as an object of exchange. Will Varner enters into a transaction with Flem Snopes which provides him the deed to the old Frenchman's place in exchange for his marriage to his pregnant daughter. Similarly, Flem Snopes trades on his knowledge of the adulterous affair between Eula and Manfred De Spain in order to remove De Spain from his bank presidency; simultaneously, De Spain trades his majority stake in the Jefferson bank in return for Eula. In each instance, Eula is subordinated to the material interests of others who manipulate her will for their own schemes. James Gray Watson has maintained that Eula is analogous to "a twenty-dollar gold piece that earned eighteen years of interest" (145).

The portraiture of Eula as a commodity in the trilogy coincides with that of Heed in Toni Morrison's novel *Love* and evidences the intersection of race and gender in both the interpersonal and social spheres.

Chapter 6

The Elliptical Narrative Prose Style of William Faulkner and Toni Morrison

Toni Morrison opens her seventh novel with the enigmatic words, "They shoot the white girl first" (*Paradise* 3). Thus readers are thrust headlong into the novel that is jumpstarted by a question that remains unanswered even at the novel's conclusion. Louis Menand, author of "The War Between Men and Women," identifies Seneca as "a white runaway" (79); however, as has been argued in the chapter "High-topped Shoes . . . ," the brogan has often been used by Faulkner as a signifier of race, or a condition of servitude. The brogan is invested with similar meaning in Morrison's oeuvres. Witness the invitation of Blacks to their Southern kin at the turn of the century, as recorded in the novel *Jazz:* "We got room now, so pack your suitcase and don't bring no high-top shoes" (32). Ron David, author of *Toni Morrison Explained: A Reader's Road Map to the Novels,* argues that an indicator of race resides in the unspoken: "Whatever you specify, I should turn the word over like a coin and look at the other side. There's nothing outlandish about that. If a writer points out the Asians and blacks and Latinas, it's a pretty sure bet that he is None of the Above. You are at the center of the world you create [. . .] and the only way I can find you is to look in the spaces between the things you specify" (179). In light of his theory that the specifier is often the obverse of that specified, David concludes that Mavis, given her remark regarding Soan, is white: "The black woman opened her arms" (43). Additional credence of David's claim is Mavis's comment on Pallas' hair, described as "thick" and "curly" (171), one that underscores a difference rather than a similarity between the two: "Mavis stopped her stroking. 'I love your hair'" (*Paradise* 182). For her part, Toni Morrison has insisted that an issue is made of race in *Paradise* for the explicit purpose of its disavowal:

> "I did that on purpose," Morrison says. "I wanted the readers to won-
> der about the race of those girls until those readers understood that
> their race didn't matter. I want to dissuade people from reading litera-
> ture in that way." And she adds: "Race is the least reliable informa-
> tion you can have about someone. It's real information, but it tells
> you next to nothing." (qtd. in Gray 67)

The mercurial identities of the females—Mavis, Pallas, Seneca, and Con-solata—in *Paradise* are consonant with the slippage that readers find in both Faulkner's *Light in August* and *Sanctuary*. On the array of unidentified pronouns, a Faulknerian trademark, Frederick R. Karl has written in *William Faulkner: American Writer* (352):

> The opening passage [of *Sanctuary*] is full of unidentified "he's,"
> some of them belonging to the unidentified Horace, some to a Negro
> murderer awaiting execution for the slashing death of his wife. The
> "he" without any identity is a key Faulkner device, not only technical
> but metaphysical—turning a common pronoun into a search for
> meaning. The "he" alone creates mystery, as the reader fumbles
> searchingly for references. We learn eventually that the initial "he" is
> Horace, but then the pronoun is shifted to the Negro murderer; yet
> even before we learn of Horace, we as readers assign "he" to the
> jailed man. There is a curious phenomenon, since Horace as a lawyer
> seems to be "free," whereas the Negro is doomed. But the crossing
> over suggests Horace plays many roles—a point Faulkner makes with
> this novel and with comparable characters throughout his middle
> work. (352)

The novels *Light in August* and *Sanctuary,* by William Faulkner; *Jazz* and *Para-dise,* by Toni Morrison, will be the focus of this chapter; more specifically, the elliptical narrative prose style of the two authors, as illuminated in their respec-tive works, that both mimics speech and invites a participatory response from readers.

William Faulkner has shed some light on the use of multiple narrators in his fiction. Queried on the title of the short story "Was," his comments under-score a common history shared by the narrators past and present:

> [T]his background which produced Issac McCaslin had to be told by
> somebody, and so this is Issac McCaslin's uncle, this Cass here is not
> old Ike, this is Ike's uncle. And "Was" simply because Ike is saying
> to the reader, I'm not telling this, this was my uncle, my great-uncle
> that told it. That's the only reason for "Was"—that this was the old
> time. (*Faulkner in the University* 38)

Evidence of a shared history is contained in the short story "Delta Autumn" of *Go Down, Moses.* The great great grandson of Carothers McCaslin, Roth Edmonds, repeats the crime of his great great grandfather, namely, that of incestuous miscegenation; Roth Edmonds has fathered a son with the granddaughter of James Beauchamp, or his great uncle, that he has refused to acknowledge. The now eighty-year-old Ike McCaslin, who has repudiated his patrimony upon discovery of the crime of the past, can only await with dread the destruction of the soil at the hands of those who have defiled it. Importantly, on the annual hunting trip that he anticipates will be one of his last, predictably, his kinsman kills a doe, an act that carries with it a theme of the apocalypse: "'We don't kill does because if we did kill does in a few years there wouldn't even be any bucks left to kill, Uncle Ike,' Wyatt said" (347). John Duvall reads Morrison's fiction as a reclamation of self that is inimical to the construction of Black identity found in Faulkner; also, as a response to *Go Down, Moses.* In *Song of Solomon* and *Go Down, Moses,* the doe, according to Duvall, assumes totemic properties for characters:

> Guitar's story would certainly be understood by Ike McCaslin who knows that the hunter must not kill does because they, more than bucks, insure that there will be deer to kill in the future. But in "Delta Autumn," doe hunting takes on a number of meanings. For one of the men, it is a way to tease Roth Edmonds about the young African-American woman with whom Edmonds has had an affair. Does, however, take on a different significance for Ike (who does not yet know of Roth's affair) in the context of America's imminent involvement in World War II. But from the protection of women and children, the metaphor returns by the story's end to the specificity of the young African-American woman. After learning that his kinsman Roth Edmonds has repeated the very act—incestuous miscegenation—that caused him, Ike, to repudiate his patrimony, he intuits that the deer Roth has killed is a doe. (84)

For his part, Faulkner has emphasized that the short story "Delta Autumn" brings full circle the cycle of incest and miscegenation begun with McCaslin that yokes together irreparably his descendants one to the other. In response to the question of whether the "incest of Roth Edmonds in 'Delta Autumn' complete[d] a cycle of incest and miscegenation begun by old McCaslin and only interrupted by the goodness of Buck and Buddy and Ike in the middle," Faulkner had responded, "Yes, it came home. If that's what you mean by complete a cycle, yes, it did" (*Faulkner in the University* 277).

Indeed, the ambiguous pronouns in Faulkner's literature inscribe the characters as chameleons, an attribute that Frederick Karl has related to the author himself: "Although the military deceptions [Faulkner] perpetuated about himself gradually lessened, he maintained artifice by way of obscure prose, hiding his traces, camouflaging himself. Like the hunter he was, Faulkner insisted on stealth: pronouns rather than names create stealthy reading" (388).

Joe Trace of Toni Morrison's *Jazz* also exudes characteristics of a chameleon. He had re-named himself after his abandonment by parents who "left him without a trace" (125): "Before I met her [Dorcas] I'd changed into new seven times. The first time was when I named my own self, since nobody did it for me, since nobody knew what it could or should have been" (123). His metamorphosis Trace compares to that of a snake shedding its skin (129): "They say snakes go blind for a while before they shed skin for the last time." His attempt during his third change (127) to re-unite with the female believed to be his mother, Wild, had been unsuccessful. Thus, Joe's pursuit of the eighteen-year-old Dorcas Manfred, the female with whom he has had an affair, replicates the fifty-year-old's desire to be re-united with the lost mother associated in his mind with redwings:

> "[Joe] hauled himself down the incline and, as he turned to go four redwings shot up from the lower limbs of a white-oak tree. Huge, isolated, it grew in unlikely soil—entwined in its own roots. Immediately Joe fell to his knees, whispering: 'Is it you? Just say it. Say anything.'" (178)

The imagery at the end of the novel, evocative of the murdered Dorcas and the female Wild, suggests a fusion of characters; concomitantly, a reclamation of self:

> Lying next to her [Violet], his head turned toward the window, he sees through the glass darkness taking the shape of a shoulder with a thin line of blood. Slowly, slowly it forms itself into a bird with a blade of red on the wing. Meanwhile Violet rests her hand on her chest as though it were the sunlit rim of a well and down there somebody is gathering gifts (lead pencils, Bull Durham, Jap Rose Soap) to distribute to them all. (224-25)

The correspondence between Dorcas and Wild has been commented upon by Missy Dehn Kubitschek in her work *Toni Morrison: A Critical Companion:* "The imagery here connects Joe with both Dorcas and Wild. At the same time, Violet is connected with the well in which her mother drowned—but the well contains, not Rose Dear's dead body, but her live spirit blessing her children with gifts" (159). Likewise, Philip M. Weinstein, author of *What Else But Love? The Ordeal of Race in Faulkner and Morrison,* has observed the twinned relationship between the eighteen-year-old Dorcas with whom Joe Trace has had an affair and Wild, the missing parent for whom his wife Violet has served as surrogate:

Orphans meeting though thirty-five years apart, [Trace] mothers this girl, fathers her, loves her as the Violet he has lost, as the woman for whom Violet was the substitute. The roles blend into each other, all of them related under the sign of loss represented by the missing Mama. (155)

More to the point, Philip M. Weinstein contends in his work that Morrison reprises with a twist in *Jazz* several of the most salient motifs in Faulkner's *Absalom, Absalom!*, namely, that of abandoned sons in search of their paternal origins (145). Witness Charles Bon of *Absalom* and Joe Trace and Golden Gray of *Jazz;* however, unlike Thomas Sutpen of *Absalom, Absalom!*, Golden Gray's father is Hunter's Hunter, a character more evocative of Sam Fathers from *Go Down, Moses* than the white scion Thomas Sutpen of *Absalom*. Weinstein elaborates on the distinctions between the two characters Charles Bon of Faulkner's *Absalom* and Golden Gray of Morrison's *Jazz:*

Morrison makes the father black, however, and that changes everything. Faulkner's wounded son looking for the authority of the white origin becomes Morrison's wounded son missing the authority of the black origin. In place of Bon's eroticized paternal investment—which drains his relationships with others of substance, which leads (when balked) to suicidal immolation—Golden Gray's commitment to the father is schizoid: hatred of the racial contamination, longing for the paternal blessing. In other words, paternity without patriarchy. (148)

Morrison's signification upon Faulkner is resonant not only in the elliptical prose style of her fiction and her reprisal of Faulknerian motifs, but as well in the catalogue of names that invites an intertextual reading of *Jazz* and *Go Down, Moses*. Witness the following: a cat in *Jazz* that is given the name dog (152), quite reminiscent of the fyce in "Bear" from *Go Down, Moses* given the name "Lion"; a sawmill town wherein Trace finds work in *Jazz* is given the name "Bear"; and the character Wild, described by Golden Gray as possessing "deer eyes" (152), calls to mind the slain doe of "Delta Autumn" that is symptomatic of modern blight. Indeed, Morrison fingers in *Jazz* the image of Faulkner's Bear, or Old Ben, that in *Go Down, Moses* is associated with a lost Eden, but in Morrison's *Jazz* becomes inseparable from shame related to a conceptualization of Blacks as inscribed by others (178-79):

A woman who frightened children, made men sharpen knives, for whom brides left food out (might as well—otherwise she stole it). Leaving traces of her sloven unhousebroken self all over the county. Shaming him before everybody but Victory, who neither laughed nor slant-eyed him when Joe told him what he believed Hunter meant by those words and especially that look.

Faulkner's extensive use of animal imagery to create character is readily apparent in the short story "Fox Hunt." The pedigreed New Yorker Harrison Blair spends two months in Carolina engaged in fox hunting, a sport that becomes a metaphor for his competitive instincts. A black horse that Steve Gawtry, a would-be rival, purports to own Blair insists on purchasing, even though the black horse is one that Gawtry, purportedly, refuses to sell. The details of this "talk story" are gleaned from conversations between Blair's chauffeur and valet, observers and, to an extent, manipulators of the action, as the valet is the one who concocts the story of the horse that results in Blair's wife being used as bait, or lure. The analogy between the female, or vixen (589), and the fox Faulkner makes clear from references to the female's hair as "brush" and eyes "red like a fox's and then brown again like a fox" (592). The outcome of the short story, the trampling of the fox by Blair in advance of the pack of hounds, hints at a role inimical to nature. As Edmond L. Volpe summarizes in *A Reader's Guide to William Faulkner: The Short Stories:*

> Faulkner uses animal imagery throughout the story ["Fox Hunt"]. Animals, in fact, are almost as predominant as people. Seldom do we catch glimpses of the principal characters except on horses. The cumulative effect of the emphasis on animals is to make us aware of man's relationship to the world of nature and his abuse of that relationship. (118)

Man's defilement of nature evinces a spiritual malaise: "By living close to the world of nature, by being forced to pit themselves against the land, human beings remain aware that they are an integral part of the natural world, with its immutable patterns in which all living things must die and return to earth. Whatever tends to blind man to this reality—any and all of these abstract forces Faulkner considers inimical" (Volpe 248-49). Recall Roth Edmonds' denudation of the great granddaughter of James Beauchamp in "Delta Autumn" that is correlated to man's denudation of nature, or fall from grace (349):

> "But He said, 'I will give him his chance. I will give him warning and foreknowledge too, along with the desire to follow and the power to slay. The woods and fields he ravages and the game he devastates will be the consequence and signature of his crime and guilt, and his punishment.'"

Antipodal to Roth Edmonds is the Bear, or Old Ben, a symbol of indestructibility that emanates from his oneness with nature, or his natural habitat: "Then it [Old Ben] was gone. It didn't walk into the woods. It faded, sank back into the wilderness without motion as he had watched a fish, a huge old bass, sink back into the dark depths of its pools and vanish without even any movement of its fins" (*Go Down, Moses* 209).

The literature by William Faulkner, in its conjuration of "the imminent loss of an Arcadian condition," is interpreted by some as representative of the pastoral tradition: "[T]his emotional foreboding, usually combined with a sense of childhood passing, is followed by a determination to re-create the lost world by some form of imaginative escape from or indictment of the new condition" (MacKethan 157). In her work *The Dream of Arcady: Place and Time in Southern Literature,* Lucinda Hardwick MacKethan examines the novels *Sartoris, Absalom, Absalom!, The Sound and the Fury,* and *Go Down, Moses* as expressions of loss and regret toward a world that Faulkner's characters wished to re-create.

Thadious M. Davis, author of *Games of Property: Law, Race, Gender, and Faulkner's* Go Down, Moses, has observed that Old Ben, the Bear, has been problematic for her precisely due to its abstractionism; however, Faulkner's work *Go Down, Moses,* interpreted by Davis against the grain, holds out new possibilities (7):

> In fact, even one of Faulkner's most celebrated textual creations seemed to me profoundly retrograde; every time I read "The Old People" and "The Bear," I configured Old Ben, the bear, with a black man's face. In my interactive participation with the narrative and in my interpretation of its deep structure, Old Ben loomed as that mighty abstraction, "The Negro," the trope par excellence of endurance and sufferance. Descriptive, symbolic language and emblematic passages intensified the association and, concomitantly, distanced me as a black reader from the text. Ensconced in the margins, I read against the grain of received critical thinking about both "The Bear" and *Go Down, Moses.*

Davis has identified implicitly a major distinction between Faulkner and Morrison, namely, their imagined audience, as can be gleaned from Faulkner's postulation of "The Negro" as Other. Weinstein agrees with the sentiment, as expressed by Davis, that Faulkner did not envision in his mind's eye a substantial Black audience for his literature:

> As I mentioned in the last chapter, [Faulkner] never envisaged a substantial black audience, and one can only wonder what, if any, difference the emergence of that possibility might have made with respect to the brutality of his language [. . .]. I say this neither to excuse his language nor to wish it were different, but to ponder—as a "might-have-been"—how he might have met that further complication. (188)

To Faulkner's credit, the author has observed in interviews being oblivious to his readership, and the claims made against Faulkner for his insensitivity to Blacks could apply to females as well inasmuch as his portrayals of females are often freighted with inculcated biases that he seeks to overthrow, thus resulting in authorial ambivalence. Witness the females in his works often associated with man's fall. In the hybrid novel-drama, *Requiem for a Nun,* Faulkner reprises characters from the novel *Sanctuary:* Temple Drake and Gowan Stevens. Temple's decision to sneak off to a ball game "because she would have to get on a train to do it" and "because [she] liked evil" (135), becomes analogous to the Fall, as it sets in motion the series of events that lead to murder, rape, and that culminate in *Requiem for a Nun* in infanticide at the hands of Nancy Mannigoe to forestall the infant's abandonment by Temple. The act of infanticide is one for which Temple bears indirect responsibility, as her decision eight years prior forged a bond with Gowan Stevens founded on guilt that the marriage has attempted to expiate. Faulkner, when asked about the symbolic role of women in his literature, "someone is felled by a woman," demurred: "and some men are improved by women. I don't think that I would make any generalization about an opinion of women—some of the best people are women" (*Lion in the Garden* 100). Asked on a separate occasion whether he envisioned a particular audience for his work, Faulkner responded that his own lofty expectations were the force behind his creations:

> [A]t one time in my life I was so busy writing, I wrote so seriously, that I didn't have time to stop and think, "Who will read this? Will he like it, or won't he like it?" Because I was so busy trying to write something that would please me, that would suit me, that would be in my estimation the best. Each time it was not, and I had no time to stop and think who will read this, what will they think, because at that time I was furiously engaged in writing the next one, hoping that that would be the one that would suit me completely, knowing it wouldn't and I would probably have to write another one as soon as that was done. *(Lion in the Garden* 125)

That having been said, the exclusion of the Black reader from Faulkner's creative consciousness, readers may look upon Morrison's fiction as revisionist to the extent that Morrison details in her novel *Paradise* "the [black] phase of the same family [the Edmonds]" that Faulkner had created in *Go Down, Moses* but had not given voice in his fiction. Faulkner had commented on the design of the work:

> "The Bear" was part of a novel. That novel was—happened to be composed of more or less complete stories, but it was held together by one family, the Negro and the white phase of the same family, same people. *The Bear* was just a part of that—of a novel. (*Faulkner in the University* 4)

It is no coincidence that the founding families of Haven are not only given names evocative of "the Negro phase of the same family," namely, Beauchamps (194, 284), but are identified as former Mississippians:

> They were extraordinary. They had served, picked, plowed and traded in Louisiana since 1755, when it included Mississippi; and when it was divided into states they had helped govern both from 1868 to 1875, after which they had been reduced to field labor. They had kept the issue of their loins fruitful for more than two hundred years. (99)

Indeed, the signification of Morrison upon Faulkner's literature has led Missy Dehn Kubitshek to define Morrison's literature as metafiction:

> Analogously, *Jazz* acknowledges the past on the meta-level of literary history. The novel constantly refers to earlier writers' works. Hunters Hunter, for example, strongly resembles a character in Faulkner's *Go Down, Moses,* and Golden Gray revisits Charles Bon in another of Faulkner's works, *Absalom, Absalom!* These examples could be multiplied indefinitely. A reader knowledgeable about the tradition of English meets an ancestral presence in virtually every section of the novel; being *Jazz*, of course, it doesn't simply reproduce these presences but redefines them in the context of its own stories.

An example of the re-definition relates to "the Negro phase of the same family," as Morrison in *Jazz* and in *Paradise* reveals shame as an impact of the familial disinheritance that Faulkner had depicted in *Go Down, Moses,* but had not explored from the perspective of those disinherited. Needless to say, the characters depicted in both Faulkner's and Morrison's works become prisms through which readers view larger society. Sutpen's rejection of Charles Bon in *Absalom, Absalom!* represents the refusal of the South to acknowledge the fraternity of Blacks. On the symbolism of the Sutpen tragedy, Ilse Dusoir Lind has argued in the article "The Design and Meaning of *Absalom, Absalom!*

> The Sutpen tragedy is the means of conveying the larger social tragedy. In its broader outlines, the Sutpen tragedy is in many ways analogous to the social. Sutpen had two sons: one white, the other Negro. He denied the Negro; fratricide resulted. The Civil War, too, was a fratricidal conflict caused by the denial of the Negro. (293)

On the other hand, the disinheritance of the founding families of their political office and personal liberties in *Paradise* becomes emblematic of prejudices founded not wholly on race, but rather on gradations of skin tone. The odyssey of the fifteen founding families was precipitated in part by the divestiture of some of their political office: "Descendants of those whose worthiness was so endemic it got three of their children elected to rule in state legislatures and county offices: who, when thrown out of office without ceremony of proof of wrongdoing, refused to believe what they guessed was the real reason that made it impossible for them to find other mental labor" (193). However, the Fairly homesteaders (189), so deemed because of their light features, had spurned those considered eight-rock because the dark features of the latter were considered an anathema, a curse that the nine founding families (189) were later to make a virtue by a similar exclusion of others unlike themselves. Through this episode in *Paradise,* Morrison reveals not only the manner in which identities are constructed, but distills as well self-hatred, as epitomized by the Fairly homesteaders, as one of the legacies of slavery (189):

> They saved the clarity of their hatred for the men who had insulted
> them in ways too confounding for language: first by excluding them,
> then by offering them staples to exist in that very exclusion. Every-
> thing anybody wanted to know about the citizens of Haven or Ruby
> lay in the ramifications of that one rebuff out of many.

The character Joe Christmas of William Faulkner's *Light in August* like-wise constructs his identity largely in response to the reaction of others toward him. Unsure of his ethnicity, Joe Christmas exists in a no-man's land. Thus he becomes a pawn in the hands of others, such as the dietician, Lucas Burch, the waitress, and Doc Hines, who utilize race both as an offensive and defensive weapon. Collectively, the characters label Joe Christmas "Negro" in order to deflect attention from themselves onto a red herring, Joe Christmas: the dietician, to protect her reputation; Lucas Burch, to avoid the suspicion of murder; the waitress, to redeem herself in the eyes of others, namely, Max and Mame (198), whose good opinion she values; and Doc Hines, to exonerate himself for murder. In these instances, race is shown by Faulkner to be a chimera insepara-ble from the interests of those insistent upon its construct. For the very reason that the ethnicity of Joe Christmas is not supplied, readers therefore are inclined to assess characters based in part upon the extent of their vitriolic response to him.

For example, "Doc Hines," the grandfather of Joe Christmas had called for his grandson's lynching upon news of the murder of Joanna Burden. Yet he is the one who had put the life of his daughter, Milly, at risk by refusing to sum-mon a doctor to preside at Joe's birth. His motives are clear; he seeks the extir-pation of both the daughter he believes has dishonored him and her son by a circus performer who has been described as Mexican (353). Doc Hines had murdered the circus performer believed to have kidnapped his daughter. Thus his label of the Mexican circus performer as "Negro" serves to exonerate him of murder. Importantly, Doc Hines was not charged with murder as the circus owner later corroborated Doc Hines' allegations. It is no accident, though, that the Negro bootlegger Lee Goodwin of *Sanctuary* is lynched after he has been falsely accused of the rape of Temple Drake and the murder of the half-wit committed by the gangster Popeye. Apparently, Faulkner associated with these acts of injustice a retributive justice, as the gangster Popeye is arrested later in Birmingham, charged with the murder of a policeman he claims not to have committed, and is hanged for that murder (308). Edmond L. Volpe confirms in his work *A Reader's Guide to William Faulkner* that the shibboleth "Negro" is expressive of the characters' own guilt, and, one might add, of the characters' own perceived shortcomings (163):

> Like the Jeffersonians who, thirty years later, automatically accept Brown's statement that Christmas is a Negro, the dietician accepts her wild designation as a fact. The shibboleth simplifies the categorizing. It curtains guilt: the anger that should be directed inward finds a convenient external object.

The prototype for Joe Christmas is Nelse Patton, a Black man who was hanged in 1908 in Jefferson, Mississippi, following his murder of Mattie McMillan, a white woman (Blotner 32). The circumstances surrounding the murder are themselves murky; however, unmistakable was the swiftness of mob law, which brooked no interference from the penal system. Rather than await court arraignment, Nelse Patton was taken peremptorily from his jail cell where he had been incarcerated, was castrated and his body mutilated before being put on public display. Faulkner would find in this image of the crucifixion a metaphor for the Black man's persecution.

The persecution of Joe Christmas is in keeping with the Christ-like nature of his persona. The identification of his age as 33 is in keeping also with the allusion. In chapter 10, Faulkner notes that he is 30 years old; in chapter two, Christmas is said to have lived in Jefferson, Mississippi, for close to three years, thus making him 33: "But even the ones who bought the whiskey did not know that Christmas was actually living in a tumble down Negro cabin on Miss Burden's place, and that he had been living in it for more than two years" (32). Volpe has summarized in his work *A Reader's Guide to William Faulkner* the affinity between Joe Christmas and Christ:

> Throughout the novel, many details evoke the story of Jesus. The day, for example, on which Hines brings Joe to the orphanage is Christmas eve, and his initials are those of Jesus Christ. The circumstances of Joe's birth and some incidents from his early years are recounted, but the years of early manhood are obscure. As in the Christ story, the final three years and the crucifixion are fully presented. Lucas Burch, who is identified as Joe's disciple, betrays his master. Wandering around after the murder, Christmas must suddenly know the day of the week, and when he discovers it is Friday, he goes directly to Mottstown to be captured. (172)

Reference has been made already to Faulkner's use of ambiguous pronouns that has the effect of making his characters uniform. More importantly, the fusion of characters serves to accentuate particular traits, such as the ones shared by Horace Benbow and Gavin Stevens of *Sanctuary*: dipsomania and fear. The two characters, on the hunt for bootleg whiskey distilled by Lee Goodwin, enter inadvertently the criminal underworld whose periphery is patrolled by the gangster Popeye. The reference to "the drinking man" in chapter one of *Sanctuary* refers to Horace Benbow (5) and points forward to Gowan Stevens (83), whose garrulousness becomes denotative of fear. The character Tommy relates the two: "I've seen you befo. Nother feller from Jefferson out hyer three-fo nights ago. I cant call his name neither. He sho was a talker, now. Kep on telling how he up and quit his wife" (46). In *Light in August,* the rumors about Hightower propagated by the community that become fact render him likewise indistinguishable from Joe Christmas:

> [Byron] believed that the town had had the habit of saying things about the disgraced minister which they did not believe themselves for too long a time to break themselves of it. 'Because always,' he thinks, 'when anything gets to be a habit, it also manages to get a right good distance away from truth and fact.' (69)

The multiple narrative perspectives in *Light in August* have a doubling function, which creates the effect of mimicry. For example, the account of Doc Hines' pursuit of Milly and her paramour coincides with McEachern's pursuit of Joe Christmas to forestall the individuals' perceived damnation at the hands of putrefaction. Given the radicalism associated with the two, it is unsurprising that females, such as the dietician and the waitress, are deemed inseparable from man's fall from grace. The emphasis on ordination also bestows upon the novel its Biblical cadence: "[Hines] found them like he had known all the time just where they would be, like him and the man that his gal told him was a Mexican had made a date to meet there. It was like he knew" (355).

Following the capture of Joe Christmas, Mr. and Mrs. "Doc" Hines make their way to Jefferson, where he has been extradited. There, in a cabin previously occupied by Lucas Burch and Joe Christmas, Lena Grove gives birth to a son. In this episode, past and present collide, as well as characters. Mrs. Hines confuses the newborn with her lost grandson Joe and seeks redemption through him for her perceived failure to protect Joe from abduction by his grandfather. Indeed, Lyall H. Powers contends in his work *Faulkner's Yoknapatawpha Comedy* that the inverted values of individuals who have taught Joe Christmas hate rather than love have been responsible for Joe's crucifixion, in addition to their own: "Love has become hatred and Joe's religious training is, like the practice of his teachers, blatantly inverted. The explanation of Joe's 'inversion' lies with those who have educated him: his Christ-likeness serves to emphasize the evil of those inverted 'Christians' responsible for driving him into the evil he does. And insofar as that evil harms those who have instilled it in him, those original evil sources (the inverted Christians) are hoist on their own petard—they are themselves victim of the evil they have done" (98). However, with 'Joey,' Lena's son, the townspeople have been given a Second Chance at redemption:

Mrs. Hines lavishes on the baby all the compensatory love she had been unable to bestow on her Milly's Joe. Significantly, it is Mrs. Hines who, in her distraction, gives Lena's baby the only name it bears in the novel, 'Joey,' confusing Lena with her own daughter, the present with the past. Willy-nilly, however, Mrs. Hines has faced her Second Chance and done so with a display of courage and conviction. (99-100)

The theme of Second Chance finds an echo in Toni Morrison's *Paradise* as well. Through the recollections of Patricia Best, the daughter of Roger Best, readers learn that the death of the mother Delia, as a result of childbirth, was due in part to the apathy of the citizenry, behavior similar to that of Doc Hines who had refused to summon a doctor during Milly's delivery of the illegitimate Joe Christmas. Similar to the motives of Doc Hines, the inaction of the citizenry in *Paradise,* in the view of Patricia Best, pertains to their aversion to miscegenation:

All the excuses were valid, reasonable. Even with their wives begging they came up with excuses because they looked down on you, Mama, I know it, and despised Daddy for marrying a wife with no last name, a wife without people, a wife of sunlight skin, a wife of racial tampering. (197)

The threat of miscegenation that the Convent women pose explains their elimination at the end of *Paradise;* however, the failure of the 8-rock men to redress a previous wrong associated with the premature death of Delia Best is tantamount to their forfeiture of the Second Chance. The novel makes clear its re-visitation of the past in the rift between the twins Deacon and Steward that duplicates, to a degree, the irreparable split between their grandfathers Coffee and Tea that was the result of Zechariah's aka Big Papa's self-reproach (302): "Few knew and fewer remembered that Zechariah had a twin, and before he changed his name, they were known as Coffee and Tea." The difference, however, between the split that involves the twins Deacon and Steward is the possibility of forgiveness despite Deacon's recoil from Steward as an assassin. As Deacon confides in the minister Richard Misner:

"I'm thinking Coffee was right because he saw something in Tea that wasn't just going along with some drunken whiteboys. He saw something that shamed him. The way his brother thought about things; the choices he made when up against it. Coffee couldn't take it. Not because he was ashamed of his twin, but because the shame was in himself. It scared him. So he went off and never spoke to his brother again." (303)

Finally, *Light in August,* by William Faulkner; *Paradise* and *Jazz,* by Toni Morrison, share characteristics of detective fiction, but with a major distinction. In the murder mystery, the detective seeks to discover the identity of the murderer. In the literature by Faulkner and Morrison, that information is a given; instead, the authors seek to answer the question *why.* Joseph Blotner, author of *Faulkner: A Biography,* describes as "Conradian" (267) Faulkner's focus on the psychology of the murderer, for example, Mink's murder of Houston and Flem in the Snopes trilogy, rather than on the murders themselves: "Faulkner described the murder at the outset and then concentrated on the murderer's psychology" (267). To the extent that the reader as well is involved in the process of recovery, or re-creation, the role of the reader is correspondent to that of the writer/creator. Edmond L. Volpe summarizes Faulkner's narrative technique in *A Reader's Guide to William Faulkner: The Short Stories:*

> Faulkner's narratives move outward from the individual, local, and particular, like the waves generated by a pebble dropped in a pond, because as investigations of the *why* of human beings, they invariably involve the investigator personally. When Faulkner specifically introduces investigators into his narratives, such as Quentin Compson in *Absalom, Absalom!* or Horace Benbow in *Sanctuary,* his investigators are involved in a process of spiritual and moral self-discovery. By extension, the reader-investigator undergoes a similar experience. (221)

Not only has Toni Morrison commented that she generally reads mystery novels when she travels (Dreifus 75), but in an interview conducted by Elissa Schappell for *The Paris Review,* Morrison described her fiction, namely, *Jazz* and *The Bluest Eye,* as resembling the detective novel:

> "What I really want is for the plot to be *how* it happened. It is like a detective story in a sense. You know who is dead and you want to find out who did it. So, you put the salient elements up front, and the reader is hooked into wanting to know, How did that happen? Who did that and why? You are forced into having a certain kind of language that will keep the reader asking those questions. In *Jazz,* just as I did before with *The Bluest Eye,* I put the whole plot on the first page. (109)

Likewise, in an interview with Anne Koenen, Toni Morrison confessed to relying upon readers to intuit the undercurrent beneath the surface of the language in her fiction, as in her reference to Milkman at the end of *Song of Solomon* of "surrendering to the air in order to ride it." She explains in the interview with Koenen:

> There's this beat in it, in my books there's always something in the blood, in the body, that's operating underneath the language, it's hard

for me to get it in there so that you don't read it. Because I lean heavily on the reader in the book, I don't say it a lot, I mean you have to
rely on the reader to make the images work. But underneath there has
to be some other thing, it's like a heartbeat, or it's like the human responses that are always on the surface in all humans. And you struggle for it, once you know what it is. (215)

The authors' reliance on flashbacks to re-create history, the use of multiple
narrative voices to show confluence, and the involvement of the reader in the
investigative and creative process are some areas whereby the narratives of William Faulkner and Toni Morrison are aligned. The echoes that are found in literature underscore for the reader the reality that art does not take place in a vac-
uum. A study of writers such as William Faulkner and Toni Morrison therefore
reveals insight not only on the literature, but the craft of fiction itself. According
to Joseph Blotner, "[Faulkner] would take from whoever suited him, from the
classics to the Bible to the Elizabethan to the moderns, in the restless experimentation and remarkable capacity for work which would finally lead to his métier"
(131).
     The idea for *A Fable,* Faulkner's "big book," had come from a remark
made by a writer at Warner Brothers following director Henry Hathaway's re-
buff of his screenwriting abilities on a World War I story of the Unknown Soldier. The line—"The only thing that would satisfy you would be if your unknown soldier was Jesus Christ"—Hathaway considered the germ for a
screenplay and enlisted Faulkner as a writer on the project (Blotner 452). The
project never materialized, but the exit line gave ferment to Faulkner's novel *A
Fable,* credit that Faulkner acknowledged upon the book's publication; he also
offered to relinquish motion picture rights to the story to Hathaway and to William Bacher, the movie producer with whom Hathaway had formed a partner-
ship. Perhaps William Faulkner best described the writing process itself when he
spoke of an artist as a magpie who "[picks] up everything" (203):

"I think that's the way the writer goes through life, through books
and through the actual living world too. That he misses very little, not
because he's made up his mind before breakfast not to miss anything
today but because those muscles work for him, and when that need
comes he digs out things that he didn't know where he saw—which
to him didn't matter, he may have stolen it—but to him that's not important. The important thing is if he uses it worthily. If he makes
some base use of it, then of course it's a shame. But he wants to—
when he steals he wants the owner that he stole from to approve of
what he did with it or not to disapprove too much. (*Faulkner in the
University* 203)

Chapter 7

Conclusion

In the chapter "What's in a Name?" the argument was advanced that Toni Morrison's *Paradise* re-creates the Biblical story of Exodus. Toni Morrison's most recent novel, *Love*, dramatizes the origin of sin, or the story of Genesis (190). The title of Faulkner's novel *Absalom, Absalom!* was inspired by the Biblical story of David in the Old Testament involving fratricide and incest. Absalom had murdered his brother Amnon as a result of Amnon's incestuous relationship with their sister Tamar. On the relevance of the title Hyatt H. Waggoner has written in *William Faulkner: From Jefferson to the World:*

> The title of the book, with its Biblical allusion, supports the hypothesis of Shreve and Quentin. Sutpen would not say "My son" to Bon as David said it to Absalom even after Absalom's rebellion. And different as he was from his father, Henry acted in the end on the same racist principle, killing Bon finally to prevent not incest but miscegenation. One meaning of Absalom then is that when the Old South was faced with a choice it could not avoid, it chose to destroy itself rather than admit brotherhood across racial lines. (165)

Faulkner's avowal of a dearth of storied content puts the author, according to Robert W. Hamblin, in the ranks of writers such as James Joyce, T.S. Eliot, Willa Cather, Ernest Hemingway, James Steinbeck, and, one might add, Toni Morrison whose literature may be characterized as "mythic" due in part to its Biblical content:

> Faulkner's insistence that there are only a relatively few basic story lines that are repeated over and over down through the centuries places him with other writers of his time—notably Joyce, Eliot, Cather, Hemingway, O'Neill, MacLeish, Steinbeck, and Warren— who interwove their poems and narratives of contemporary life with ancient stories that have survived from primitive folklore, Greek or Roman mythology, or the Bible. Eliot gave this distinctly modern way of writing a name, calling it "the mythical method," and Faulkner became one of the method's greatest practitioners. (282)

For her part, Toni Morrison does not subscribe to the view that her literature is identifiable with that written by James Joyce or William Faulkner although she admits to being flattered by the comparison. In a 1983 interview with Nellie McKay, Morrison expressed the need for a new kind of criticism more culturally based, as the model for what she has attempted to achieve in her literature is found most commonly in music, namely, jazz (152):

> We have no systematic mode of criticism that has yet evolved from us, but it will. I am not *like* James Joyce; I am not *like* Thomas Hardy; I am not *like* Faulkner. I am not *like* in that sense. I do not have objections to being compared to such extraordinarily gifted and facile writers, but it does leave me sort of hanging there when I know that my effort is to be *like* something that has probably only been fully expressed in music, or in some other culture-gen that survives almost in isolation because the community manages to hold on to it. Sometimes I can reflect something of this in my novels. Writing novels is a way to encompass this—this something. (152)

Morrison's attempt to distance herself from Faulkner, despite the many references to him, on the basis of her distinctive role as reader and writer John Duvall considers disingenuous, particularly in light of Morrison's project *Playing in the Dark* that sprang from her stance as a writer reading rather than as a reader reading:

> My point is, simply, that when Morrison claims, as she does in *The Paris Review* interview, that her classroom technique of Faulkner proceeds from being "fascinated by what it means to write like" Faulkner, she is reading the same way she reads Cather and Hemingway—as a writer reading. It may be useful and enabling fiction for Morrison to see her novels as unmarked by Faulkner. Nevertheless, the rhetorical separation between reader and writer that Morrison wishes to maintain in her critical discourse largely collapses. (81)

Morrison has gone on to remark in the McKay interview and elsewhere that the improvisational nature of jazz, its distinctive melodic voices, and its rootedness in the African American tradition are among some of the features that her novels share with jazz. In an interview with Elissa Schappell of *The Paris Review,* Toni Morrison spoke of her novel *Jazz* and its improvisational style (116-17):

> *Jazz* was very complicated because I wanted to re-present two con-
> tradictory things—artifice and improvisation, where you have an art-
> work, planned, thought through, but at the same time appears in-
> vented, like jazz. I thought of the image being a book. Physically a
> book, but at the same time, it is writing itself. Imagining itself. Talk-
> ing. Aware of what it is doing. It watches itself think and imagine.
> That seemed to be to be a combination of artifice and improvisa-
> tion—where you practice and plan in order to invent. Also the will-
> ingness to fail, to be wrong, because jazz is performance. In a per-
> formance, you make mistakes, and you don't have the luxury of
> revision that a writer has; you have to make something out of a mis-
> take, and if you do it well enough it will take you to another place
> where you never would have gone had you not made that error.

Exemplary of the improvisational performance of the novel *Jazz* is the attempt by the narrator to re-imagine the quest of Golden Gray for his lost father
Henry LesTroy, "a man of no consequence, except a tiny reputation as a tracker
based on one or two escapades signaling his expertise in reading trails" (149), as
motivated not by the intent of patricide, but rather by the need for self-
validation:

> What was I thinking of? How could I have imagined him so poorly?
> Not noticed the hurt that was not linked to the color of his skin, or the
> blood that beat beneath it. But to some other thing that longed for au-
> thenticity, for a right to be in this place, effortlessly without needing
> to acquire a false face, a laughless grin, a talking posture. (160)

Unique to the novel *Love,* by Toni Morrison, is likewise Morrison's implicit view of art as performance. The intradiegetic narrator, one who is involved
in the narrative action she narrates and who thereby dissolves the distance between the reader and the narrator, speaks in a self-reflexive manner of the tale
she embarks on in the novel, a tale that features the Cosey women Heed, Christine, and May, all yoked by their relationship to Cosey, respectively, as wife,
granddaughter, and daughter-in-law. L. also articulates the instructional value of
her tale; it is to serve as a cautionary one "to scare wicked females and correct
unruly children" (10); its aesthetic value, though, she deems "trash."

A chef at Cosey's Hotel and Resort and later at Maceo's, L. had died, so to
speak, "with her boots on"; she had died while smothering pork chops at Maceo's (189). L's identity in the novel as chef is important as, a signature feature
of American female artists, such as Gwendolyn Brooks and Sylvia Plath, the
domestic artist is endowed with creative properties often associated with the
storyteller. The novel *Love,* a ghost story, is protean as, similar to the tune of the

jazz artist, it diverges from its original conceptualization as one "to scare wicked females and correct unruly children" and becomes rather a celebratory one of the enduring bonds of female friendship, namely, between Heed and Christine, that withstand betrayal—whites' betrayal of blacks, blacks' betrayal of blacks, and men's betrayal of women—loss, and abandonment (199-200). The female collectivism is magnified despite the alignment of some of the females, namely, Vivian (Junior's mother) with the males, namely, Vivian's brothers, who terrorize her daughter.

Contrapuntal to *Love* is the jazz album. The classic jazz album *Kind of Blue,* by Miles Davis, was entirely improvisational, as the musicians tapped to perform—John Coltrane on tenor saxophone; Julian "Cannonball' Adderley on alto; pianist Bill Evans; pianist Wynton Kelley; bassist Paul Chambers; and drummer Jimmy Cobb—had not previously performed ensemble the selections. Quincy Troupe, co-author of *Miles: The Autobiography,* writes:

> Miles told me that when he recorded *Kind of Blue,* and to get closer to a certain way of group playing he felt he needed on the album, he didn't write out the parts for the musicians. But instead, he brought into the New York studio musical sketches of what everyone was supposed to play, because he wanted a lot of spontaneity and improvisation in their playing. He hoped in this way that they might come close to the interplay he remembered seeing and hearing between the dancers and musicians of the *Ballet Africaine.* (122)

On the signature sound of jazz artists, a uniqueness that resonates as well in the literature of some African American authors, Toni Morrison had the following to say in the 1993 interview with Elissa Schappell of *The Paris Review:*

> In so much of contemporary music everybody sounds alike. But when you think about the difference between Duke Ellington and Sidney Bechet or Satchmo or Miles Davis. They don't sound anything alike, but you know that they are all black performers, because of whatever that quality is that makes you realize, "Oh yes, this is part of something called the African-American music tradition." (117)

The sentiment of Toni Morrison is echoed by musicians in their assessment of the signature sound of other musicians. For example, Wynton Marsalis has described the sound of Miles Davis as a potpourri of disparate musical voices that includes, among others, Thelonious Monk. According to Marsalis, Miles Davis learned from Monk that he could use harmonic ideas newly arrived in a spare, telling way (*The Adventure: Jazz*). Similarly, Quincy Troupe describes Davis as "a portal, a doorway or entry point to the wide range of African American music":

> A great trumpet player, composer, and bandleader, a restless, contro-
> versial, and innovative musician in a career of almost fifty years,
> Davis crossed geographical, genre, and generational borders and pro-
> duced a music that blurred and eventually erased musical catego-
> ries—classical, jazz, rock, rhythm and blues, pop, fusion, funk, world
> music, hip-hop—with stunning originality. (119)

On the same note, John Gennari, in his article "Miles and the Jazz Critics," describes the eclecticism of Miles Davis as an amalgam of contradictory impulses:

> One of the hallmarks of Miles Davis's power as a black artist was his
> facility at absorbing, managing, and manipulating his white influ-
> ences, both in the sound of his music and in the shaping of his career.
> Davis was deeply rooted in the blues and an heir to a tradition of
> black trumpeters that included Louis Armstrong, Freddie Webster,
> Ray Nance, Clark Terry, Rex Stewart, Harry Edison, Buck Clayton,
> Fats Navarro, and Dizzy Gillespie. (70)

The eclecticism associated with jazz is found also in Morrison's fiction.
Discussion of Toni Morrison's literature, namely, *Tar Baby,* has revealed the
influence of oral literature, or folktales, on her craft. Likewise, Betty Fussell has
spoken of blues and jazz among the developmental influences on Morrison's
craft: "In her novels, Morrison seeks to restore the oral language of black people, the mix of blues and jazz and gossip and tales" (285). Other African American authors, among them Ernest Gaines, have credited oral literature, in addition
to the blues and jazz, as a major influence on their art. For example, the repetition that one finds in Southern speech, "I said this; he said that," similar to the
call-and-response of jazz musicians, Ernest Gaines has aimed to emulate in his
literature (Interview with Kay Bonetti). Comparatively, the melodic technique of
jazz trumpeter Miles Davis, made analogous to a Matisse painting "where a single line can suggest a full three-dimensional volume" involves, according to
Martha Boyle, repetition:

> Davis's way with melody also involved repetition, though not in the
> minimalist sense. In his best music, notes Wynton Marsalis, Davis
> repeats a "sweet" melodic motive only as long as it takes to squeeze
> the sweetness out, then drops it and hunts for another. In his pre-
> fusion music this development of the motive related closely to
> Davis's awareness of harmonic structure, even within the loose
> boundaries of modal improvisation. (162)

Joseph Blotner in his work *William Faulkner* details the twin personas of
the artist: "A great artist was both an imitator and an innovator, but he [she] was also a
solitary who avoided groups and schools. He [she] should write poetry as a preparation
for writing prose, but he [she] should be prepared for hostile reactions to both and for
lack of recognition of his true merit" (Blotner 106). Albeit Blotner addresses his

comments specifically to William Faulkner, they are applicable as well to Toni Morrison. As an artist, Morrison models herself after the jazz musician; that is, she utilizes the method of antagonistic cooperation associated with the jazz musician; similarly, as is true of the jazz artist, there is the obsession with "making it new."

Dana A. Williams relates in the work *"In the Light of Likeness Transformed": The Literary Art of Leon Forrest* the influence of gospel, blues, and jazz on the craft of Leon Forrest; the jazz method of composition, antagonistic cooperation, is said by Williams to figure prominently in the literature by Forrest. Williams argues that to the extent that antagonistic cooperation is found in scenes in the novel *Divine Days,* by Forrest, it is found also in texts by different authors, namely, Ralph Ellison and Toni Morrison: "[Forrest] acknowledges that this antagonistic cooperation occurs between texts as well, admitting that his quest is to outplay the masters he riffs on, quarrels with, and celebrates as he invokes their work and their artistry" (15).

Such antagonistic cooperation is found in fiction by modernists William Faulkner and Toni Morrison, two writers with whom Forrest shares a connection. As an editor at Random House, Morrison was responsible for Forrest's first publication *There Is a Tree More Ancient Than Eden* (5 Williams); Forrest has identified Faulkner as having influenced his craft:

> Faulkner was certainly a strong influence, in general. [He] showed me a way of breaking open the sentence structure and opening it up so you could go for broke. Also, Faulkner's sensitivity to black life in a general way and his understanding of some aspects of the complexity of these relationships [. . . .] I think the best of Faulkner is involved with black life[. . . .] Faulkner also is very helpful in terms of clues. You can mention what he did with Rev. Shegog's sermon, for example. I have to go beyond that. There's certainly competition as Faulkner himself said, "The young guy, if he is worth his salt, he wants to be the old guy." (qtd. in Williams, 24)

Attention was paid in an earlier chapter to Toni Morrison's knack for reversal of racial stereotypes often found in the literature by Faulkner. The "high-topped shoe," or the brogan, rather than a symbol of shame, becomes in literature by Morrison, one of pride. In her later work, there is every indication that Morrison is intent on "making it new"; the generic shoe, which has assumed iconic status in Faulkner, assumes brand-name specificity in the literature by Morrison. The correlation would be the Timberland boot that has assumed brand-name status among those in the hip-hop community. In the most recent literature by Toni Morrison, the brand name, huaraches, has become the moniker for those belonging to the middle-class. It makes a lone appearance in *Love;* the purchase by Heed, following her marriage to Cosey, signals her ascendancy to the middle-class; also, the shoe, huaraches, makes a single appearance in the novel *Paradise.*

Identifiable with the 16-year-old Pallas, daughter of a lawyer for black crossover entertainers, are the material objects that link her to the bourgeoisie. Her apparel is nothing less than the genuine article: 18-caret earrings, custom-made jeans, and expensive leather Huaraches, "not that plastic or straw stuff" (312). In a vision by the estranged mother, Dee Dee, following the Convent massacre, it is the expensive Huaraches that Pallas has returned to claim from the guest bedroom, Huaraches left behind on her first and last visit to her mother.

In a study that examines the literary import of shoes, it bears remarking that with the exception of Parisian Yanturni and Italian shoemaker André Perugia, perhaps no other shoemaker of the twentieth century has achieved the prominence of Moroccan-born Manola Blahnik, who has been described as both sculptor and craftsman. His "Manolas," "cult objects" (McDowell 162), are collectible objects d'art (McDowell 171). A three-time recipient of the 1997 Fashion Designers of America Award, Blahnik's distinction as an artist as well as shoe designer is clear from the citation on the 1997 award: "'Blahnik has done for footwear what Worth did for couture, making slippers into objects of desire, collectibles for women'" (McDowell 171). Indeed, the renown of shoemaker Blahnik underscores a theme of chapters one and two, namely, the intersection between shoes and caste. In the words of Colin McDowell, "[F]ootwear [has] become the supreme statement in fashionable appearance, saying more about the wearer than all but the most extreme fashion designer's creations" (165).

Not only is innovation associated with the jazz artist, but also the music of jazz and blues artists is linked inextricably to African American history and culture. Viewed as "a crucible of black cultural memory, agency, and autonomy" (69 Gennari), the music produced during the turbulent 1960s was reflective of the racial tensions during that era. According to Quincy Troupe: "The entire country was changing. It was the beginning of the radical sixties, and there was an angrier, less melodic, more fragmented mood afoot across the nation. [. . .] In New York, the discordant and dissonant music of Coleman and his partner Don Cherry, Cecil Taylor, Archie Shepp, Albert Ayler, and Eric Dolphy, to name just a few, were beginning to be recognized by prominent jazz critics" (123). On the historical relevance of the blues to African American culture, Ernest Gaines, in the 1986 interview with Kay Bonetti, observed that the blues renditions by Bessie Smith and Ma Rainey of the Great [Louisiana] Flood of 1927, a few years before the Depression, are as vivid as any poem and have had more impact on him emotionally than any other medium.

By the same token, the inspiration for the fiction by African American authors has been the lives of African Americans. Ralph Ellison in the article "Richard Wright's Blues," describes the blues as "an autobiographical chronicle of personal catastrophe expressed lyrically" (78-79). With respect to the autobiography, Maya Angelou's *I Know Why the Caged Bird Sings* is filled with catastrophic events. Maya Angelou was raped at the age of eight years old by her mother's live-in boyfriend. At fifteen, she lived in an abandoned car in southern

California following a dispute with her father's live-in girlfriend that resulted in an artificial knife wound to the side. And at the age of sixteen (266), she became a teen mother. Yet the travail of Maya and other individuals is mitigated by music. In *I Know Why the Caged Bird Sings,* Maya had written of the commencement speaker Donleavy who had spoken of the improvements the students at Central High, the white school, could expect, "the newest microscopes and chemistry equipment for their laboratory" (174). Meanwhile students at Lafayette County Training School could expect "the only colored paved playing field in that part of Arkansas" (176). The frontal assault to the esteem of the graduates, however, is mitigated by the words of the Negro national anthem that accentuate a historical consciousness. The author pays tribute to poets, preachers, and musicians alike whose words have had a transformative impact: "It may be enough, however, to have it said that we survive in exact relationship to the dedication of our poets (include preachers, musicians and blues singers) (180).

Toni Morrison has paid a similar homage to folk culture. She has proclaimed in the article "Rootedness: The Ancestor as Foundation" the power of literature to heal. In that capacity, it functions in a manner similar to jazz. For a scattered community that is increasingly without the oral histories, tales, and sayings transmitted from generation to generation by elders, Morrison considers that literature has to fill that void. Too, since the music that once defined African American culture is no longer exclusively its own, other media, according to Morrison, have to be sought to supply the saving grace found in music for a disasporic people: "So another form has to take that place, and it seems to me that the novel is needed by African-Americans now in a way that it was not needed before—and it is following along the lines of the function of novels everywhere" (340).

For his part, William Faulkner also recognized the value of music, namely, its ability to remind individuals of their hopes and capacities. In interviews, Faulkner has aligned the three, the writer, the artist, and the musician, for their link to those precepts deemed immutable:

> It is the writer's duty to show that man has an immortal soul. The writer, the artist, the musician is the one factor which can show him the shape of his hope and aspirations of the future by reminding him of what he has accomplished in the past. (*Lion in the Garden* 202)

Moreover, the alternating pattern of *The Wild Palms,* by William Faulkner, has its origin in music, as Faulkner himself has acknowledged. In effect, he tells two stories in the novel, one of a man who risked everything for love; the other, who attempted to escape it (*Lion in the Garden* 54). The contrapuntal structure of the novel underscores the antithesis between, respectively, Harry Wilbourne and the tall convict who has been incarcerated for train robbery:

> To tell the story I wanted to tell, which was the one of the intern and the woman who gave up her family and husband to run off with him.

To tell it like that, somehow or another I had to discover counterpoint
for it, so I invented the other story, its complete antithesis, to use as
counterpoint. And I did not write those two stories and then cut into
the other. I wrote them, as you read it, as the chapters. The chapter of
the "Wild Palms," chapter of the river story, another chapter of the
"Wild Palms," and then I used the counterpoint of another chapter of
the river story, I imagine as a musician would do to compose a piece
of music in which he needed a balance, a counterpoint. *(Lion in the
Garden 132)*

Another indirect link of Faulkner to the Black cultural tradition is found in
the use of a Black vernacular by both the Black and white characters in *The
Sound and the Fury*. John T. Matthews traduces in his article "Whose America?
Faulkner, Modernism, and National Identity" that this anomaly, in its disruption
of standard speech patterns, is modernist in its application: "The use of dialect
permitted modernist writers to signal their dissent from Victorian bourgeois mores, from
the social privilege undergirding standard English, and from the imperialist powers that
employed it as the instrument of colonial subjugation" (74). Matthews further contends that Faulkner's replication of dialect in his fiction propels front and center
the dichotomy of an author profiteering from the folk culture of a disaffected
people derided in the literature itself: "The enormous richness of black folk culture,
an imaginative wealth that many modernists recognized as the only legitimate source of
cultural renewal and authenticity in the machine age, that richness could not be appropri-
ated without triggering yet another round of thieving masquerade" (83).

Herein lies a major difference between the literature by Faulkner and African American authors, specifically, Toni Morrison, namely, the element of syn-
copation, or the absence of an expected beat that creates an opening for new
voices (Williams 15). In *Light in August*, Faulkner describes the odyssey of
Lena Grove in search of Lucas Burch and the benevolence she inspires in others.
Contrastingly, in *Paradise*, the fate of one of the female walkers, the 16-year-old
Pallas, is rape. The fifteen hospital admissions of Mavis Albright in *Paradise*,
four of which were for childbirth, and the use of sunglasses as camouflage on
the cloudy days she drives the children to White Castle's are clear indicators that
her husband Frank is an abuser. Moreover, Seneca, another of the Convent
women and an orphan, had been molested by her foster brother. Also, as the
men track as quarry the Convent women, those considered the cause of the
community's strife or the "juvenile restlessness" (142), unmistakable is the
irony of their assumed roles of predators; they have become the very enemy
from whom they had sought protection of the females (18). Toni Morrison has
related in interviews the educative function of her fiction (75):

I wanted to write books that ran the whole gamut of women's sexual
experiences. I didn't like the imposition that had been placed on
black women's sexuality in literature. They were either mothers,

mammies, or whores. And they were not vulnerable people. [. . .] But
at the same time I wanted to say, "you can still be prey."

Henry Louis Gates, Jr. in his work *Signifying Monkey* distinguishes between pastiche and parody and cites Count Basie's tune "Signify" as an example
of pastiche. Evocative of the genres ragtime, boogie woogie, etc., the tune "Signify" became a synecdoche for the tradition it encompasses:

> Throughout his piece ["Signify"], Basie alludes to styles of playing
> that predominated in black music between 1920 and 1940. These
> styles include ragtime, stride, barrel-house, boogie-woogie, and the
> Kansas City "walking bass" so central to swing in the thirties.
> Through these allusions, Basie has created a composition character-
> ized by pastiche. He has recapitulated the very tradition out of which
> he grew and from which he descended. (124)

Parody, on the other hand, likewise revises; however, in contrast to pastiche,
which affirms, parody challenges: "Pastiche is an act of literary 'naming'; parody is an act of 'calling out of one's name'" (124).

In light of Gates' distinction, it may be argued that *Love,* by Toni Morrison, is a parodic response to *Absalom, Absalom!,* by William Faulkner; the marriage between the fifty-two-year-old Bill Cosey and eleven-year-old child bride
Heed the Night in *Love* represents a reductio ad absurdum of the marriage proposal of fifty-nine-year-old Colonel Thomas Sutpen to his twenty-year-old sister-in-law, Rosa Coldfield in *Absalom, Absalom!* Not only does the marriage
between Cosey and Heed fail to produce the progeny Cosey seeks, as Heed is
ruled barren, but his second marriage proves disastrous as the Cosey women—
the wife Heed, the daughter-in-law May, and the granddaughter Christine—
battle one another for the favor and affection of Cosey. The upshot is that they
reduce Cosey's life to *"a cautionary lesson in black history. . . : a dream is just a
nightmare with lipstick" (201).*

The characters Rosa Coldfield, Heed the Night, and Christine of *Absalom,
Absalom!* and *Love,* respectively, are linked not only by the theme of incest, but
also by vulnerability inseparable from their violation. Rosa Coldfield, who was
made an orphan by her father's suicide, had come to live at Sutpen's Hundred
while the men had gone off to battle. Confronted upon the return of Sutpen from
battle and his desperation to thwart time, Rosa Coldfield is rendered defenseless
in the face of his fury. Similarly, Christine observes, after being re-united with
her friend Heed, that Heed was "too young to decide" either for or against marriage to her grandfather and guardian Bill Cosey, who has been described as
omnipotent, or in a manner similar to Thomas Sutpen: "He was the Big Man
who, with no one to stop him, could get away with it and anything else he
wanted" (*Love* 133). Likewise, Colonel Sutpen is deified in *Absalom, Absalom!*
Wash Jones considers Sutpen "the fine figure of the man. . . . If God Himself

was to come down and ride the natural earth, that's what He would aim to look like" (282). Only after Sutpen's impregnation of Wash's granddaughter and Sutpen's repudiation of her for spawning a female did Jones consider the fates of suicide and murder as preferable to the destruction of his illusions: "*Better if his kind too had never drawn the breath of life on this earth. Better that all who remain of us be blasted from the face of it than that another Wash Jones should see his whole life shredded from him and shriveled away like a dried shuck thrown onto the fire*" *(290)*. Collectively, the white scion Thomas Sutpen of *Absalom, Absalom!*, by William Faulkner, and Bill Cosey of *Love*, by Toni Morrison, become symbols of the suppression not only of the female voice but the voices of those deemed subordinate or Other by patriarchal society. Moreover, Toni Morrison in *Love* is critical not only of patriarchy, but the collusion of women in their own subordination: "[Morrison's] target, however, seems to be patriarchy and the ways women have accommodated it by mistaking entrapment for *love*. All in all, the women of this novel are helpless in Cosey's world and have no ability to make change inside marriages, low-wage employment, prostitution and, especially, girlhood. They fight petty domestic wars. More than loving Billy Cosey, they obeyed him" (Thulani 3). To wit, *Love, The Bluest Eye, Sula, Jazz, Tar Baby, Song of Solomon, Beloved*, and *Paradise* become demonstrative not only of the "concord of sensibilities" that Ralph Ellison has associated with the African American tradition, but, in their evocation of Faulkner, the jazz tradition as well.

Finally, the argument of a Faulknerian intertext in Morrison's fiction should not in any way raise questions regarding Morrison's genius. Instead, as John Duvall has averred in his work *The Identifying Fictions of Toni Morrison*, a juxtaposition of the two writers enhances the reading of their respective works, as Morrison's revisionist approaches to Faulkner invite a fresh reading of Faulkner and vice versa: "[H]er fiction and literary criticism may cause one to rethink Faulkner in a fundamental way" (75). Such a "rethinking" emerges from a reconsideration of Faulkner's relationship with Callie Barr, one that becomes a prism from which one might view Faulkner's attitudes toward race.

Critics have been at pains often to reconcile Faulkner's defense of a racialist past with the writer's defense of it. That love-hate relationship with the South is embodied in Quentin Compson of *Absalom, Absalom!*. That conflict is represented squarely in Faulkner's relationship with the Black female Faulkner affectionately referred to in interviews as his foster mother (*Lion in the Garden* 184). The book *Go Down, Moses* was dedicated to her memory; Faulkner delivered the eulogy at her funeral, and the headstone on her grave was encrypted with the words "Mammy/ Her white children bless her" (Blotner 413). Following the 1949 Nobel Prize for Literature, Faulkner used a portion of the funds from the award to further the education of Mississippian James McGlowan, "One Oxford Negro," and approached him to teach Callie Barr her letters (Blotner 535). Interestingly, Stephen Oates has described Faulkner's dichotomous relationship with the South that linguistically yokes together the contraries:

> Yet [Faulkner] loved Mississippi [. . .] remembering childhood Christmases when he had to stay in bed until dawn, the car rides to Memphis, his first sweetheart, Mammy Callie and Uncle Ned. He loved "all of it even while he had to hate some of it because he knows now that you don't love because: you love despite; not for the virtues, but despite the faults." (263)

Daniel J. Singal traces the split in Faulkner to the collision of nineteenth century Victorianism and twentieth century modernism that Faulkner sought to embrace (12). From another perspective, Faulkner's split self seems more privately based, as Faulkner seemed torn by conflicting loyalties to members of a group that segregationist ideology dictated that he revile. In the 1993 interview with Charlie Rose, Toni Morrison had spoken candidly of the confusion produced in the psyche of youth indoctrinated by racism; youth no longer trust their instincts. That self-doubt may account for the contradictoriness often found in Faulkner's body of work. Thus a juxtaposition of the two writers invariably enhances the reading of their respective works. In the words of Duvall, "[A] discussion of Faulkner's influence on Morrison [. . .] suggest[s] how reading Morrison reshapes the way one reads Faulkner" (75).

References

Preface

Barthelemy, Anthony. "Brogans." Benstock and Ferriss 179-96.

Benstock, Shari, and Suzanne Ferriss, ed. *Footnotes: On Shoes*. New Brunswick: Rutgers UP, 2001.

Davis, Thadious M. *Games of Property: Law, Race, Gender, and Faulkner's* Go Down, Moses. Durham and London: Duke UP, 2003.

Dussere, Erik. *Balancing the Books: Faulkner, Morrison, and the Economics of Slavery*. New York and London: Routledge, 2003.

Gates, Henry Louis, Jr. *The Signifying Monkey: A Theory of Afro-American Literary Criticism*. New York: Oxford UP, 1988.

Gray, Richard. *The Life of William Faulkner: A Critical Biography*. Oxford: Blackwell, 1994.

Jones, Bessie, W., and Audrey Vinson. "Interview with Toni Morrison." Taylor-Guthrie 171-87.

Karl, Frederick R. *William Faulkner: American Writer*. New York: Weidenfeld, 1989.

Kennedy, John. Review of *Paradise*, by Toni Morrison. *Antioch Review* 58 (summer 2000): 377.

Kolmerten, Carol A., Stephen M. Ross, and Judith Bryant Wittenberg, ed. *Unflinching Gaze: Morrison and Faulkner Re-Envisioned*. Jackson: UP of Mississippi, 1997.

Kubitschek, Missy Dehn. *Toni Morrison: A Critical Companion*. Westport: Greenwood, 1988.

LeClair, Thomas. "The Language Must Not Sweat: A Conversation with Toni Morrison." Taylor-Guthrie 119-28.

McKay, Nellie. "An Interview with Toni Morrison." Taylor-Guthrie 138-55.

McKee, Patricia. *Producing American Races: Henry James, William Faulkner, Toni Morrison*. Durham: Duke University P, 1999.

Morrison, Toni. *Paradise*. New York: Knopf, 1998.

Powers, Lyall H. *Faulkner's Yoknapatawpha's Comedy*. Ann Arbor: U of Michigan P, 1980.

Tate, Claudia. "Interview with Toni Morrison." Taylor-Guthrie 156-70.

Taylor-Guthrie, Danille, ed. *Conversations with Toni Morrison*. Jackson: UP of Mississippi, 1994.

Introduction

Babb, Valerie Melissa. *Ernest Gaines*. Boston: Twayne, 1991.

Carmean, Karen. *Ernest J. Gaines: A Critical Companion*. Westport, Ct: Greenwood Press, 1998.

Dussere, Erik. *Balancing the Books: Faulkner, Morrison, and the Economics of Slavery*. New York: Routledge, 2003.

Ellison, Ralph. *Shadow and Act*. New York: Random House, 1964.

Faulkner, William. *Absalom, Absalom!*. New York: Vintage, 1936.

————. *Faulkner in the University: Class Conferences at the University of Virginia 1957-58.* Ed. Frederick L. Gwynn and Joseph L. Blotner. New York: Random House, 1959.

————. *Go Down, Moses.* New York: Random, 1940.

————. *The Sound and the Fury.* 1929. Norton Critical Edition. Ed. David Minter. New York: Norton, 1994.

Garrett, George P., Jr., "The Influence of William Faulkner." *Georgia Review* 18 (winter 1964): 419-27.

Gray, Paul. "Paradise Found." *Time* 19 January 1998: 63-68.

Irwin, John T. *Doubling and Incest/Repetition and Revenge: A Speculative Reading of Faulkner.* Baltimore: John Hopkins UP, 1975.

Karl, Frederick R. *William Faulkner: American Writer (A Biography).* New York: Weidenfeld, 1989.

Matus, Jill. *Toni Morrison.* Manchester: Manchester UP, 1998.

Menand, Louis. "The War Between Men and Women." *The New Yorker* 12 January 1998: 78-82.

Morrison, Toni. *Love.* New York: Alfred A. Knopf, 2. *Paradise.* New York: Knopf, 1998.

Weinstein, Philip M. *What Else But Love?: The Ordeal of Race in Faulkner and Morrison.* New York: Columbia UP, 1996.

Chapter 1: "High-topped Shoes"

Angelou, Maya. *I Know Why the Caged Bird Sings.* New York: Random House, 1969.

Babb, Valerie Melissa. *Ernest Gaines.* Boston: Twayne, 1991.

Barthelemy, Anthony. "Brogans." In *Footnotes: On Shoes.* Ed. Shari Benstock & Suzanne Ferris. New Brunswick: Rutgers UP, 2001. 179-196.

Bogumil, Mary L. *Understanding August Wilson.* Columbia: Univ. of South Carolina Press, 1999.

Davis, Thadious. *Faulkner's "Negro": Art and the Southern Context.* Baton Rouge: Louisiana State UP, 1983.

Dussere, Erik. *Balancing the Books: Faulkner, Morrison, and the Economics of Slavery.* New York and London: Routledge, 2003.

Dyson, Michael Eric. "The Culture of Hip-Hop." *The Michael Dyson Reader.* New York: Basic Civitas Books, 2004. 401-10.

Ellison, Ralph. "On Bird, Bird-Watching, and Jazz." *Shadow and Act.* New York: Random House, 1964. 221-32.

Faulkner, William. *As I Lay Dying.* New York: Random House, 1957.

————. "Evangeline." In *Uncollected Stories of William Faulkner.* Ed. Joseph Blotner. New York: Random House, 1979. 583-609.

————. *Intruder in the Dust.* New York: Random House, 1948.

————. *Light in August.* Intro. by Cleanth Brooks. New York: Random House, 1968.

————. "Miss Zilphia Gant." In *Uncollected Stories of William Faulkner.* Ed. Joseph Blotner. New York: Random House, 1979. 368-81.

————. "Mountain Victory." In *Collected Stories of William Faulkner.* New York: Random House, 1934. 745-77.

————. *Sanctuary.* New York: Random House, 1931.

————. *The Wild Palms.* New York: Random House, 1939.

Gaines, Ernest J. *Of Love and Dust*. New York: Dial Press, 1967.

Gray, Richard. G. *The Life of William Faulkner: A Critical Biography*. Oxford: Blackwell, 1994.

Harris, Trudier. *The Novels of Toni Morrison*. Knoxville: U of Tennessee P, 1991.

Hurston, Zora Neale. *Their Eyes Were Watching God*. 1937. New York: Harper, 1990.

Karl, Frederick Robert. *William Faulkner: American Writer* (A Biography). New York: Weidenfeld & Nicolson, 1989.

McKelly, James C. "Hymns of Sedition: Portraits of the Artist in Contemporary African-American Drama." *Arizona Quarterly* 48.1 (spring 1992): 87-107.

Morrison, Toni. *Beloved*. New York: Knopf, 1987.

⸻. *Jazz*. New York: Knopf, 1992.

⸻. *Paradise*. New York: Knopf, 1998.

⸻. *Song of Solomon*. New York: New American Library, 1977.

⸻. *Sula*. New York: New American Library, 1973.

Pilkington, John. *The Heart of Yoknapatawpha*. Jackson: UP of Mississippi, 1981.

Powers, Lyall H. *Faulkner's Yoknapatawpha Comedy*. Ann Arbor: U of Michigan P, 1980.

Singal, Daniel J. *William Faulkner: The Making of a Modernist*. Chapel Hill: U of North Carolina P, 1997.

Volpe, Edmond L. *A Reader's Guide to William Faulkner: The Short Stories*. New York: Syracuse UP, 2004.

Wilson, August. *Ma Rainey's Black Bottom: A Play in Two Acts*. New York: Plume, 1981.

Wolfe, Peter. *August Wilson*. New York: Twayne, 1999.

Chapter 2: The Symbolic Implications of Incest

The Bible.

Bouson, J. Brooks. *Quiet as It's Kept: Shame, Trauma, and Race in the Novels of Toni Morrison*. Albany: State University of New York P, 2000.

Bruccoli, Matthew. *Some Sort of Epic Grandeur: The Life of F. Scott Fitzgerald*. New York: Harcourt Brace Jovanovich, 1981.

Camus, Albert. *The Myth of Sisyphus and Other Essays*. Trans. Justin O'Brien. New York: Knopf, 1955. Originally published in France as *Le Mythe de Sisyphe* (Paris: Gallimard, 1942).

Davis, Thadious M. *Games of Property: Law, Race, Gender, and Faulkner's* Go Down, Moses. Durham: Duke UP, 2003.

Donaldson, Scott. *Hemingway vs. Fitzgerald: The Rise and Fall of a Literary Friendship*. New York: Overlook, 1999.

Faulkner, William. *Absalom, Absalom!* New York: Random House, 1931.

⸻. *Faulkner in the University: Class Conferences at the University of Virginia 1957-58*. Ed. Frederick L. Gwynn and Joseph L. Blotner. New York: Vintage, 1959.

⸻. *Go Down, Moses*. New York: Random House, 1940.

⸻. *Light in August*. New York. Random House, 1936.

⸻. *Sanctuary*. New York: Random House, 1931.

⸻. *The Sound and the Fury*. 1929. Ed. David Minter. Norton Critical Ed. 2nd ed. New York: Norton, 1994.

Fitzgerald, F. Scott. "Babylon Revisited." *The Short Stories of F. Scott Fitzgerald.* Ed. and with Preface by Matthew J. Bruccoli. New York: Charles Scribner's Sons, 1989. 616-33.
————. *The Crack-Up.* Ed. Edmund Wilson. New York: New Directions, 1945.
————. *The Great Gatsby.* 1925. Preface and Notes by Matthew J. Bruccoli. New York: Macmillan, 1992.
————. *Tender is the Night.* New York: Charles Scribner's Sons, 1933.
Gates, Henry Louis, Jr. *The Signifying Monkey: A Theory of Afro-American Literary Criticism.* New York: Oxford UP, 1988.
Irwin, John T. *Doubling and Incest/Repetition and Revenge: A Speculative Reading of Faulkner.* Baltimore and London: John Hopkins UP, 1975.
Karl, Frederick R. *William Faulkner: American Writer (A Biography).* New York: Weidenfeld & Nicolson, 1989.
Kennedy, John. Review of *Paradise,* by Toni Morrison. *The Antioch Review* 58.3 (summer 2000): 377.
Koenen, Anne. "'The One Out of Sequence': An Interview with Toni Morrison." *History and Tradition in Afro-American Culture.* Ed. Gunter H. Lenz. Frankfurt: Campus, 1984. 207-221.
Lehan, Richard D. *F. Scott Fitzgerald and the Craft of Fiction.* With a Preface by Harry T. Moore. Carbondale: Southern Illinois UP, 1966.
Lind, Ilse Dusoir. "The Design and Meaning of *Absalom, Absalom!* " In *William Faulkner: Four Decades of Criticism.* Ed. Linda Welshimer Wagner. n.p.: Michigan State UP, 1973. 272-97.
Morrison, Toni. *The Bluest Eye.* New York: Washington Square Press, 1970.
————. *Love.* New York: Knopf, 2003.
————. *Paradise.* New York: Knopf, 1998.
Parker, Robert Dale. *Faulkner and the Novelistic Imagination.* Urbana: U of Illinois P, 1985.
Pelzer, Linda C. *Student Companion to F. Scott Fitzgerald.* Student Companions to Classic Writers. Westport, Connecticut: Greenwood P, 2000.
Powers, Lyall H. *Faulkner's Yoknapatawpha Comedy.* Ann Arbor: U of Michigan P, 1980.
Reames, Kelly. *Toni Morrison's Paradise: A Reader's Guide.* New York: Continuum, 2001.
Reaves, Gerri. "The Slip in the Ballet Slipper: Illusion and the Naked Foot." *Footnotes: On Shoes.* Ed. Shari Benstock and Suzanne Ferris. New Brunswick: Rutgers UP, 2001. 251-71.

Chapter 3: What's in a Name?

Angelou, Maya. *I Know Why the Caged Bird Sings.* New York. Random House, 1969.
Baldwin, James. *Go Tell It on the Mountain.* New York: Dell, 1952.
The Bible.
Benston, Kimberly W. "'I Yam What I Am': Naming and Unnaming in Afro-American Literature." *Black American Literature Forum* 16.1 (1982): 3-11.
Bogumil, Mary L. *Understanding August Wilson.* Columbia: U of South Carolina P, 1999.

Ellison, Ralph. "Hidden Name and Complex Fate: A Writer's Experience in the United States." *Shadow and Act.* New York: Random House, 1964. 144-66.

Fabre, Michel. "Fathers and Sons in Baldwin's *Go Tell It on the Mountain."James Baldwin: A Collection of Critical Essays.* Ed. Keneth Kinnamon. Englewood Cliffs, N.J.: Prentice-Hall, 1974. 120-38.

Gaines, Ernest J. *The Autobiography of Miss Jane Pittman.* New York: Bantam, 1971.

Hurston, Zora Neale. *Jonah's Gourd Vine.* 1934. New York: Harper, 1990.

————. *Moses, Man of the Mountain.* 1939. New York: HarperCollins, 1991.

————. *Their Eyes Were Watching God.* 1937. New York: Harper, 1990.

King, Sigrid. "Naming and Power in Zora Neale Hurston's *Their Eyes Were Watching God." Critical Essays on Zora Neale Hurston.* Ed. Gloria L. Cronin. New York: G.K. Hall, 1998. 115-27.

Koenen, Anne. "'The One Out of Sequence': An Interview with Toni Morrison". *History and Tradition in Afro-American Culture.* Ed. Gunter H. Lenz. Frankfurt: Campus, 1984. 207-20.

Meisenhelder, Susan Edwards. *Hitting a Straight Lick with a Crooked Stick: Race and Gender in the Work of Zora Neale Hurston.* Tuscaloosa: U of Alabama P, 1999.

Morris, Milton D. "Democratic Politics and Black Subordination." *A Turbulent Voyage: Readings in African American Studies.* Ed. Floyd W. Hayes III. San Diego: Collegiate Press, 1992.

Morrison, Toni. *Paradise.* New York: Knopf, 1997.

Wilson, August. *Joe Turner's Come and Gone.* New York: Plume, 1988.

Wolfe, Peter. *August Wilson.* New York: Twayne, 1999.

Chapter 4: The Influence of African Folktales on Selected Literature

Angelou, Maya. *I Know Why the Caged Bird Sings.* New York: Random House, 1969.

Brewer, J. Mason. *American Negro Folklore.* Illustrations by Richard Lowe. Chicago: Quadrangle Books, 1968.

Brylowski, Walter. *Faulkner's Olympian Laugh: Myth in the Novels.* Detroit: Wayne State UP, 1968.

Cather, Willa. *O Pioneers!* 1912. New York: Vintage, 1992.

Chesnutt, Charles W. *The Conjure Woman.* 1899. Ann Arbor: U of Michigan P, 1969.

Chesnutt, Helen M. *Charles Waddell Chesnutt: Pioneer of the Color Line.* Chapel Hill: U of North Carolina P, 1952.

Courlander, Harold. *A Treasury of Afro-American Folklore: The Oral Literature, Traditions, Recollections, Legends, Tales, Songs, Religious Beliefs, Customs, Sayings, and Humor of Peoples of African Descent in the Americas.* New York: Crown, 1976.

————. *A Treasury of African Folklore: The Oral Literature, Traditions, Myths, Legends, Epics, Tales, Recollections, Wisdom, Sayings, and Humor of Africa.* New York: Marlowe & Company, 1996.

Davis, Thadious M. *Games of Property: Law, Race, Gender, and Faulkner's Go Down, Moses.* Durham: Duke UP, 2003.

Dorson, Richard M. Collected with Introduction and Notes by. *American Negro Folktales.* New York: Fawcett, 1956.

Doty, William G. "Native American Tricksters: Literary Figures of Community Transformers." *Trickster Lives: Culture and Myth in American Fiction.* Ed. Jeanne Campbell Reesman. Athens: U of Georgia P, 2001.

Ellison, Ralph. "Change the Joke and Slip the Yoke." *Shadow and Act.* New York: Random House, 1964. 45-59.

Faulkner, William. *As I Lay Dying.* New York: Random House, 1930.

———. *Faulkner in the University: Class Conferences at the University of Virginia 1957-1958.* Ed. Frederick L. Gwynn and Joseph L. Blotner. New York: Knopf, 1959.

———. *Lion in the Garden: Interviews with William Faulkner 1926-1962.* Ed. James B. Meriwether and Michael Millgate. New York: Random House, 1968.

———. *The Reivers (A Reminiscence).* New York: Random House, 1962.

Gates, Jr., Henry Louis and Sieglinde Lemke. Introduction. *The Complete Stories.* HarperCollins, 1995. ix-xxiii.

Gates, Jr., Henry Louis. *The Signifying Monkey: A Theory of Afro-American Literary Criticism.* New York: Oxford UP, 1988.

Greene, Robert. *The 48 Laws of Power.* New York: Penguin, 2000.

Homer. *The Odyssey.* Trans. Robert Fitzgerald. *Literature of the Western World: The Ancient World Through the Renaissance.* Vol. 1. 4th ed. Compilers Brian Wilkie and James Hurt. Upper Saddle River, New Jersey: Prentice Hall, 1977. 275-596.

Hughes, Langston, and Arna Bontemps, Ed. *The Book of Negro Folklore.* New York: Dodd, Mead and Company, 1958.

Hurston, Zora Neale. "The Bone of Contention." *The Complete Stories.* Intro. by Henry Louis Gates, Jr., and Sieglinde Lemke. New York: HarperCollins, 1995. 209-20.

———. *Every Tongue Got to Confess: Negro Folk-tales from the Gulf States.* Foreword by John Edgar Wideman. New York: HarperCollins, 2002.

———. "High John De Conquer." *The Complete Stories.* New York: HarperCollins, 1995. 139-48.

———. *Mules and Men.* Preface by Franz Boas with a new Foreword by Arnold Rampersad. New York: Harper, 1935.

———. *Seraph on the Suwanee.* 1948. With a Foreword by Hazel V. Carby. New York: HarperCollins, 1991.

———. *Their Eyes Were Watching God.* 1937. New York: Harper, 1990.

Karl, Frederick R. *William Faulkner: American Writer* (Biography): New York: Weidenfeld & Nicolson, 1989.

Kubitschek, Missy Dehn. *Toni Morrison: A Critical Companion.* Westport: Greenwood P, 1998.

LeClair, Thomas. "The Language Must Not Sweat: A Conversation with Toni Morrison." Taylor-Guthrie, 119-28.

Lowe, John. *"Jump at the Sun": Zora Neale Hurston's Cosmic Comedy.* Urbana: U of Illinois P, 1994.

Minter, David. *William Faulkner: His Life and Work.* Baltimore and London: John Hopkins UP, 1980.

Morrison, Toni. *Tar Baby.* New York: Knopf, 1981.

Naylor, Gloria. "A Conversation: Gloria Naylor and Toni Morrison." Taylor-Guthrie, 188-222.

Ngugi wa Thiong'o. *A Grain of Wheat.* London: Heinemann, 1967.

Nyberg, David. *The Varnished Truth: Truth Telling and Deceiving in Ordinary Life.* Chicago: Univ. of Chicago P, 1993.

O'Connor, Flannery. *Collected Works*. New York: Library of America, 1988.
Pilkington, John. *The Heart of Yoknapatawpha*. Jackson: UP of Mississippi, 1981.
Powers, Lyall H. *Faulkner's Yoknapatawpha Comedy*. Ann Arbor: U of Michigan P, 1980.
Reesman, Jeanne Campbell. "Introduction." *Trickster Lives: Culture and Myth in American Fiction*. Athens: U of Georgia P, 2001.
Ruas, Charles. "Toni Morrison." Taylor-Guthrie, 93-118.
Singal, Daniel Joseph. *William Faulkner: The Making of a Modernist*. Chapel Hill: U of North Carolina P, 1997.
Smith, Jeanne Rosier. *Writing Tricksters: Mythic Gambols in American Ethnic Literature*. Berkeley: U of California P, 1997.
Taylor-Guthrie, Danille, ed. *Conversations with Toni Morrison*. Jackson: UP of Mississippi, 1994.
Wilson, Judith. "A Conversation with Toni Morrison." Taylor-Guthrie, 129-37.

Chapter 5: Snopesism as a Form of Tricksterism

Blotner, Joseph. *Faulkner: A Biography*. One vol. New York: Random House, 1984.
Dorson, Richard M., comp. *American Negro Folktales*. Greenwich: Fawcett, 1956.
Faulkner, William. *Selected Letters of William Faulkner*. Ed. Joseph Blotner. New York: Random House, 1977.
———. *Snopes: The Hamlet; The Town; The Mansion*. Intro. by George Garrett. New York: Modern Library Edition, 1994.
Gray, Richard. *The Life of William Faulkner: A Critical Biography*. Oxford: Blackwell, 1994.
Morrison, Toni. *Love*. New York: Knopf, 2003.
Powers, Lyall H. *Faulkner's Yoknapatawpha Comedy*. Ann Arbor: U of Michigan P, 1980.
Singal, Daniel J. *William Faulkner: The Making of a Modernist*. Chapel Hill: U of North Carolina P, 1997.
Volpe, Edmond L. *A Reader's Guide to William Faulkner*. New York: Farrar Straus, 1964.
Watson, James Gray. *The Snopes Dilemma: Faulkner's Trilogy*. Coral Gables: U of Miami P, 1968.

Chapter 6: The Elliptical Prose Style of Faulkner and Morrison

David, Ron. *Toni Morrison Explained: A Reader's Road Map to the Novels*. New York: Random House, 2000.
Davis, Thadious M. *Games of Property: Law, Race, Gender and Faulkner's Go Down, Moses*. Durham: Duke UP, 2003.
Dreifus, Claudia. "Chloe Wofford: Toni Morrison." *The New York Times Magazine* 11 September 1994: 73-75.
Duvall, John M. *The Identifying Fictions of Toni Morrison: Modernist Authenticity and Postmodern Blackness*. New York: Palgrave, 2000.
Faulkner, William. *Absalom, Absalom!* 1936. New York: Random House, 1964.

————. *Faulkner in the University: Class Conferences at the University of Virginia 1957-58.* Ed. Frederick L. Gwynn and Joseph L. Blotner. New York: Random House, 1959.

————. *Go Down, Moses.* New York: Random House, 1942.

————. *Light in August.* 1932. New York: Random House, 1968.

————. *Lion in the Garden: Interviews with William Faulkner 1926-1962.* Ed. James B. Meriwether and Michael Millgate. New York: Random House, 1968.

————. *Requiem for a Nun.* New York: Random House, 1951.

————. *Sanctuary.* 1931. New York: Random House, 1958.

Gray, Paul. "Paradise Found." *Time* 19 January 1998: 63-68.

Karl, Frederick R. *William Faulkner: American Writer.* New York: Weidenfeld and Nicholson, 1989.

Koenen, Anne. "The One Out of Sequence": An Interview with Toni Morrison. *History and Tradition in Afro-American Culture.* Ed. Gunter H. Lenz. Campus: Frankfurt, 1984.

Kubitschek, Missy Dehn. *Toni Morrison: A Critical Companion.* Westport: Greenwood Press, 1998.

Lind, Ilse Dusoir. "The Design and Meaning of *Absalom, Absalom!*" *William Faulkner: Four Decades of Criticism.* Ed. Linda Welshimer Wagner. n.p. Michigan State UP, 1973. 272-97.

MacKethan, Lucinda Hardwick. *The Dream of Arcady: Place and Time in Southern Literature.* Baton Rouge: Louisiana State UP, 1980.

Menand, Louis. "The War Between Men and Women." *The New Yorker* 12 January 1998: 78-82.

Morrison, Toni. *Jazz.* New York: Knopf, 1992.

————. *Paradise.* New York: Knopf, 1998.

Powers, Lyall H. *Faulkner's Yoknapatawpha Comedy.* Ann Arbor: U of Michigan P, 1980.

Schappell, Elissa. "Toni Morrison: The Art of Fiction CXXXIV" *The Paris Review* 128.35 (fall 1993): 82-125.

Volpe, Edmond L. *A Reader's Guide to William Faulkner.* New York: Farrar, Straus and Company, 1964.

————. *A Reader's Guide to William Faulkner: The Short Stories.* New York: Syracuse UP, 2004.

Weinstein, Philip M. *What Else But Love? The Ordeal of Race in Faulkner and Morrison.* New York: Columbia UP, 1996.

Chapter 7: Conclusion

Angelou, Maya. *I Know Why the Caged Bird Sings.* New York: Random House, 1969.

The Adventure: Jazz (Episode 9). PBS Video, 2000. 120 minutes.

Davis, Thulani. "Not Beloved. Review of *Love,* by Toni Morrison. *Nation* 277.20 (December 2003): 1-3. Academic Search Premier. EBSCO. St. Cloud State University Lib. 7 January 2005.

Dreifus, Claudia. "Chloe Wofford/Toni Morrison." *The New York Times Magazine* 11 September 1994: 73-75.

Duvall, John M. *The Identifying Fictions of Toni Morrison: Modernist Authenticity and Postmodern Blackness.* New York: Palgrave, 2000.

Early, Gerald, ed. *Miles Davis and American Culture.* St. Louis: Missouri Historical Society Press, 2001.

Faulkner, William. *Lion in the Garden: Interviews with William Faulkner 1926-1962.* Ed. James B. Meriwether and Michael Millgate. New York: Random House, 1968.

———. *The Wild Palms.* New York: Random House, 1939.

Fussell, Betty. "All That Jazz." Taylor-Guthrie. 280-87.

Gaines, Ernest. Interview with Kay Bonetti. Columbia, Mo: American Audio Prose Library, 1986.

Gennari, John. "Miles and the Jazz Critics." Early, 66-77.

Hamblin, Robert W. "'Like a Big Soft Fading Wheel': The Triumph of Faulkner's Art." Kartiganer and Abadie, 272-84.

Kartiganer, Donald M., and Ann J. Abadie, Ed. *Faulkner at 100: Retrospect and Prospect (Faulkner and Yoknapatawpha, 1997).* Jackson: UP of Mississippi, 2000.

Matthews, John T. "Whose America? Faulkner, Modernism, and National Identity." Kartiganer and Abadie, 70-92.

McDowell, Colin. *Manola Blahnik.* New York: HarperCollins, 2000.

McKay, Nellie. "An Interview with Toni Morrison." Taylor-Guthrie, 138-55.

Morrison, Toni. Interview with Charlie Rose. PBS. 1993.

———. *Jazz.* New York: Knopf, 1992.

———. *Love.* New York: Knopf, 2003.

———. *Paradise.* New York: Knopf, 1998.

———. "Rootedness: The Ancestor as Foundation." *Black Women Writers 1950-1980: A Critical Evaluation.* Ed. Marie Evans. New York: Anchor/Doubleday, 1984.

Oates, Stephen B. *William Faulkner: The Man and the Artist* (A Biography). New York: Harper, 1987.

Schappell, Elissa. "Toni Morrison: The Art of Fiction CXXXIV." *The Paris Review* 128.35 (fall 1993): 82-125.

Taylor-Guthrie, Danille, ed. *Conversations with Toni Morrison.* Jackson: UP of Mississippi, 1994.

Troupe, Quincy. "From *Kind of Blue* to *Bitches Brew.*" Early, 118-28.

A Selected Bibliography

Angelou, Maya. *I Know Why the Caged Bird Sings.* New York: Random House, 1969.

The Adventure: Jazz (Episode 9). PBS Video, 2000. 120 minutes.

Babb, Valerie Melissa. *Ernest Gaines.* Boston : Twayne, 1991.

Baldwin, James. *Go Tell It on the Mountain.* New York: Dell, 1952.

Barthelemy, Anthony. "Brogans." In *Footnotes: On Shoes.* Ed. Shari Benstock & Suzanne Ferris. New Brunswick: Rutgers UP, 2001. 179-96.

Benston, Kimberly W. "'I Yam What I Am': Naming and Unnaming in Afro-American Literature." *Black American Literature Forum* 16.1 (1982): 3-11.

Blotner, Joseph. *Faulkner: A Biography.* One volume. New York: Random House, 1984.

Bogumil, Mary L. *Understanding August Wilson.* Columbia: U of South Carolina P, 1999.

Bouson, J. Brooks. *Quite as It's Kept: Shame, Trauma, and Race in the Novels of Toni Morrison.* Albany: State University of New York P, 2000.

Brewer, J. Mason. *American Negro Folklore.* Illus. Richard Lowe. Chicago: Quadrangle Books, 1968.

Bruccoli, Matthew. *Some Sort of Epic Grandeur: The Life of F. Scott Fitzgerald.* New York: Harcourt Brace Jovanovich, 1981.

Brylowski, Walter. *Faulkner's Olympian Laugh: Myth in the Novels.* Detroit: Wayne State UP, 1968.

Camus, Albert. *The Myth of Sisyphus and Other Essays.* Trans. Justin O'Brien. New York: Knopf, 1955. Originally published in France as *Le Mythe de Sisyphe* (Paris: Gallimard, 1942).

Carmean, Karen. *Ernest J. Gaines: A Critical Companion.* Westport, Ct: Greenwood Press, 1998.

Cather, Willa. *O Pioneers!* 1912. New York: Vintage, 1992.

Chesnutt, Charles W. *The Conjure Woman.* 1899. Ann Arbor: U of Michigan P, 1969.

Chesnutt, Helen M. *Charles Waddell Chesnutt: Pioneer of the Color Line.* Chapel Hill: U of North Carolina P, 1952.

Courlander, Harold. *A Treasury of Afro-American Folklore: The Oral Literature, Traditions, Recollections, Legends, Tales, Songs, Religious Beliefs, Customs, Sayings, Songs, and Humor of Peoples of African Descent in the Americas.* New York: Crown, 1976.

———. *A Treasury of African Folklore: The Oral Literature, Traditions, Myths, Legends, Epics, Tales, Recollections, Wisdom, Sayings, and Humor of Africa.* New York: Marlowe & Company, 1996.

David, Ron. *Toni Morrison Explained: A Reader's Road Map to the Novels.* New York: Random House, 2000.

Davis, Thadious. *Faulkner's "Negro": Art and the Southern Context.* Baton Rouge: Louisiana State UP, 1983.

———. *Games of Property: Law, Race, Gender, and Faulkner's* Go Down, Moses. Durham: Duke UP, 2003.

Davis, Thulani. "Not Beloved. Review of *Love*, by Toni Morrison." *Nation* 277.20 (December 2003): 1-3. Academic Search Premier. EBSCO. St. Cloud State Univ. Lib. 7 January 2005.

Donaldson, Scott. *Hemingway vs. Fitzgerald: The Rise and Fall of a Literary Friendship.* New York: Overlook, 1999.

Dorson, Richard M., comp. *American Negro Folktales.* Greenwich: Fawcett, 1956.

Doty, William G. "Native American Tricksters: Literary Figures of Community Transformers." *Trickster Lives: Culture and Myth in American Fiction.* Ed. Jeanne Campbell Reesman. Athens: U of Georgia P, 2001.

Dreifus, Claudia. "Chloe Wofford: Toni Morrison." *The New York Times Magazine* 11 September 1994: 73-75.

Dussere, Erik. *Balancing the Books: Faulkner, Morrison, and the Economics of Slavery.* New York and London: Routledge, 2003.

Duvall, John M. *The Identifying Fictions of Toni Morrison: Modernist Authenticity and Postmodern Blackness.* New York: Palgrave, 2000.

Dyson, Michael Eric. "The Culture of Hip-Hop." *The Michael Dyson Reader.* New York: Basic Civitas Books, 2004. 401-10.

Early, Gerald, ed. *Miles Davis and the American Culture.* St. Louis: Missouri Historical Society Press, 2001.

Ellison, Ralph. "On Bird, Bird-Watching, and Jazz." *Shadow and Act,* 221-32.

———. "Change the Joke and Slip the Yoke." *Shadow and Act,* 45-59.

———. "Hidden Name and Complex Fate: A Writer's Experience in the United States." *Shadow and Act,* 144-66.

———. *Shadow and Act.* New York: Random House, 1964.

Faulkner, William. *Absalom, Absalom!.* New York: Random House, 1936.

———. *As I Lay Dying.* New York: Random House, 1957.

———. "Evangeline." In *Uncollected Stories of William Faulkner.* Ed. Joseph Blotner. New York: Random House, 1979. 583-609.

———. *Faulkner in the University: Class Conferences at the University of Virginia 1957-58.* Ed. Frederick L. Gwynn and Joseph L. Blotner. New York: Random House, 1959.

———. *Go Down, Moses.* New York: Random House, 1940.

———. *Intruder in the Dust.* New York: Random House, 1948.

———. *Light in August.* 1932. New York: Random House, 1968.

———. *Lion in the Garden: Interviews with William Faulkner 1926-1962.* Ed. James B. Meriwether and Michael Millgate. New York: Random House, 1968.

——. "Miss Zilphia Gant." In *Uncollected Stories of William Faulkner*. Ed. Joseph Blotner. New York: Random House, 1979. 368-81.

——. *Mosquitoes*. New York: Liveright, 1955.

——. "Mountain Victory." In *Collected Stories of William Faulkner*. New York: Random House, 1934. 745-77.

——. *The Reivers* (A Reminiscence). New York: Random House, 1962.

——. *Requiem for a Nun*. New York: Random House, 1951.

——. *Sanctuary*. 1931. New York: Random House, 1968.

——. *Selected Letters of William Faulkner*. Ed. Joseph Blotner. New York: Random House, 1977.

——. *Snopes: The Hamlet; The Town, The Mansion*. Intro. by George Garrett. New York: Modern Library, 1994.

——. *The Sound and the Fury*. 1929. Norton Critical Edition. Ed. David Minter. New York: Norton, 1994.

——. *The Wild Palms*. New York: Random House, 1939.

Fitzgerald, F. Scott. "Babylon Revisited." *The Short Stories of F. Scott Fitzgerald*. Ed. And with Preface by Matthew J. Bruccoli. New York: Charles Scribner's Sons, 1989. 616-33.

——. *The Crack-Up*. Ed. Edmund Wilson. New York: New Directions, 1945.

——. *The Great Gatsby*. 1925. Preface and Notes by Matthew J. Bruccoli. New York: Macmillan, 1992.

——. *Tender is the Night*. New York: Charles Scribner's Sons, 1933.

Fussell, Betty. "All That Jazz." Taylor-Guthrie, 138-55.

Gaines, Ernest J. *The Autobiography of Miss Jane Pittman*. New York: Bantam, 1971.

——. Interview with Kay Bonetti. Columbia, Mo.: American Audio Prose Library, 1986.

——. *Of Love and Dust*. New York: Dial Press, 1967.

Garrett, George P., Jr. "The Influence of William Faulkner." *Georgia Review* 18 (winter 1964): 419-27.

Gates, Henry Louis, Jr., and Sieglinde Lemke. Introduction. *The Complete Stories*. New York: HarperCollins, 1995. ix-xxiii.

Gates, Henry Louis, Jr. *The Signifying Monkey: A Theory of Afro-American Literary Criticism*. New York: Oxford UP, 1988.

Gray, Paul. "Paradise Found." *Time* 19 January 1998: 63-68.

Gray, Richard G. *The Life of William Faulkner: A Critical Biography*. Oxford: Blackwell, 1994.

Greene, Robert. *The 48 Laws of Power*. New York: Penguin, 2000.

Harris, Trudier. *The Novels of Toni Morrison*. Knoxville: U of Tennessee P, 1991.

Homer. *The Odyssey*. Trans. Robert Fitzgerald. *Literature of the Western World: The Ancient World Through the Renaissance*. Vol. One. 4th ed. Comp.

Brian Wilkie and James Hurt. Upper Saddle River, New Jersey: Prentice Hall, 1977. 275-596.

Hughes, Langston, and Arna Bontemps, Eds. *The Book of Negro Folklore.* New York: Dodd, Mead and Company, 1958.

Hurston, Zora Neale. "The Bone of Contention." *The Complete Stories.* Intro. by Henry Louis Gates, Jr., and Sieglinde Lemke. New York: HarperCollins, 1995. 209-20.

————. *Every Tongue Got to Confess: Negro Folk-tales from the Gulf States.* Foreword by John Edgar Wideman. New York: HarperCollins, 2002.

————. "High John De Conquer." *The Complete Stories.* New York: HarperCollins, 1995. 139-48.

————. *Jonah's Gourd Vine.* 1934. New York : Harper, 1990.

————. *Moses, Man of the Mountain.* 1939. New York: HarperCollins, 1991.

————. *Mules and Men.* Preface by Franz Boas with a new Foreword by Arnold Rampersad. New York: Harper, 1935.

————. *Seraph on the Suwanee.* 1948. With a Foreword by Hazel V. Carby. New York: HarperCollins, 1991.

————. *Their Eyes Were Watching God.* 1937. Urbana: U of Illinois P, 1978.

Irwin, John T. *Doubling and Incest/Repetition and Revenge: A Speculative Reading of Faulkner.* Baltimore: John Hopkins UP, 1975.

Jones, Bessie W., and Audrey Vinson. "An Interview with Toni Morrison." Taylor-Guthrie 171-87.

Karl, Frederick R. *William Faulkner: American Writer (A Biography).* New York: Weidenfeld and Nicolson, 1989.

Kartiganer, Donald M., and Ann J. Abadie, ed. *Faulkner at 100: Retrospect and Prospect (Faulkner and Yoknapatawpha, 1997).* Jackson: UP of Mississippi, 2000.

Kennedy, John. Review of *Paradise,* by Toni Morrison. *The Antioch Review* 58.3 (summer 2000): 377.

King, Sigrid. "Naming and Power in Zora Neale Hurston's *Their Eyes Were Watching God." Critical Essays on Zora Neale Hurston.* Ed. Gloria L. Cronin. New York: G.K. Hall, 1998. 115-27.

Koenen, Ann. "'The One Out of Sequence': An Interview with Toni Morrison." *History and Tradition in Afro-American Culture.* Ed. Gunter H. Lenz. Frankfurt: Campus, 1984. 207-221.

Kolmerten, Carol A., Stephen M. Ross, and Judith Bryant Wittenberg, Ed. *Unflinching Gaze: Morrison and Faulkner Re-Envisioned.* Jackson: UP of Mississippi, 1997.

Kubitschek, Missy Dehn. *Toni Morrison: A Critical Companion.* Westport: Greenwood Press, 1998.

LeClair, Thomas. "The Language Must Not Sweat: A Conversation with Toni Morrison." Taylor-Guthrie, 119-28.

Lehan, Richard D. *F. Scott Fitzgerald and the Craft of Fiction.* With a Preface by Harry T. Moore. Carbondale: Southern Illinois UP, 1966.

Lind, Ilse Dusoir. "The Design and Meaning of *Absalom, Absalom!.* " In *William Faulkner: Four Decades of Criticism.* Ed. Linda Welshimer Wagner. n.p.: Michigan State UP, 1973. 272-97.

Lowe, John. *"Jump at the Sun":Zora Neale Hurston's Cosmic Comedy.* Urbana: U of Illinois P, 1994.

MacKethan, Lucinda Hardwick. *The Dream of Arcady: Place and Time in Southern Literature.* Baton Rouge: Louisiana State UP, 1980.

Matus, Jill. *Toni Morrison.* Manchester: Manchester UP, 1998.

McDowell, Colin. *Manola Blahnik.* New York: HarperCollins, 2000.

McKay, Nellie. "An Interview with Toni Morrison." Taylor-Guthrie 138-55.

McKee, Patricia. *Producing American Races: Henry James, William Faulkner, Toni Morrison.* Durham: Duke UP, 1999.

McKelly, James C. "Hymns of Sedition: Portraits of the Artist in Contemporary African-American Drama." *Arizona Quarterly* 48.1 (spring 1992): 87-107.

Meisenhelder, Susan Edwards. *Hitting a Straight Lick with a Crooked Stick: Race and Gender in the Works of Zora Neale Hurston.* Tuscaloosa: U of Alabama P, 1999.

Menand, Louis. "The War Between Men and Women." *The New Yorker* 12 January 1998: 78-82.

Minter, David. *William Faulkner: His Life and Work.* Baltimore and London: John Hopkins UP, 1980.

Morris, Milton D. "Democratic Politics and Black Subordination." *A Turbulent Voyage: Readings in African American Studies.* Ed. Floyd W. Hayes III. San Diego: Collegiate Press, 1992.

Morrison, Toni. *Beloved.* New York: Knopf, 1987.

———.*The Bluest Eye.* New York: Washington Square Press, 1970.

———. Interview with Charlie Rose. PBS. 1993.

———. *Jazz.* New York: Alfred A. Knopf, 1992.

———. *Love.* New York: Knopf, 2003.

———. *Paradise.* New York: Knopf, 1998.

———. "Rootedness: The Ancestor as Foundation." *Black Women Writers 1950-1980: A Critical Evaluation.* Ed. Marie Evans. New York: Anchor/Doubleday, 1984.

———. *Song of Solomon.* New York: New American Library, 1977.

———. *Sula.* New York: New American Library, 1973.

———. *Tar Baby.* New York: Random House, 1981.

Naylor, Gloria. "A Conversation: Gloria Naylor and Toni Morrison." Taylor-Guthrie, 188-222.

Ngugi wa Thiong'o. *A Grain of Wheat.* London: Heinemann, 1967.

Oates, Stephen. *William Faulkner: The Man and the Artist* (A Biography). New York: Harper, 1987.

O'Connor, Flannery. *Collected Works*. New York: Library of America, 1988.
Parker, Robert Dale. *Faulkner and the Novelistic Imagination*. Urbana: U of Illinois P, 1985.
Pelzer, Linda C. *Student Companion to F. Scott Fitzgerald*. Student Companions to Classic Writers. Westport, CT: Greenwood Press, 2000.
Pilkington, John. *The Heart of Yoknapatawpha*. Jackson: UP of Mississippi, 1981.
Powers, Lyall H. *Faulkner's Yoknapatawpha Comedy*. Ann Arbor: U of Michigan P, 1980.
Reames, Kelly. *Toni Morrison's* Paradise: *A Reader's Guide*. New York: Continuum, 2001.
Reaves, Gerri. "The Slip in the Ballet Slipper: Illusion and the Naked Foot." *Footnotes: On Shoes*. Ed. Shari Benstock and Suzanne Ferris. New Brunswick: Rutgers UP, 2001. 251-71.
Reesman, Jeanne Campbell. "Introduction." *Trickster Lives: Culture and Myth in American Fiction*. Athens: U of Georgia P, 2001.
Ruas, Charles. "Toni Morrison." Taylor-Guthrie, 93-118.
Samuels, Wilfred D., and Clenora Hudson-Weems. *Toni Morrison*. New York: Twayne, 1990.
Schappell, Elissa. "Toni Morrison: The Art of Fiction CXXXIV." *The Paris Review* 128.35 (fall 1993): 82-125.
Singal, Daniel J. *William Faulkner: The Making of a Modernist*. Chapel Hill: U of North Carolina P, 1997.
Smith, Jeanne Rosier. *Writing Tricksters: Mythic Gambols in American Ethnic Literature*. Berkeley: U of California P, 1997.
Tate, Claudia. "Interview with Toni Morrison." Taylor-Guthrie 156-70.
Taylor-Guthrie, Danille, ed. *Conversations with Toni Morrison*. Jackson: UP of Mississippi, 1994.
Troupe, Quincy. "From *Kind of Blue* to *Bitches Brew.*" Early, 118-28.
Volpe, Edmond L. *A Reader's Guide to William Faulkner*. New York: Farrar, Straus and Company, 1964.
———. *A Reader's Guide to William Faulkner: The Short Stories*. New York: Syracuse UP, 2004.
Watson, James Gray. *The Snopes Dilemma: Faulkner's Trilogy*. Coral Gables: U of Miami P, 1968.
Weinstein, Philip M. *What Else But Love?: The Ordeal of Race in Faulkner and Morrison*. New York: Columbia UP, 1996.
Williams, Dana. *"In the Light of Likeness Transformed": The Literary Art of Leon Forrest*. Columbus: Ohio State UP, 2005.
Wilson, August. *Ma Rainey's Black Bottom: A Play in Two Acts*. New York: Penguin, 1981.
———. *Joe Turner's Come and Gone*. New York: Penguin, 1988.
Wilson, Judith. "A Conversation with Toni Morrison." Taylor-Guthrie, 129-37.

Wolfe, Peter. *August Wilson*. New York: Twayne, 1999.

Index

Biographical Note

Tommie Lee Jackson, professor of English at St. Cloud State University, St. Cloud, Minnesota, is the author of *Existentialist Fiction of Ayi Kwei Armah, Albert Camus, and Jean-Paul Sartre* (1997) and *An Invincible Summer: Female Diasporan Authors* (2001). She holds a Ph.D. from the University of Nebraska at Lincoln.

CPSIA information can be obtained at www.ICGtesting.com
Printed in the USA
BVOW071040130713

325786BV00001B/23/P